4 plus 1

Five Plays for
Young Actors

Ron Blicq

*For Heidi
Best wishes!
Ron*

4 plus 1

Five Plays for Young Actors

This book is the first of a two-volume set of 12 plays written by the same author. As its title implies, it features one- and two-act plays written especially for actors who are 7 to 16 years old. All the plays have been successfully produced.

The second volume is titled *Seven Plays with a Light Touch* and will be published early in 2015. It will contain one-act plays primarily for adult actors and audiences (although two of the plays have teens in principal roles). The plays range in length from 8 minutes to 55 minutes.

Another adult two-act play by the same author, titled *Closure*, was chosen as Best Canadian Play and published by Samuel French in 2008. It is available directly from Samuel French or can be ordered from any bookstore (or online from Amazon).

All of the plays in this book are available for production by both professional and amateur theater groups. However, because they are copyright, approval has to be obtained first from the publisher (see page 275 for details.)

First published in Canada in 2014 by
R-Group Publications, 569 Oxford St, Winnipeg MB R3M 3J2
(a Division of The Roning Group Inc)
rgrouppubs@gmail.com

Copyright © 2014 Ron S. Blicq
First Edition

ISBN
978-1-4602-5122-5 (Paperback)
978-1-4602-5123-2 (eBook)
978-1-4602-5121-8 (Hardcover)

Produced by

FriesenPress, Inc
Suite 300 – 852 Fort Street
Victoria, BC, Canada, V8W 1H8

Distributed to the trade by The Ingram Book Company

Cover photographs
Upper front cover: *The Railway Children* - John Gaisford
Lower front cover and back cover:
Adventures with a Psammead – John Fitzgerald

Acknowledgments

This book and its five plays would not have been possible if it had not been for the many people who helped me create and perform stories suitable for young audiences. On this page I want to thank all of you who have so generously given much of yourselves to ensure our audiences have had a happy experience. In so doing you clearly reinforced my belief that writing for young actors and young audiences is not only viable but also a very real pleasure.

I would like to list everyone here but, as there are so many of you, will you please forgive me if I just say a very big **Thank You**? ("You" are the over 150 actors, directors, stage managers, sound and light technicians, stage crews, and countless front-of-house staff I have had the pleasure to work with.)

I also want to recognize how much I appreciated the trust that the Guernsey Amateur Dramatic and Operatic Club *(GADOC)* in the British Channel Islands invested in me, as a new and relatively unknown playwright, when they chose to produce my as yet unperformed plays. Indeed, they produced both *The Popsicle-Stick Wand* and *The Railway Children* in the very first year of our collaboration and did a magnificent job. Then just a few years later they produced *Adventures with a Psammead* with equal success.

In Winnipeg I shall never forget the tremendous effort by the six actors who worked so hard to make the two "Popsicle-Stick Wand" plays we produced at the Winnipeg Fringe Theatre Festival such fun for the audiences. And for me!

Thank you so much, all my friends.

Books by the Same Author

Theatre
Closure
Five Plays for Young Actors
Seven Plays With a Light Touch

Novels/Biography
Choosing Home
The Spirit of Giving
Au Revoir, Sarnia Chérie
(Good-bye, Dear Guernsey)
You Will Write, Won't You?

Education
On The Move
Technically-Write!
Administratively-Write!
Communicating at Work
Guidelines for Report Writing

Contents

"Children at play are not playing about; their games should be seen as their most serious-minded activity."

Michel Eyquero de Montaigne
1533-1592

About the Plays

When planning this book I based my selection of plays on three premises: they must be suitable for performance by actors in the 7- to 15-year-old age range; they must already have been performed successfully; and I must have *seen* young actors performing in them. I felt the latter was particularly important, since it would permit me to evaluate each play's suitability for young people, both as performers and as audience.

Sitting in the audience also presented me with a welcome surprise: in each case I was astonished by the quality of the young performers' acting and their enthusiasm in portraying their different roles. This, in turn, supported my long-established view that young actors should perform young peoples' roles, rather than have adult actors pretend they are children.

All the plays I have selected are new, in that they were written over the last decade. Two are completely original, written specifically for performance at two consecutive Fringe Theatre Festivals in Winnipeg, Canada. The remaining three are adaptations from well-known stories and novels that have been popular for generations.

There are three one-act plays, each about 40-50 minutes in length. They are followed by two full-length plays of 70-80 minutes each, plus an additional 15 minutes for an intermission between the acts.

~~~

So, what is the significance of "4 plus 1," which I have placed above the book's title: *Five Plays for Young Actors*? It's because there is a common thread—an element of wizardry—among the first four plays that is not evident in the fifth play.

In the first two plays the wizardry affects two girls and two boys, all approximately 12 years old, and is created by an elderly man they meet beside a local beach. He introduces himself as "Miracle the Magician" and encourages them to use Popsicle sticks to make their own wands (which he enables with temporary magic powers). They then experience a series of adventures that tickle the imagination of young audiences.

The third play is based on the traditional tale of *Puss in Boots*, which I have modified so that Puss has unique magic powers. He uses them subtly, gradually persuading the King to approve the marriage between Puss's penniless master Darren and the King's daughter—the Princess—even though early in the play we have heard the King insist their union would be totally inappropriate and must never occur.

Interaction with the audience is an integral component in each of the one-act plays.

I have based the fourth play, *Adventures with a Psammead*, on the story *Five Children and It,* written by the well-known novelist Edith Nesbit. Five children discover an ancient "sand wizard" who has magic powers, which he uses to grant the children's sometimes unusual requests. Their wishes may seem logical, but they have unexpected and often exciting results.

The fifth play is also based on a Nesbit story, this time the most well-known of all her novels: *The Railway Children.* Over the past three decades the story has twice been made into successful films, yet only over the past ten years has it been performed with any degree of frequency as a stage play. Three children living temporarily in a country cottage discover the local railway line and have a glorious and sometimes wild series of adventures.

Three of the five plays were produced originally by a renowned amateur theatre group on the British Island of Guernsey, while two were performed first by a drama group in Winnipeg, Canada. In each case, the major characters were children, and they were played by young actors of an age commensurate with those of the child or teen they were playing, ranging from 7 up to 15 years of age.

I have found that young audiences identify much more readily with the youthful characters they see on stage, when the actors are the correct age for the role they are playing and are of a comparable age to the critical audience they are facing. Too often, I have seen 20- to 30-year-old adult actors emulating children who are supposedly 8 to 15 years old. When this happens, although the audience may be happily entertained, they are less likely to believe they are watching real people and the situations the performers encounter are credible.

Film-makers regularly engage young actors of the correct age to perform as children. However, they have a distinct advantage in that they can shoot a scene over and over until the actors portray their characters in exactly the way the director wants. It is very different for a play performed on the stage, because the director has to invest great faith in the young actors and trust them to consistently provide a strong performance.

My experience may seem rare, but I have seen many young actors who, although they may kibitz about annoyingly during rehearsals, turn in inspiring performances when the production goes "live" and they are facing an audience. I have learned to trust them!

I had the good fortune to be drawn into the first production of each play in this book, either as consulting author or director, from which I have been able to prepare the Production Notes that follow immediately after each script. They describe issues we encountered during the planning stages and over several rehearsals, and the adjustments we had to make. I hope these notes will be helpful for future directors as they gear up to produce their interpretations of the plays.

Ron Blicq
May 2014

Five Plays for Young Actors

Play No. 1

The Popsicle-Stick Wand

Synopsis

It's mid-summer and four children—two girls and two boys between the ages of 10 and 12—arrive at a local beach planning to fish and swim. There they meet an elderly man who turns out to be a magician, with whom they make friends.

While the magician is having a nap, one of the boys steals his wand and practices doing magic tricks with it. When the other three children discover what he has done they demand that he return it, but he eludes them by using the wand to make himself invisible. A 'blind' chase ensues, onstage and into the audience, during which the invisible boy commands the wand to 'freeze' one of the girls chasing him. The remaining two children wake the magician and ask him to help.

The magician has the children search for discarded Popsicle sticks, which he helps them glue together to make a temporary wand. He has a girl hold the wand while he casts a magic spell to enable it. Yet when she tries to use the wand, she finds she has insufficient 'command power.' So she enlists the audience's help to give her commands greater strength, which is achieved by having two of the children 'work' the audience.

A unique twist is that, to undo a magic command, the original command has to be said backwards; for example: "Abracadabra" has to be said as "Arba Arbadac," and "Freeze Alison" becomes "Zeerf Nosila," and so on. It's the role of the two children working the audience to teach the children and adults in front of them how to say the commands backwards.

The Set

The action takes place on a stretch of grassland between a road and a rocky beach. There are large boulders at downstage right, one of which can be moved. There is a tall tree at stage left, with branches that move and leaves that shake. Upstage, there are a

5

bench and a street lamp on the right, and a seesaw (teeter-totter) between the center and stage left.

The director has the option to tailor the production by replacing the names of cities and towns referred to in the play with local names.

Length of Play   Approximately 40 minutes

The Characters

Alison	)	
Jennifer	)	*ages between*
Jonathan	)	*10 and 12*
Bumpy-Bumpy *(male)*	)	
Miracle the Magician		age 60

Production History

The first production of the play was in the UK, by the Guernsey Amateur Dramatic and Operatic Club (GADOC), on May 23, 2003, as part of the GADOC 55th One-Act-Play Festival. John Gaisford directed the play and acted as Miracle the Magician.

The young actors in the UK production were *(from the top):*

Kim Le Marchant
  (Jennifer)

Adele Sales
  (Alison)

Michael Sullivan
  (Bumpy-Bumpy)

Jack Lucas
  (Jonathan)

Author photo

The first North American production of *The Popsicle-Stick Wand* was presented by R-G Productions from July 21 to 29, 2006, as part of the Winnipeg Fringe Theatre Festival. The play was directed by the author.

The Popsicle-Stick Wand

A rehearsal moment in the Winnipeg Production.   *Author photo*

The actors are *(from left to right)*:

John Chase	*Miracle the Magician*
Alysha Barrie	*Alison*
Scott Austin	*Jonathan*
Lexi Carvey	*Jennifer*
Kevin Carruthers	*Bumpy-Bumpy*

There are character descriptions for each role, starting on page 41. Notes about the two productions start on page 43.

Some Script Guidelines

Throughout the script, two symbols are used occasionally at the end of a piece of dialogue to indicate how the sentence ends:

... An ellipsis at the end of a statement means the speaker just trails off and leaves his or her thought hanging in the air (possibly accompanied by a shrug).

— A dash at the end of a statement means the speaker is interrupted by the next speaker, so that the first speaker's statement is incomplete. Sometimes there is an italicized continuation of the statement *(within brackets)* immediately following the dash, to help the actor sense where the sentence was going.

7

Script: *The Popsicle-Stick Wand*

© *2003, Ron Blicq*

(At curtain up, MIRACLE *the Magician is lying between two large rocks at stage right, one of his feet wedged between them. Behind the rocks, upstage, is the entrance to the beach. In front of it is a bench-seat and, beside it, an old-fashioned lamp standard with a lamp at the top. Center upstage is a seesaw [teeter-totter]. To stage left there is a large tree, mostly offstage but with its upper branches protruding onto the stage. The* CHILDREN *can be heard approaching offstage left. They are carrying fishing gear, a soccer ball, towels, and a picnic cooler. All wear swimsuits with shorts over them.)*

*(*BUMPY-BUMPY *enters walking backwards, facing and followed by* ALISON, *then* JONATHAN *and* JENNIFER, *who carry the picnic cooler between them.)*

BUMPY-BUMPY: The best place to fish is out in the Whiteshell.

JENNIFER: My grandfather likes to take his boat out to Gimli, fish off Willow Island.

JONATHAN: Off the pier is better.

ALISON: Yeah, but they're always guys swimming there, jumping off the harbor wall.

BUMPY-BUMPY: Y-e-a-h!

ALISON: It's not really allowed.

BUMPY-BUMPY: Well, what else is there to do?

ALISON: At Gimli? Lots!

JENNIFER: The best place we've fished is at Waskesiu, in Prince Albert National Park. *(Waskesiu is pronounced 'Woss-ka-soo'.)*

(They stop center stage and put their towels, soccer ball, fishing gear, the picnic cooler, etc, on the grass.)

*(*ALISON *and* JONATHAN *jump on the seesaw, with Alison stage left and Jonathan stage right.)*

8

(MIRACLE *moans.*)

BUMPY-BUMPY: Yeah, but it's so far to drive. Bor-ing!

JONATHAN: Well, personally, I like this beach. It's—

ALISON: Sshh! Did you hear that?

JENNIFER: Hear what?

ALISON: A cry. Like a moan.

(They listen.)

BUMPY-BUMPY: No. You're imagining it.

MIRACLE: *(soft, weary)* Oooh. Help me.

ALISON: Listen!

MIRACLE: Can you help me?

JONATHAN: There's someone there!

ALISON: Sounds like they're hurt.

(They search. BUMPY-BUMPY *discovers* MIRACLE.*)*

BUMPY-BUMPY: Hey! It's an old man.

(The others run up.)

Are you hurt, mister?

MIRACLE: *(hoarsely)* Oh, thank goodness you've come. I shouted and shouted—

JENNIFER: Looks like he's broken his leg.

MIRACLE: But no-one answered. I've been here all night.

ALISON: What happened?

JONATHAN: Can I help you up?

MIRACLE: Oh, no. Thank you. You can't. My foot is stuck. I slipped on the rocks.

(The CHILDREN *peer at his foot.* ALISON *fetches a towel; with* JENNIFER*'s help she places it under* MIRACLE*'s head.)*

BUMPY-BUMPY: *(to* JONATHAN*)* Help me pull this rock back.

MIRACLE: If you could just release my foot.

9

(JONATHAN and BUMPY-BUMPY *pull on the rock. It doesn't move.)*

JONATHAN: Alison! Jennifer! Help us pull.

(ALISON and JENNIFER *pull on* JONATHAN's *and* BUMPY-BUMPY's *waists.)*

BUMPY-BUMPY: Okay... Pull! ... Again!

(The rock doesn't move. JONATHAN's *hands slip on the rock and the four children fall back.)*

ALISON: Perhaps we should call the police.

JENNIFER: Or the paramedics.

MIRACLE: Oh, no! No. You see, I had my wa – er – my stick with me. It flew out of my hand when I fell. If you could just find it for me.

JONATHAN: Which way did it go?

MIRACLE: I don't know. I was falling and—

BUMPY-BUMPY: Come on. It can't be far.

(The CHILDREN *hunt.)*

JONATHAN: *(calls to* MIRACLE*)* Is it like a walking stick?

MIRACLE: No, smaller.

JENNIFER: *(approaches with a thick branch)* Is this it?

MIRACLE: No. Just a thin stick. About 40 centimeters long, with colored bands around it.

BUMPY-BUMPY: *(carrying Miracle's wand)* Would this be it?

MIRACLE: Oh, yes! Thank you. Thank you.

(The CHILDREN *gather around him.)*

ALISON: It's pretty.

MIRACLE: Yes. Yes, I suppose it is. I'd never thought of it like that. ... Now. If you wouldn't mind, I must ask you to do something for me. Would you stand over there, by that tree.

(The CHILDREN *hesitate.)*

MIRACLE: Only for a moment.

JONATHAN: *(after a brief pause)* Come on, then.

(The CHILDREN *follow him to the tree.)*

JENNIFER: *(whispers to* ALISON*)* Do you think he's...?

ALISON: *(whispers)* I don't know. He does seem a bit strange.

MIRACLE: Just one more thing: Will you all turn your backs to me. Please. I won't be long.

(The CHILDREN *hesitate again, then face away from* MIRACLE.*)*

*(*MIRACLE *points his wand toward the rock.)*

Abracadabra. Rock: move left.

(The rock starts to move then slips back.)

Oh dear! **Abracadabra. Rock: move left!**

(The rock moves slowly aside. BUMPY-BUMPY *sneaks a peek, sees what happens.* MIRACLE *stands up unsteadily, brushes himself off, and slips the wand into one of his cloak's deep pockets.)*

It's all right now. You can turn around.

*(*MIRACLE *and the* CHILDREN *meet center stage.)*

JENNIFER: You're free!

JONATHAN: How did you do that?

BUMPY-BUMPY: Where's your stick?

MIRACLE: Oh. In my pocket. For safety.

BUMPY-BUMPY: Can I see it?

ALISON: That's not very polite, Bumpy-Bumpy.

BUMPY-BUMPY: Are you a wizard?

MIRACLE: Well, I suppose you could call me that.

JENNIFER: That stick is a wand?

BUMPY-BUMPY: He used it to move the rock!

ALISON: You weren't supposed to look!

JONATHAN: Is that how you got free?

BUMPY-BUMPY: He moved the rock! The four of us couldn't! *(to* MIRACLE*)* Are you really a wizard?

MIRACLE: I prefer to call myself a magician.

JENNIFER: Do you do magic acts? Like perform on the stage?

MIRACLE: Oh, no. I'm a very private magician.

ALISON: I've never seen you before.

MIRACLE: You wouldn't have. I arrived only yesterday. I've come to see what it would be like to live here.

ALISON: You mean, you will stay?

MIRACLE: I'd like to. But I can only do that if you can all keep a secret. I don't want anyone to know who I am. Or that I am a magician. You see, I like to keep myself as a very private kind of person

JONATHAN: Of course. No problem.

BUMPY-BUMPY: My lips will be sealed!

*(*JENNIFER *and* ALISON *nod their heads in agreement.)*

MIRACLE: Well, if we are to be friends, it would be nice if I could know your names. Mine is Miracle.

ALISON: Miracle?

MIRACLE: Miracle the Magician.

ALISON: I'm Alison.

*(*MIRACLE *shakes* ALISON*'s hand, and then shakes with the others in turn.)*

MIRACLE: Alison.

ALISON: And this is Jennifer.

MIRACLE: Jennifer. How do you do?

JENNIFER: Hi.

JONATHAN: I'm Jonathan.

MIRACLE: Jonathan.

BUMPY-BUMPY: And I'm Bumpy-Bumpy.

MIRACLE: How do you do, Bumpy-Bumpy. May I ask: what is the derivation of your name?

BUMPY-BUMPY: Well... it's...um...

JENNIFER: His real name is Bertrand Bermandson. We just shortened it to Bumpy-Bumpy.

MIRACLE: Ah, I see. "Bumpy-Bumpy." Unusual, but appropriate.

(Slight pause.)

JENNIFER: I don't want to be impolite, but... I mean, now you know us—

BUMPY-BUMPY: Jennifer wants to see your wand.

MIRACLE: Well, now we're friends, I can't see any harm. Just for once.

(MIRACLE pulls the wand from his cloak and hands it to JENNIFER. They ALL peer at it.)

ALISON: I didn't really believe, before, about wizards and, like, magic.

MIRACLE: Now you do?

ALISON: I guess.

JONATHAN: Can you show us?

MIRACLE: Show you what?

JONATHAN: How it works?

(MIRACLE takes the wand, waves it around.)

MIRACLE: You mean, like this?

BUMPY-BUMPY: Like you did before.

JENNIFER: Oh, please!

(MIRACLE points the want at the top of the lamp standard.)

MIRACLE: Abracadabra. Lamp: get bright!

(The lamp lights up. MIRACLE lowers the wand slowly.)

Now, lamp: get dim!

(The lamp dims slowly with the wand's movement.)

BUMPY-BUMPY: It's as easy as that?

MIRACLE: When you know the right words.

BUMPY-BUMPY: Abracadabra?

MIRACLE: Right. And then you give a command. *(he points to the lamp.)* Lamp: now get brighter.

(The lamp brightens to full strength.)

JONATHAN: Can you make yourself invisible?

MIRACLE: If I wanted to, I suppose I could. I've never really had occasion to—

BUMPY-BUMPY: Show us!

ALISON: Bumpy!

MIRACLE: One day, perhaps. But, you know, I don't want to interrupt your fishing plans. And after last night's adventure, I think a little nap would suit me. So, if you don't mind...

(MIRACLE places the wand in an inside pocket of his cloak, takes it off, folds it, and lays it on the rock. The CHILDREN collect their fishing gear and the ball.)

JENNIFER: Thank you for showing us.

ALISON: Oh, yes. It was incredible.

MIRACLE: Well, thank you.

(The CHILDREN exit upstage right, saying "See you later," "Bye-bye," etc. MIRACLE responds, waves.)

(MIRACLE stretches out the towel that previously supported his head and lies down on it, beside the rock.)

(The lights dim to about 20% to indicate a short passage of time, then come up again with the scene unchanged.)

(We hear the children's voices in the background.)

(BUMPY-BUMPY enters stealthily from upstage right, checks he is unobserved, searches for the wand around MIRACLE, and then reaches for the cloak.)

The Popsicle-Stick Wand

JONATHAN: *(calling, voice over)* I'll get a towel!

(BUMPY-BUMPY jumps behind the rock, squats down, peers around it. JONATHAN enters, picks up a towel, walks over to and peers at the sleeping MIRACLE, then exits toward the beach.)

(BUMPY-BUMPY stealthily works his way toward MIRACLE. He kneels, lifts Miracle's cloak, searches in the pockets, and pulls out Miracle's wand. He refolds the cloak, checks MIRACLE is still asleep, then creeps toward midstage.)

BUMPY-BUMPY: *(waving the wand in the air)* Ah-ha! Abracadabra! Abracadabra! Abracadabra!

(He points the wand toward the lamp.)

Now. Abracadabra. Lamp, go dim!

(Nothing happens.)

O-h-h...! *(with greater intensity)* **Abracadabra. Lamp: go dim!**

(The lamp dims. He raises the wand.)

Now go bright.

(The lamp lights up again.)

Ha, ha! I can do it.

(BUMPY-BUMPY checks that MIRACLE still sleeps, then points the wand at the bench.)

Abracadabra. Bench: fall over!

(The bench topples over and lies on its back.)

(BUMPY-BUMPY searches then waves his wand at the seesaw.)

Ah! The seesaw! Abracadabra. Seesaw: follow my wand!

(The lower end of the seesaw rises and the upper end drops to the ground, following the wand's movement.)

That's so cool!

(He continues to make the seesaw rise and fall.)

15

(JONATHAN, JENNIFER and ALISON enter from the beach. JONATHAN carries a pail and the ball. JENNIFER carries a towel. JONATHAN sees the fallen bench, rights it, and rests the ball on it. They watch Bumpy-Bumpy, who has not heard them enter.)

ALISON: Bumpy-Bumpy! What are you doing?

BUMPY-BUMPY: Look at this, will you! It works! *(points to the lamp)* Abracadabra. Lamp: go dim.

(BUMPY-BUMPY lowers the wand and the lamp slowly extinguishes.)

JONATHAN: That's Miracle's wand!

BUMPY-BUMPY: Watch the seesaw. Abracadabra. Seesaw: follow my wand!

(The seesaw follows the wand's movements.)

JENNIFER: Cool!

ALISON: How did you get it? The wand?

BUMPY-BUMPY: I…er…I borrowed it.

JENNIFER: You asked him?

BUMPY-BUMPY: Well, no, not exactly…

JENNIFER: Then you stole it!

BUMPY-BUMPY: Oh, no. He wouldn't mind. I didn't want to wake him.

JONATHAN: Give it here!

(BUMPY-BUMPY shakes his head, backs away. JONATHAN shouts to the others.)

Get him!

(THEY chase BUMPY-BUMPY but he eludes them, runs around the seesaw and bench, then eventually stands under the tree branches, where he turns the wand toward the others and speaks rapidly.)

BUMPY-BUMPY: Abracadabra!

(ALISON, JENNIFER and JONATHAN stop. There is a brief pause, then BUMPY-BUMPY turns the wand toward himself.)

BUMPY-BUMPY: *(continuing)* Abracadabra! Make me invisible!

(There is a puff of smoke; when it clears he is no longer visible.)

ALISON: Oh, no!

(JENNIFER lunges forward and paws the air where Bumpy-Bumpy was standing.)

JENNIFER: I touched him! He went that way, I think *(points to the rocks.)*

BUMPY-BUMPY: *(voice over, center stage)* I'm over here!

(The CHILDREN search, arms outstretched.)

(from stage right) Now I'm here!

(The ball bounces off the bench. JENNIFER squeals. JONATHAN retrieves the ball and places it beside the picnic cooler.)

BUMPY-BUMPY: *(voice over)* I'm like the invisible man!

(The three CHILDREN, their arms outstretched, close toward the bench.)

(stage left) It's like you're trying to 'Pin the Tail on the Donkey!'

(The chasers, with arms outstretched, cross to stage left.)

But I'm over here now! *(from stage right)*

(The chasers swing around, face stage right.)

JONATHAN: We'll make a line.

JENNIFER: How?

JONATHAN: Stand one on each side of me. Now, stretch out your arms. Walk forward. Move your arms up and down as you go.

(The chasers advance in a line from stage left to stage right, "feeling" and touching with outstretched fingertips.)

BUMPY-BUMPY: *(voice over, stage right)* You'll not find me like that! No way!

(There is the sound of bumping stage right, as if someone is running up three or four steps. Then silence. The children reach the rocks.)

JONATHAN: Nothing.

ALISON: I didn't even feel him, like if he rushed past.

JENNIFER: Sssh! We don't want to wake Miracle.

ALISON: I think we should.

JONATHAN: He'll know what to do.

JENNIFER: I'd rather get his wand back to him while he's still asleep. I mean, he trusted us.

ALISON: Yeah. You're right.

JONATHAN: But how?

BUMPY-BUMPY: *(voice over, behind the audience)* Exactly! How're you going to catch me, if you can't see me?

JONATHAN: He's way up there?

(The chasers shade their eyes against the light, peer up to the back of the theater.)

BUMPY-BUMPY: What're you doing that for? You can't see me. I'm invisible!

(JENNIFER draws JONATHAN and ALISON into a huddle. They whisper, nod, look up toward the back of the theater. They break apart and JENNIFER steps to stage front.)

JENNIFER: Could we have the house lights up, please?

(Pause; the house lights come up. JENNIFER and JONATHAN each step to a front corner of the stage and look at ALISON, who steps to stage front, center. She addresses the audience.)

ALISON: Look. We need your help. Can you help us? *(pause)* Oh, thank you. Now, Jennifer's going to walk up one aisle, and Jonathan will walk up the other. If you're sitting in an aisle seat, we need you to put your arms out in the aisle—like this *(stretches her arms out to the side, horizontally),* so if Bumpy-Bumpy tries to run past you, you'll feel him.

(JONATHAN and JENNIFER also stretch their arms out to the side when Alison says "like this".)

BUMPY-BUMPY: *(voice over)* You think that'll work? Don't kid yourselves!

ALISON: *(shouts to BUMPY-BUMPY)* It will. Just you wait! *(to the audience)* Are you ready? Hands out in the aisle? Oh, good! *(to JENNIFER and JONATHAN)* Off you go!

(JONATHAN and JENNIFER walk up the aisle steps, their arms outstretched, ad-libbing as they go: "Did you feel him?" "Could you hear him breathing?" They reach the top and walk across the back row of seats (if they are unoccupied.)

ALISON: *(continuing, to JONATHAN and JENNIFER)* Nothing?

JONATHAN: Nothing.

JENNIFER: I didn't feel anything, either.

ALISON: Oh, no! *(to the audience)* You can put your arms down now. *(to JONATHAN and JENNIFER)* Stay up there, so he can't escape, in case he's hiding in a seat. *(to the audience)* If there's an empty seat next to you, just feel around in it. Don't be afraid. Bumpy-Bumpy won't bite!

(There is a bumping sound as though someone is running down three or four steps at stage left.)

BUMPY-BUMPY: *(voice over, stage left)* I'm not that hungry!

ALISON: You're here?

BUMPY-BUMPY: *(voice over)* Right! And you can't find me!

ALISON: How did you get past Jennifer? Past Jonathan?

BUMPY-BUMPY: *(voice over)* Ah! That's my secret. I've got the wand, remember?

JENNIFER: We're coming back.

JONATHAN: Wait for us!

> *(JONATHAN and JENNIFER run down the aisles. ALISON pulls them together and they huddle and whisper. The house lights dim.)*

ALISON: He's by the tree.

JONATHAN: We'll pretend to go the other way, then run back and corner him. Okay?

ALISON: Okay. *(loud, so Bumpy-Bumpy will hear)* Right. By the rocks, then.

> *(They start toward the rocks, arms outstretched, After several steps, at a signal from JONATHAN, they swing around and run toward the tree.)*

JENNIFER: I touched him!

JONATHAN: Round here, I think.

> *(The branches of the tree bend and wave progressively upward.)*

ALISON: No. Look at the tree! He's climbing into the branches.

BUMPY-BUMPY: Ha, ha! You'll never catch me up here!

JONATHAN: Oh, that's what you think!

> *(JONATHAN makes as if he is about to climb the tree.)*

ALISON: No, Jonathan! He'll just move about.

JENNIFER: Too dangerous. I've got a better idea.

> *(JENNIFER beckons to ALISON and JONATHAN. They huddle while JENNIFER whispers to them. Then JONATHAN and ALISON encircle the tree with their arms and shout up at Bumpy-Bumpy. Concurrently, JENNIFER edges around the upstage edge of the stage, moving toward MIRACLE.)*

(The following actions overlap.)

JONATHAN: There's no way you can get down now!

ALISON: We're bound to catch you.

BUMPY-BUMPY: *(voice over)* I can wait.

ALISON: You'll get hungry!

BUMPY-BUMPY: *(voice over)* So will you!

ALISON: But we've got sandwiches!

BUMPY-BUMPY: *(voice over)* So what! I'll make my own. I'll use the wand.

(ALISON scampers over to the picnic cooler and kneels beside it; she opens it, rummages around inside.)

(JENNIFER shakes MIRACLE's shoulder.)

JENNIFER: Miracle! Miracle!

MIRACLE: Who calls me?

JENNIFER: Miracle: Wake up!

MIRACLE: Oh, it's you, Jennifer.

JENNIFER: Sssh! We've got a problem.

(JENNIFER whispers to MIRACLE. He glances over to the tree and then at ALISON.)

(ALISON holds up a sandwich.)

ALISON: See!

BUMPY-BUMPY: *(voice over)* Abracadabra—

MIRACLE: *(shouts)* Keep moving, Alison! You, too, Jonathan. Don't be a sitting target!

BUMPY-BUMPY: *(voice over)* Abracadabra. Freeze Alison!

(ALISON is frozen, caught in mid-action as she returns the sandwich to the cooler.)

JENNIFER: Oh, Alison!

(JENNIFER starts to run toward ALISON, but MIRACLE pulls her back.)

MIRACLE: No, Jennifer! He'll freeze you too!

> *(MIRACLE draws her behind the rock. JONATHAN hides behind the tree, upstage left.)*
>
> *(MIRACLE suddenly stands up, faces the tree, raises and points his arms to the upper part of the tree; he speaks rapidly and with great intensity.)*
>
> **Arba Arbadac! Elbasid Dnaw!**

BUMPY-BUMPY: *(voice over)* Ouch! The wand is hot!

MIRACLE: Good! *(to JENNIFER)* I've disabled my wand. He can't use it any more.

JENNIFER: But what about Alison?

MIRACLE: I'm sorry, I can't help her. I have used up all my energy.

> *(JENNIFER and JONATHAN run to ALISON, touch her, but she remains motionless.)*

JONATHAN: Alison! Can you hear me?

> *(Pause.)*

JENNIFER: Blink an eyelid if you can.

> *(ALISON does not move.)*
>
> *(to MIRACLE)* You can't...?

MIRACLE: No. I'm sorry.

JONATHAN: We can't leave her like that!

JENNIFER: Isn't there anything we can do?

MIRACLE: Not without a wand. I don't know any other wizards here. ... But, you know, perhaps there is a way. Do you have any Popsicle sticks?

JONATHAN: Popsicle sticks?

MIRACLE: To make a temporary wand. It's been done before, under similar circumstances. You will have to search around. There might be some near the beach.

JONATHAN: You want us to look for Popsicle sticks?

(Miracle nods. JENNIFER and JONATHAN search, scuffing their feet over the ground. JENNIFER picks up a Popsicle stick.)

JENNIFER: I've got one!

MIRACLE: Good! Keep looking. I can manage with just two.

(The search continues.)

JONATHAN: Here!

(JONATHAN holds his Popsicle stick out to MIRACLE.)

MIRACLE: Give it to Jennifer.

(MIRACLE reaches for his cloak and pulls a roll of Scotch tape from an inside pocket.)

(to JENNIFER) Lay the two sticks end to end, but so the ends overlap about an inch.

(MIRACLE winds Scotch tape around the stick overlap.)

(JONATHAN goes to ALISON, bends down to look her in the face, then pats her shoulder.)

JONATHAN: It's all right, Alison. We'll soon have you back with us. *(calls)* Miracle! Do you think she can hear me?

MIRACLE: Oh, I doubt it. But it's worth trying; you never know.

(MIRACLE takes the Popsicle-stick 'wand' in both hands, wiggles it; it holds firm.)

There! That will do.

(MIRACLE hands the wand to JENNIFER.)

(JONATHAN rests a hand on ALISON's shoulder.)

JONATHAN: Just a little longer, Ali.

JENNIFER: That's a wand?

MIRACLE: It will be. When I enable it.

(JENNIFER holds the wand out for MIRACLE to take.)

No! It's your wand. A temporary wand. A magician can own only one. Now: hold it out toward me. Keep it horizontal.

(MIRACLE steps back and holds his hands out toward the wand.)

MIRACLE: *(continuing)* Abracadabra. Enable new wand!

(Nothing happens; JONATHAN stands beside JENNIFER.)

(MIRACLE addresses the sticks with greater emphasis.)

Abracadabra. Enable new wand!

(The sticks tremble uncontrollably. JENNIFER shrieks.)

JENNIFER: Oh! It's getting warm! Almost hot!

MIRACLE: Good! That means the spell's working.

JONATHAN: *(touching the wand)* But will it work?

MIRACLE: *(to JENNIFER)* Try. Test it.

(JENNIFER holds the wand out to JONATHAN.)

JENNIFER: You do it.

MIRACLE: No, no. A temporary wand can be used only by the person who held it when it was created.

JENNIFER: But…how?

JONATHAN: Bumpy-Bumpy made the seesaw go up and down.

MIRACLE: Alright, try that. Point your wand toward the lower end of the seesaw. Right! Now, say: "Abracadabra. Seesaw: follow my wand."

JENNIFER: Abracadabra. Seesaw: follow my wand.

(Nothing happens.)

MIRACLE: More emotion, my dear. More emotion.

JENNIFER: I'll try. **Abracadabra. Seesaw: follow my wand!** Oh! It's getting warm.

MIRACLE: Lift it up. Slowly.

(The seesaw follows the wand, up and down.)

JONATHAN: It's working!

JENNIFER: Oh, my!

JONATHAN: Cool!

MIRACLE: Right! Now let's put your wand to work.

JONATHAN: You mean, release Alison?

MIRACLE: Definitely.

(JENNIFER stands in front of ALISON, points the wand at her.)

JENNIFER: Like this?

MIRACLE: No, Jennifer. You'll frighten her when she comes to. Stand beside her.

(JENNIFER moves to one side of ALISON.)

JENNIFER: But what do I say?

MIRACLE: What did Bumpy-Bumpy say?

(JENNIFER shakes her head.)

JONATHAN: I think it was: "Abracadabra. Freeze Alison."

JENNIFER: *(points the wand at ALISON)* Abracadabra. Unfreeze Alison.

(ALISON does not move.)

MIRACLE: Hmmm. In the world of wizardry, if we want to undo a spell, sometimes we have to reverse the command. Particularly with a temporary wand.

JONATHAN: You mean, say it backwards?

MIRACLE: Yes.

JENNIFER: All of it?

MIRACLE: Yes. All the words.

JENNIFER: Abracadabra, too?

MIRACLE: Try it.

JENNIFER: Abra is ... er... Arba...

JONATHAN: Arbadac!

MIRACLE: You've got it! Now: "Freeze Alison".

JENNIFER: Freeze... um ... Zeerf?

MIRACLE: Yes, yes!

JONATHAN: Nosila!

JENNIFER: Nosila?

JONATHAN: That's Alison backwards: Nosila.

JENNIFER: It doesn't sound like her!

JONATHAN: Well, it is! And she won't think it's funny.

JENNIFER: Alright.

> *(JENNIFER points the wand at* ALISON.*)*
>
> Arba Arbadac. Zeerf Nosila!
>
> *(The wand shakes in her hand, but* ALISON *does not move.)*
>
> It's warm!

MIRACLE: Do it again! But more emotion this time.

JENNIFER: **Arba Arbadac. Zeerf Nosila!**

> *(The wand shakes violently.* ALISON *starts to move;* JENNIFER *places both hands on the wand.)*

JENNIFER: I can't hold it!

> *(The wand flies to the ground;* ALISON *freezes again;* JENNIFER *rubs her hands together.)*

MIRACLE: You'll need some help.

> *(The "help" comes from* JONATHAN *and the audience, who chant the words with* JENNIFER. *The following sequence needs some ad-libbing.)*
>
> *(*MIRACLE *walks downstage, faces the audience.)*
>
> Can you help us unfreeze Alison?
>
> *(*MIRACLE *acknowledges the response, then turns to* JENNIFER.*)*
>
> Point your wand toward the rocks, over there.

JENNIFER: Will it be cool enough?

MIRACLE: Oh, yes. It'll be fine.

> *(JENNIFER picks up the wand, points it at the rocks.)*
>
> Now say this after me: Abracadabra.

JENNIFER: Backwards?

MIRACLE: No. This time you're giving a new command.

JENNIFER: Okay. Abracadabra.

MIRACLE: Make two signs.

JENNIFER: Make two signs.

MIRACLE: Now you have to say what kind of signs you want: "Arba Arbadac."

JENNIFER: Arba Arbadac.

MIRACLE: "Zeerf Nosila."

JENNIFER: Zeerf Nosila.

MIRACLE: Now say all of it.

JENNIFER: *(points the wand at the rocks)* Abracadabra. Make two signs: Arba Arbadac, Zeerf Nosila.

(There is a growing whooshing sound. Two large pieces of card fly in from behind the rocks and land midstage.)

JONATHAN: It worked!

(JONATHAN and MIRACLE each pick up a sign. Miracle's sign says "Abracadabra" on one side and "Arba Arbadac" on the other; Jonathan's sign says "Freeze Alison" on one side and "Zeerf Nosila" on the other; the words are in audience-readable-size letters.)

MIRACLE: *(to JONATHAN)* I'll need your help too.

(MIRACLE walks to downstage center right and points to downstage center left.)

You stand there.

(MIRACLE turns to the audience in front of him.)

All of you on this side, you have to say "Abracadabra" backwards, like this.

(He holds up the sign showing Abracadabra, then turns it around.)

"Arba Arbadac." Try it: Arba Arbadac.

(Audience response.)

That's fine, but we need more emotion! Again: Arba Arbadac.

MIRACLE: *(continuing)* Good! *(to* JONATHAN*)* Now you.

JONATHAN: *(to the audience in front of him)* All of you on this side, I want you to say "Freeze Alison" backwards.

*(*JONATHAN *holds up the sign "Freeze Alison," then turns it around.)*

"Zeerf Nosila." Say it with me: Zeerf Nosila.

(Audience response; he looks at MIRACLE.*)*

Is that all right?

MIRACLE: Louder, I think.

JONATHAN: *(to audience)* Can you do it again? Zeerf Nosila.

(Audience response. JONATHAN *turns to* MIRACLE.*)*

How was that?

MIRACLE: Fine! So now we're ready. Jennifer: you give the commands—not too quickly—and we'll all say it with you.

(He gestures to the audience.)

Are you ready?

(Audience response; he turns back to JENNIFER.*)*

MIRACLE: Right, Jennifer! Point your wand at Alison. Now say it.

JENNIFER: Arba Arbadac. Zeerf Nosila!

*(*MIRACLE *and* JONATHAN *say the words with her and encourage the audience to say the same.* ALISON *starts to move but freezes again.)*

MIRACLE: Once more. Louder this time! Lots of emotion!

JENNIFER: **Arba Arbadac. Zeerf Nosila!**

*(*ALISON *unfreezes and looks up at the tree.* MIRACLE *and* JONATHAN *applaud.)*

*(*ALISON *digs into the basket, picks up a second sandwich pack, and holds both packs aloft.)*

ALISON: See, Bumpy-Bumpy! We brought our own sandwiches. Lots of them!

28

BUMPY-BUMPY: *(voice over)* It doesn't matter anymore! Not now!

(ALISON lowers the sandwiches into the cooler.)

JENNIFER: *(to* MIRACLE) Why is she…?

MIRACLE: *(to* JENNIFER *and* JONATHAN*)* Alison doesn't know she has missed anything. *(to* ALISON*)* You were asleep, my dear: just for a little while.

ALISON: Asleep?

MIRACLE: It was a spell. It will never happen again.

ALISON: Oh. I didn't feel anything.

(The tree branches shake.)

JONATHAN: Bumpy-Bumpy's trying to escape!

JENNIFER: Oh, no!

*(JONATHAN *and* JENNIFER *run to the tree.)*

ALISON: *(to* MIRACLE*)* Is it okay?

MIRACLE: He can't harm you now. He's lost his power. Come on.

JONATHAN: *(calls up into the tree)* You'd better come down now, Bumpy-Bumpy.

BUMPY-BUMPY: *(voice over)* Oh, no. No way.

ALISON: We won't hurt you.

BUMPY-BUMPY: *(voice over)* Uh-uh!

MIRACLE: Then we will have to bring him down. Or rather, you will, Jennifer.

JENNIFER: But what do I say?

MIRACLE: What do you think?

JENNIFER: "Come down"?

MIRACLE: To where?

JONATHAN: You could send him to Nodnol.

ALISON: Nodnol?

MIRACLE: Nodnol is London, said backwards. To undo a spell, Jennifer has to say the instruction backwards. *(to* JENNIFER*)* Somewhere closer, I think.

JENNIFER: How about Otnorot?

ALISON: Otnorot?

JENNIFER: That's Toronto. Backwards.

ALISON: A-h-h. I see…

JONATHAN: I think Wen Kroy would be better.

ALISON: Wen Kroy?… Umm… New York!

> *(They laugh.)*

> No. I think we should send him to Wocsom.

JONATHAN: Wocsom?

ALISON: Moscow!

MIRACLE: Oh, well done, Alison. *(to* JENNIFER*)* No, I think we'll just bring him down here.

JENNIFER: So I say: "Come to me"?

> *(*MIRACLE *nods;* JENNIFER *rehearses.)*

> Arba Arbadac. Ipmub-Ipmub Muck oot eem!

MIRACLE: Perfect! But you'll need help. Let's make two more signs.

JENNIFER: Okay! *(points her wand toward the rocks)* Abracadabra. Make two signs: Ipmub-Ipmub, Muck oot eem!

> *(The whooshing noise builds, the wand shakes and two signs fly in from behind the rocks and land center stage.)*

ALISON: That's so cool!

> *(*JONATHAN *picks up "Ipmub-Impub" and* ALISON *picks up "Muck oot eem." * ALISON *holds up her sign.)*

ALISON: "Muck oot eem." That's "Come to me."

JONATHAN: *(holds up his sign)* And "Ipmub-Ipmub" is Bumpy-Bumpy backwards.

MIRACLE: *(to the audience)* We need your help again. On this side I'll be Abracadabra.

(MIRACLE holds up the sign "Arba Arbadac.")

Jonathan will take the middle, and Alison will take all of you on that side.

(JONATHAN moves downstage center; ALISON moves downstage left.)

Now, let's rehearse.

>> The rehearsal is ad-libbed here, as before, and then: <<

MIRACLE: Jennifer, back away from the tree a bit, to get a better angle.

(JENNIFER backs about 2 meters [8 feet] and points the wand at the upper branches of the tree.)

JENNIFER: *(to JONATHAN)* Are you ready?

JONATHAN: Yes. Ready.

JENNIFER: You, too, Ali?

ALISON: Ready.

BUMPY-BUMPY: *(voice over, stage left)* But I'm not!

JONATHAN: You don't have a choice, Bumpy-Bumpy.

BUMPY-BUMPY: *(voice over)* I don't like this at all.

MIRACLE: Jennifer will try to bring you down gently. Won't you Jennifer?

JENNIFER: I don't know how, but I'll try.

MIRACLE: That's the idea.

JENNIFER: *(gestures to the audience)* Are all of you ready?

(Audience response.)

Right, then! Let's do it.

(She continues in unison with the actors and audience.)

Arba Arbadac. Ipmub-Ipmub: Muck oot eem! *(speaking alone)* Gently, if possible.

(The wand shakes and the leaves and branches move. There is a crash and a cloud of dust rises from the ground at the foot of the tree.)

BUMPY-BUMPY: *(voice over)* Ouch! Oh, my leg.

JENNIFER: Jump on him!

(ALISON and JONATHAN feel for and then jump on the [imaginary] invisible Bumpy-Bumpy. They face each other, spaced some 1.3 meters [4 feet] apart.)

BUMPY-BUMPY: *(voice over)* Oh-h-h.

JONATHAN: I've got his legs!

ALISON: I'm holding his hands.

BUMPY-BUMPY: *(voice over)* Oh, my bum hurts!

MIRACLE: Jennifer: can you fetch my cloak? Please.

(JENNIFER fetches the cloak, hands it to MIRACLE. He holds it in front of the "invisible" BUMPY-BUMPY who, hidden by the cloak, crawls in and lies down between JONATHAN and ALISON.)

When I place my cloak over him, I want you to jump on it and hold him down. Ready?

ALISON: Ready!

JONATHAN: Okay!

(MIRACLE lowers his cloak and ALISON and JONATHAN jump on it.)

BUMPY-BUMPY: Oh, ouch! Let me out!

MIRACLE: Not quite yet, my lad. *(to JENNIFER)* Can you make him visible again?

JENNIFER: I think so. I say: "Make Bumpy-Bumpy visible"?

MIRACLE: You've got the idea!

ALISON: But backwards, surely?

MIRACLE: Quite right, my dear.

JENNIFER: *(to herself, practicing)* Arba Arbadac. Kame… Ipmub-Ipmub…elbisiv. *(to MIRACLE)* I think I've got it.

32

MIRACLE: Excellent.

(JENNIFER *moves to the side of* JONATHAN *and* ALISON, *and points the wand at the cloak.*)

JENNIFER: **Arba Arbadac. Kame Ipmub-Ipmub elbisiv!**

(*The wand shakes and the cloak bumps around.*)

Is he there?

(JONATHAN *and* ALISON *each lift a corner of the cloak.*)

JONATHAN: Yes!

ALISON: I can see a hand.

MIRACLE: Good. Lift off the cloak.

(*They stand and do so, revealing a now pathetic* BUMPY-BUMPY *lying on the ground.* JONATHAN *holds the cloak.*)

Stand up, my boy.

(BUMPY-BUMPY *does so, painfully.* MIRACLE *takes his wand from him.*)

I don't think you will need this any more.

BUMPY-BUMPY: I'm sorry, Miracle. I'm really sorry.

MIRACLE: I think you should be saying that to your friends, don't you?

BUMPY-BUMPY: Sorry...sorry.

MIRACLE: Especially Alison.

BUMPY-BUMPY: Sorry, Alison.

ALISON: I didn't feel anything. Really I didn't.

BUMPY-BUMPY: Well...

MIRACLE: *(to* JONATHAN*)* Let me have my cloak.

(MIRACLE *slips his arms into the cloak and slides his wand into a pocket.*)

Now, I have an idea. But first, Bumpy-Bumpy, will you sit beside the picnic cooler? Go on!

(BUMPY-BUMPY *shuffles to the cooler.*)

33

(MIRACLE *turns to the other children.*)

MIRACLE: *(continuing)* You know, I think you've all earned an ice cream. Why don't you come with me?

(JONATHAN, ALISON and JENNIFER ad-lib acknowledgment and move toward upstage right.)

(BUMPY-BUMPY stands up and is about to follow.)

(MIRACLE rests a hand on JENNIFER's arm.)

One more thing before we go. Jennifer, will you point your wand at the picnic cooler. Go on! I want you to say: "Abracadabra. Stay."

JENNIFER: Backwards?

MIRACLE: No. You're opening an instruction.

JENNIFER: *(nods, points the wand)* Abracadabra. Stay.

MIRACLE: Again.

JENNIFER: **Abracadabra. Stay!**

(A spotlight above stage center illuminates the cooler, Bumpy-Bumpy, and about 3 feet around him.)

MIRACLE: Good! I felt the spell go through. Come on.

ALISON: What was that for?

JENNIFER: What does it do?

MIRACLE: A-h-h. You'll see. Later.

(MIRACLE and the three CHILDREN exit.)

(BUMPY-BUMPY starts to follow but stops at the edge of the spotlit area [he has bumped into an invisible wall]. He feels the wall, and pats it to left and right.)

BUMPY-BUMPY: Oh, no. Oh, no! I'm trapped.

(BUMPY-BUMPY reaches up as high as he can, but still feels the wall. He sinks to the ground and reaches into the cooler.)

I guess I might as well have one of those sandwiches. *(he takes a bite.)* Ugh! Liver sausage. I hate liver sausage!

34

(The lights dim briefly to indicate a passage of time. When they come up BUMPY-BUMPY *is sitting with his elbows resting on the closed cooler and his chin resting on his hands.)*

*(*MIRACLE *and the three* CHILDREN *enter carrying partly eaten candy bars.)*

MIRACLE: Well, my friends, it's time I was on my way. But two things before I go. First: what you have seen today remains only with the four of you: you are to tell no one else. Can you promise me that? Jonathan?

(As Miracle speaks, ALISON *walks toward* BUMPY-BUMPY*, holding an unopened chocolate bar out to him. He reaches for it, their hands almost touch, and then her hand bumps into the barrier. She reaches up, feels the barrier, and shrugs.* BUMPY-BUMPY *nods, sits.* ALISON *returns to the group.)*

JONATHAN: Oh, yes. I'll tell no one.

MIRACLE: Alison?

ALISON: Oh, yes, Miracle. And, really, I didn't see everything.

MIRACLE: Jennifer?

JENNIFER: Who would believe me!

MIRACLE: Bumpy-Bumpy?

BUMPY-BUMPY: Yes, definitely. Never, never.

MIRACLE: Good. If word gets out, I'll know right away. Then I'll make myself invisible and leave on the next Greyhound bus for Calgary. Now, you wouldn't want that, would you?

(The CHILDREN *laugh, say "No," "Definitely not," "You're our friend," etc.)*

MIRACLE: Now, Jennifer, I think it would be best if I disable your wand.

JENNIFER: Oh. Do you have to?

*(*JENNIFER *holds the wand out to* MIRACLE.*)*

MIRACLE: No, you hold it. *(he strokes the wand lightly)* Arba Arbadac. Elbasid tub eno erom lleps.

JONATHAN: Abra Cadabra... Disable ... but I didn't get the rest.

MIRACLE: You will. *(to* JENNIFER*)* Actually, your wand is still enabled. I've allowed you just one more spell. One wish. But only one!

JENNIFER: Oh, that's wonderful, Miracle! Thank you.

MIRACLE: Use it wisely, mind.

JENNIFER: Oh, I will.

MIRACLE: Just be careful, because as soon as you use it, the wand will automatically disable. You will never be able to use it again.

*(*JENNIFER *nods in agreement)*

So, good-bye, my friends. May I visit you again, when you are on another fishing expedition?

(The CHILDREN *respond with "Good-bye, Miracle," "Thanks for ice cream/chocolate bar," and "Oh, yes!" etc., as* MIRACLE *shakes* JONATHAN'*s and then* ALISON'*s hand; When he turns to* JENNIFER, *she jumps forward and gives him a hug.*

*(*MIRACLE *walks through the 'invisible wall' and shakes* BUMPY-BUMPY'*s hand.)*

Don't lose your sense of fun, Bumpy-Bumpy! Just know how to contain it.

BUMPY-BUMPY: Oh, I will. I promise.

*(*MIRACLE *crosses to stage left, lifts an arm in a brief wave, and exits. [If possible, there will be a puff of smoke and he will disappear.])*

*(*ALISON *and* JONATHAN *crowd around* JENNIFER.*)*

ALISON: Now *you're* a magician!

JENNIFER: Well, hardly...

(During the following conversation, BUMPY-BUMPY *feels his way around the wall. Then he sits beside the picnic cooler, rests his head on his hands, and watches the others.)*

ALISON: *(to* JENNIFER*)* So, what are you going to wish for?

JONATHAN: New fishing tackle? For all of us?

JENNIFER: Oh, I don't know. Miracle didn't say how soon I have to use it.

ALISON: How about that puppy you've always wanted?

JENNIFER: Oh, yes! That's a great idea!

JONATHAN: What a waste! You can go to the Pound and get a puppy for nothing.

ALISON: No you can't. You have to pay for the pup's shots.

JENNIFER: I wouldn't mind a new bike. *(to* ALISON*)* That Norco I showed you at the Bike Center last week.

ALISON: The one with the mileage and speed thing built into the handlebars?

JENNIFER: My parents would never buy me a bike like that.

JONATHAN: A bike's a bike! Go for a smartphone, like the new Nabuchi.

JENNIFER: Can I watch movies on it?

JONATHAN: Sure you can! You could include a voucher for twenty movie rentals into the wish.

ALISON: Make it a hundred!

JENNIFER: No. What I'd really like is an airline ticket, so I could visit my sister in New Zealand.

ALISON: See her new baby?

JENNIFER: Oh, yes. I'd love to do that.

JONATHAN: Just you? Not your parents?

JENNIFER: Well, yeah I guess…

ALISON: A family holiday?

JENNIFER: Yeah, but then I wouldn't be sharing it with you.

ALISON: It's *your* wish, Jen.

JENNIFER: Not really. We were all involved.

JONATHAN: D'you want my opinion? I think we should put it to a vote. *(points to the audience)* See what they think.

JENNIFER: Ask *them*?

ALISON: They helped us before.

(Some ad-libbing may be necessary in the following sequence. One of the young actors may have to ask for the house lights to come up.)

JONATHAN: *(to the audience)* How many of you think Jennifer should wish for a smartphone, like the new Nabuchi? Put your hands up.

(He counts quickly.)

About … *(says the number).*

(ALISON steps forward.)

ALISON: My turn! How many of you would like Jennifer to wish for that new bike: the special one?

(ALISON counts quickly.)

Hmmm… about *(says the number).*

(JENNIFER steps forward.)

JENNIFER: Do you think I should wish for the airline tickets? See my sister in New Zealand?

(She counts quickly and says the number.)

JONATHAN: So it looks like you're going to wish for…. *(he inserts words to match the largest count).*

JENNIFER: Shall I do it then?

JONATHAN: You heard what they said. *(to the audience)* You agree, don't you? Jennifer should make her wish? Now?

(JONATHAN encourages the audience to respond. He turns to JENNIFER.)

There!

(BUMPY-BUMPY jumps up and feels the walls. ALISON notices.)

(NOTE: At this point the dialogue can go in one of two directions. If someone in the audience shouts that Bumpy-Bumpy is still trapped, the dialogue between the two horizontal lines below is omitted and the cast ad-lib a response.)

(If no child in the audience shouts out a warning, then the following occurs.)

JENNIFER: Okay.

(She faces the audience, holds the wand out in front of her, speaks loudly.)

Abra Cadabra. I wish for—

ALISON: *(shouts)* No! You can't!

(JENNIFER and JONATHAN turn toward ALISON.)

ALISON: Look at Bumpy-Bumpy: he can't get out!

JONATHAN: Oh, yes, he can. You saw Miracle: he walked straight up to Bumpy-Bumpy.

(JONATHAN walks toward BUMPY-BUMPY, bumps into the invisible wall, and falls back.)

How did Miracle do that?

ALISON: He's a magician, Jonathan. A wizard! *(to JENNIFER)* No, Jen. I'm sorry. *This* has to be your wish.

JENNIFER: You mean, Bumpy-Bumpy?

BUMPY-BUMPY: Can you let me out?

JONATHAN: Should we? *(it's a joke)*

ALISON: I guess we have to.

JENNIFER: Miracle's a lot smarter than I thought! I don't really have a spell of my own, do I?

(Slight pause.)

JONATHAN: What did Miracle have you say, when you zapped the cooler?

JENNIFER: Just one word: "Stay."

ALISON: Did you say Bumpy-Bumpy's name? Or "picnic cooler"?

JENNIFER: N-o-o-o.

JONATHAN: Then you have to say just the one word, but backwards.

JENNIFER: I'll try.

(JENNIFER points the wand at BUMPY-BUMPY.)

Arba Arbadac. Yates! Did that do it?

(BUMPY-BUMPY puts a hand on the "wall," shakes his head.)

JONATHAN: Miracle kept saying "More emotion."

JENNIFER: Right! *(steps back and points the wand at BUMPY-BUMPY)* **Arba Arbadac. Yates!** *(The wand shakes in her hand.)* Oh!

(The spotlight extinguishes.)

(BUMPY-BUMPY feels for the invisible wall by sticking a foot outside the 'enclosure,' then leaps forward, throwing his hands in the air.)

BUMPY-BUMPY: Yeh!

(JONATHAN and ALISON run to him, grab his hands; all three are laughing, dance around; simultaneously, the lights dim but a spotlight comes up on JENNIFER, who holds up a single Popsicle stick in each hand. She shakes her head in wonder.)

JENNIFER: Just two Popsicle sticks…!

(The lights dim to black.)

E N D

Character Sketches

Jennifer

Jennifer is an outgoing, happy young woman, always ready with a smile and a genuinely cheerful greeting. As a student she shines, and particularly in debating and drama. Yet normally she does not push herself forward, preferring to be an active member of the debating team and drama group rather than be the leader.

Jennifer is quietly adventurous, always ready to try new approaches when making presentations and preferring to be around or with people rather than on her own. Occasionally she tends to act and speak spontaneously without thinking too closely about the possible outcome, sometimes with an unexpected result that surprises her.

Alison

Alison also is a cheerful young woman, but in a much more reserved way. At first, newcomers think she is shy; yet once she gets to know and accept a new friend, she becomes a very true companion. She enjoys life, but inwardly more than outwardly.

She is a B+ student, but she has to work hard to achieve it. She tends to think a problem or a situation through very carefully before making a decision or voicing her opinion. She does not like, even inadvertently, to do or say anything that might hurt someone's feelings. She is admired (and liked) for her sensibility and sensitivity.

Jonathan

Jonathan is a soccer player and an ardent supporter of the local soccer team. He is outgoing, adventurous, and definitely not a "stay at home and read a book" person. This does not imply he does not like reading; it just means he is very particular in his choice: he especially likes books that focus on computer games.

He loves fishing, but not on his own: he prefers to share the adventure with his special friends. He is loyal, open-minded, trusting, and fairly outspoken – sort of midway between Jennifer and Alison. He is particularly friendly with Alison, whom he trusts and respects for her stability and fairness. Jonathan is easy-going and takes life as it comes.

Bumpy-Bumpy

His real name is Bertrand Bermandson, which several years ago his friends shortened to the nickname "Bumpy-Bumpy." The name has stuck ever since, and he does not mind.

Bumpy-Bumpy is mischievous, but in a nice way. Adults who do not know him tend to think he is a bit of a truant, which is not so, although Bumpy-Bumpy tends to promote the image. He is not a particularly good student, not because he is incompetent but because he is *bored* with the sometimes dull way that interesting subjects are taught at school.

He loves to question and to conduct experiments (he does better in Science than most other subjects), and often he pushes himself into apparently extravagant or unnecessary situations, because his mind keeps questioning why and how. He likes his three friends because they accept him the way he is, whereas many other children—and particularly their parents—think he is a bit of a ragamuffin. (His nickname does not help!) In some ways he is quite shy, but intentionally acts boisterously so as not to let it show.

Miracle the Magician

Miracle is an unusual magician/wizard, because he has always maintained a low profile. He is very skilled, and proud of his skills. Even though he is in his 60s, he has not until this year felt that his age is depriving him of some of his capabilities as a wizard.

He is well-educated and has a strong control of the language: he speaks carefully and thoughtfully, and rarely lets himself become flustered. He is particularly fond of children and his lack of pretentiousness means he relates well with them; he has taken a particular liking to the four friends he has just acquired. He is charmed by Jennifer's smile and openness, by Alison's reserve and genuine friendliness, by Jonathan's outgoing personality, and even by Bumpy-Bumpy's mischievousness.

Production Notes

The first production of *The Popsicle-Stick Wand* occurred as an entry into a one-act play festival on the Island of Guernsey in the British Channel Islands. The UK setting required some script emendations to "fit" the location, with the primary change being made to the play's title. Because Popsicles are not known in the UK, and Lolly's are (they also are on a stick), I changed the title to *The Lolly-Stick Wand*. Other changes were made in the names of towns and beaches, using some names from within the island itself, and some from mainland England (for example, 'Toronto' was changed to 'Cobo Bay' and became 'Oboc Yab'). The children's names, and that of the magician, remained the same.

Creating the magic effects was simple in some cases and more difficult in others. For example, commanding the wand to dim and then bring up the streetlamp was achieved by having the stage manager operate an off-stage dimmer control. But making the seesaw (teeter-totter) rise up and down on its own required a more innovative approach.

The seesaw was constructed with one end slightly lighter than the other, so that when the seesaw was at rest the lighter end would always be elevated. To the higher point we attached a black piece of fine fishing line, which hung straight down to a ring set in a black-painted piece of wood that protruded out from the black curtain at the back of the stage. The fishing line was then fed to a second ring, offstage, behind the curtain, where the stage manager could pull on it to make the seesaw rise and fall. (The seesaw had to be positioned well upstage to achieve this, but still needed space for actors to walk between it and the back curtain.) To help create the illusion of magic, and distract the audience from thinking the seesaw axle was cranked from behind the stage, early in the play we had two of the actors walk right around the seesaw and then ride it in a natural way.

When Bumpy-Bumpy is supposedly "invisible," the actor stands behind stage and speaks from stage left or right when he is supposedly on one side of the stage or the other. For the moments when he is supposed to be at the back of the audience, we installed a loudspeaker behind the last row (or under a vacant seat) and covered it with a heavy cloth to conceal it and partly muffle the words. The actor then spoke into a behind-stage microphone. We created a similar effect when Bumpy-Bumpy was in the tree.

Adults frequently ask me why I chose the strange name of "Bumpy-Bumpy" for the mischievous boy. (It's interesting that children never question the name: they just accept it as being perfectly natural.) So, for the benefit of adults accompanying a young audience, its derivation is described in the dialogue.

I chose the name "Alison" for the girl who would be 'frozen,' so that when the audience would help unfreeze her, it would be easy to convert it to the backward version: *Nosila.* This would have been less easy with Jennifer's name, because backwards it would have been *Refinnej.*

An unexpected outcome also evolved as the seven performances at the Winnipeg Fringe Festival progressed. After the closing scene, children in the audience would run up to the actors, who would still be on stage, and ask questions about saying their own names backwards. Then some parents wrote reviews of the play, in which they specifically commented on how their children—and soon their children's friends—tried reversing many words in their vocabularies. They also mentioned that children were asking their parents to buy Popsicles, which they devoured quickly so they could make their own wands!

I was fascinated by how well the young actors, both in Guernsey and Winnipeg, adapted to their roles and how well they played them. Early in the rehearsals I found that during ordinary conversation they were referring to each other by their character names. I found this an invaluable approach, especially when having to give sometimes critical advice.

The big "unknown" was how effectively the young actors playing Alison and Jonathan (who in the Guernsey production was only 9), would be able to work the audience when they had to encourage them to help Jennifer give her commands. I need not have worried!

I was astounded by their professionalism, both in Guernsey and Winnipeg, when they stepped to the front of the stage, one on each side, with the large-letter signboards in their hands, and confidently persuaded the audience to help. My reaction was echoed by the Festival Adjudicator in the UK, who when commenting on the performance said this:

> "The sequence in which Jonathan and Alison 'worked' the audience and persuaded them to chant the spells could be a hazardous business at the best of times, let alone when playing in a drama festival. But it was done with great aplomb by the two young performers, who demonstrated a confidence in working with their audience that most adults would find hard to muster."

He then awarded the Elaine Ralls Memorial Trophy to Jack Lucas and Adele Sales, for creating the magic moment during the Festival that most captured his and the audience's attention. That, to me, was a magic moment in itself!

Preparing for the Contest

In **Battle of the Wands,** *the four children have to demonstrate to Miracle the Magician how well they can perform magic tricks. Alison (played by Alysha Barrie) has "frozen" Jonathan (Scott Austin) and now has to bring him back to his normal self.*

Author photo

Play No. 2

Battle of the Wands
Return of the Popsicle-Stick Wand

Synopsis

One year has passed since Miracle the Magician first met Alison, Jennifer, Jonathan and Bumpy-Bumpy (in Play No. 1), and since then they have become fast friends, have met frequently, and have had many adventures together. Now, however, Miracle has decided it is time to retire, and he wants to appoint someone to take his place, someone to become "Miracle the Magician 2." Not surprisingly, he can think of no better person to be his replacement than one of his four friends (any one of them).

So he invites them to meet him at the beach where they first met. When they arrive, he tells them there is to be a contest, and each is to show him how well they can perform a magic trick with four new Popsicle-stick wands he will help them make.

But Miracle's great-niece Savannah arrives, decides she is entitled to be his successor, and ruins the tricks the contestants are trying to perform. When Bumpy-Bumpy discovers what she is doing, he challenges her to a "Battle of the Wands."

The ensuing battle proves who really is entitled to become Miracle the Magician 2.

The Set

The scene is set in a grassy area with an entrance to a beach upstage right and an entrance from a road to the local town upstage left. The stage is bare except for

- three large rocks downstage right,
- a bench-seat upstage right,
- an old-fashioned lamp standard with a lamp at the top, upstage center right,
- a seesaw (teeter-totter) upstage center left,
- a patch of grass (a green carpet—optional) mid-stage left, and

- a folded garden chair, beside the grass, center-stage left.

Note re Location

The director has the option to tailor the production by replacing the names of cities and towns referred to in the play with local names.

Magic Effects

All the magic effects used in the first play will occur again, but there will be more for the sequel: a thunderstorm; a toy bear that climbs a lamp-post; shoes that dance on a bench; and a "visible" invisible boy.

Length of Play: Approximately 50 minutes.

The Characters

Battle of the Wands features the same characters as in *The Popsicle-Stick Wand,* plus one additional young character— Savannah—who is a trouble-maker:

Alison	)
Jennifer	) *ages between*
Jonathan	) *11 and 13*
Bumpy-Bumpy *(male)*	)
Savannah	age 15
Miracle the Magician	age 61

There are brief descriptions of each character, starting on page 96.

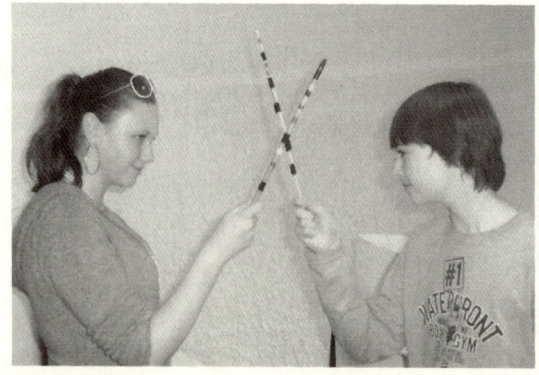

Savannah *(Megan Wilson)* and Bumpy-Bumpy *(Kevin Carruthers)* rehearsing their battle to decide who will become *Miracle the Magician 2*
Author photo

Production History

Jennifer, Alison, Jonathan and Bumpy-Bumpy are now one year older than they are in *The Popsicle-Stick Wand*, and the intervening twelve months have provided them with time, under Miracle the Magician's guidance, to practice their skills in using Popsicle-stick wands to perform magic tricks. Their skill becomes a core feature in the new play.

The two plays were produced successively, one year apart, as part of the *KidsFringe* venue of the *Winnipeg Fringe Theatre Festival*. The first performance of *Battle of the Wands* occurred on July 20th, 2007, with the following cast:

Alison	*Alysha Barrie*
Jennifer	*Lexi Carvey*
Jonathan	*Scott Austin*
Bumpy-Bumpy	*Kevin Carruthers*
Savannah	*Megan Wilson*
Miracle the Magician	*John Chase*

The play was directed by the author.

Some Script Guidelines

Throughout the script, two symbols are used occasionally at the end of a piece of dialogue to indicate how the sentence ends:

- ... An ellipsis at the end of a statement means the speaker just trails off and leaves his or her thought hanging in the air (possibly accompanied by a shrug).

- — a dash at the end of a statement means the speaker is interrupted by the next speaker and the first speaker's statement is incomplete. Sometimes there is an italicized continuation of the statement *(within brackets)* immediately following the dash, to help the actor sense where the sentence was going.

v.o. means 'voice over'

Notes about the production start on page 99.

Script: *Battle of the Wands*
Return of the Popsicle-Stick Wand

© 2006, Ron Blicq

(Before the audience enters, four Popsicle sticks have been placed at different points on stage [only three of which are found by the four children – the fourth is there as a reserve, in case insufficient are drawn later from the audience]. Another seven or eight Popsicle sticks have been placed in the auditorium, around and under the seats, ideally in the first four or five rows.)

(At curtain up the stage is unlit. MIRACLE stands at stage center facing the audience. He raises his arms sideways so that his cloak spreads out like a bat's wings, accompanied by rising music. A spotlight highlights MIRACLE. He lowers his arms and the music fades.)

MIRACLE: Oh, hello, everyone. I doubt whether you have met me before, so let me introduce myself. I'm Miracle the Magician—well, I'm a wizard really—and I came to live in xxxx *(name of local city or town)* just one year ago. That's when I first met four very special people—right over there, by those rocks.

(He points to the rocks stage right.)

Oh! Of course. You can't see them. Can you?

(He pulls a wand from his cloak and points it stage right.)

Abracadabra. Sun: shine on the rocks.

(Lights come up over the rocks and spread full-stage.)

There! That's where I first met Alison, Jennifer, Jonathan and Bumpy-Bumpy – who you will meet today. They are going to perform magic tricks for you. Only they don't know it yet: it's going to be a surprise!

(JENNIFER enters upstage left, reading a letter.)

This is Jennifer, for whom I made a Popsicle-stick wand last year. Hello, Jennifer!

JENNIFER: Oh, hi, Miracle.

MIRACLE: You got my invitation?

JENNIFER: Yes. *(holds up the letter)* What's the special occasion you are talking about?

MIRACLE: Ah! You'll see. When you're all here.

JENNIFER: The others were right behind me.

(JONATHAN and ALISON enter from upstage left, carrying a picnic cooler between them, a drinks flask, and a soccer ball. They place them center stage.)

ALISON: Hi, Miracle. Hi, Jen.

JONATHAN: Hello, Miracle.

MIRACLE: Hello, Alison; hello, Jonathan.

JENNIFER: Where's Bumpy-Bumpy?

JONATHAN: He ran ahead, down to the beach.

ALISON: *(to JENNIFER)* Has Miracle told you why we're here?

JENNIFER: No. He said to wait.

ALISON: Oh.

MIRACLE: As soon as Bumpy-Bumpy is here, then I'll tell you. … Ah! There he is.

(BUMPY-BUMPY enters upstage right. He carries two beach towels, which he lays over the back of the bench. He crosses to the others.)

BUMPY-BUMPY: Hi, Miracle. We're having a picnic?

MIRACLE: You could call it that! But, first, we have some business to attend to.

ALISON: Business?

BUMPY-BUMPY: Magic business?

MIRACLE: In a way.

JONATHAN: Special tricks?

MIRACLE: W-e-l-l. That's up to you.

JENNIFER: Oh, Miracle! Tell us!

MIRACLE: Alright. Perhaps you should sit down.

(MIRACLE *opens up the garden chair and sits in it. The* CHILDREN *sit around him.*)

BUMPY-BUMPY: We're having another party?

JONATHAN: Like the one in July?

ALISON: *(to* MIRACLE*)* You made your own fireworks. With your wand! They were so cool!

(Murmurs of agreement.)

(SAVANNAH *sneaks in from downstage right, hides behind the rocks, and listens.*)

MIRACLE: We'll picnic afterward. First, though, I have to tell you something. You see, I have decided it's time for me to retire and—

JENNIFER: You're retiring?

JONATHAN: You're not going to leave us, are you?

MIRACLE: No, no. Nothing like that. It's just that, before I retire, I have to appoint a new Miracle the Magician. To take my place.

ALISON: Oh, no. We want you.

MIRACLE: It will be someone you know.

(The CHILDREN *ask "We know?" - "Who?" - "Tell us," etc.)*

It will be one of you.

BUMPY-BUMPY: One of us?

MIRACLE: You are my special friends. I know one of you will make a very special magician.

SAVANNAH: Huh!

JENNIFER: Which one?

MIRACLE: That is up to you. There is to be a competition. A contest.

JENNIFER: You want all four of us to enter?

MIRACLE: Absolutely. Any one of you could be the next Miracle the Magician.

ALISON: You mean, you'd want *me* to be a magician?

JENNIFER: Or me?

MIRACLE: Certainly. Or Jonathan. Or Bumpy-Bumpy.

BUMPY-BUMPY: Cool!

JONATHAN: Yeah!

MIRACLE: You are all quite capable.

JONATHAN: What sort of contest?

MIRACLE: Each of you has to show me how good you are at performing magic tricks.

JENNIFER: What kind of tricks?

MIRACLE: That's up to you. You choose.

ALISON: When? When will we—

MIRACLE: Today.

ALISON: Today!

MIRACLE: As soon as you're ready.

JENNIFER: But we don't have any wands!

MIRACLE: What did you do last year? Right here.

BUMPY-BUMPY: Made one from Popsicle sticks!

JONATHAN: Ah!

(JONATHAN stands, turns upstage, searches.)

MIRACLE: You've got the idea, Jonathan!

(Comments from JENNIFER ["Of course!"]), ALISON ["Ah!"], and BUMPY-BUMPY ["Me, too."]. They search. JONATHAN, JENNIFER and BUMPY-BUMPY each find a Popsicle stick, saying "Here's one," or "I've got one." They turn to MIRACLE.)

JONATHAN: There are only three.

ALISON: I haven't even got one!

JENNIFER: What do we do now?

MIRACLE: You're on your own, my friends. You can't ask me. I'm the judge.

(Pause. In a concerted movement both BUMPY-BUMPY *and* JONATHAN *each offers his Popsicle stick to* JENNIFER.*)*

BUMPY-BUMPY: Here, take mine.

JONATHAN: At least we have enough to make one wand.

*(*JENNIFER *takes* BUMPY-BUMPY*'s stick.)*

JENNIFER: Thanks.

MIRACLE: You'll need this.

*(*MIRACLE *pulls a roll of tape from his cloak and hands it to* ALISON.*)*

ALISON: Thank you, Miracle. *(to* JENNIFER*)* Okay: now overlap the two ends.

*(*BUMPY-BUMPY *and* JONATHAN *continue to search.* ALISON *binds the tape around the sticks, tests its strength, and hands it back to* JENNIFER.*)*

MIRACLE: Now, let me enable it. Hold it out in front of me.

*(*BUMPY-BUMPY *and* JONATHAN *return.* MIRACLE *holds his hands over the wand.)*

Abracadabra: Enable Jennifer's wand!

JENNIFER: Oh! It's warm. Almost hot!

MIRACLE: Then it's enabled.

JENNIFER: Oh, that's awesome, Miracle.

JONATHAN: Do we have to share it?

MIRACLE: Oh, no. You each must have your own.

ALISON: But how?

MIRACLE: Find more Popsicle sticks.

ALISON: There aren't any!

MIRACLE: Have you looked everywhere?

(Slight pause. BUMPY-BUMPY *points to the audience.)*

BUMPY-BUMPY: Maybe they have some?

(The CHILDREN *address the audience.)*

JONATHAN: Would any of you have a Popsicle stick with you?

(They wait for an answer.)

ALISON: Look around your seat, will you?

JENNIFER: Wait a minute.

*(*JENNIFER *points her wand at front row center and slowly raises it.)*

Abracadabra. House lights: come on!

(The house lights come on as her wand rises.)

JONATHAN: Your wand works, Jen!

BUMPY-BUMPY: *(to the audience)* Can you see if there's a Popsicle-stick under your seat?

(Some ad-lib here, as the audience finds Popsicle sticks and the four CHILDREN *go in to retrieve them. There are remarks like: "Oh, that's cool!", "That's great!" "Another one!" "Thank you."* JONATHAN, ALISON *and* BUMPY-BUMPY *work together with children in the audience, to assemble and tape their wands: "Hold both ends," "Get the tape tight," "Keep them still," etc.)*

ALISON: Miracle: could you enable mine? Please.

MIRACLE: Right. I'll do them all together. Hold them out in front of me.

*(*MIRACLE *holds his hands over the three wands.)*

Abracadabra. Enable three Popsicle-stick wands.

ALISON: Mine's warm!

JONATHAN: So's mine!

MIRACLE: Then they're enabled.

BUMPY-BUMPY: Mine isn't. It's still cold.

MIRACLE: Hmmm. *(examines the wand)* Let's try again.

(BUMPY-BUMPY *holds the wand out in front of* MIRACLE.)

MIRACLE: *(continuing)* **Abracadabra. Enable Bumpy-Bumpy's wand!**

BUMPY-BUMPY: Wow! It's hot!

MIRACLE: Good! That means it's strong. Now: test it.

BUMPY-BUMPY: Sure.

(BUMPY-BUMPY *walks to center downstage, points the wand high in the auditorium, then lowers it slowly.)*

Abracadabra: Dim the house lights.

(The house lights dim in concert with the wand's movement.)

It works! Thanks, Miracle.

MIRACLE: *(to* ALISON *and* JONATHAN*)* Alright, you two. Test yours.

JONATHAN: Right.

(JONATHAN *crosses to center stage, points his wand to the foot of the street lamp.)*

Street lamp, get bright!

(Nothing happens. JONATHAN *shakes his wand at the lamp.)*

Get bright!

(Nothing happens.)

SAVANNAH: Hah!

ALISON: *(in a half-whisper)* Jonathan: haven't you forgotten something? The command words!

JONATHAN: A-h-h! Abracadabra! Abracadabra. Lamp: get bright!

(The lamp brightens as JONATHAN *raises his wand.)*

Now, lamp get dim.

(The lamp dims and extinguishes.)

It works, Miracle! Thanks.

ALISON: Now it's my turn.

(ALISON walks to center upstage and faces the seesaw. She points her wand at it and raises it slowly.)

Abracadabra. Seesaw: follow my wand.

(The seesaw rises slowly and then drops gently back onto the ground. The other CHILDREN clap.)

JENNIFER: That's cool, Ali!

SAVANNAH: *(in a stage whisper to the audience)* They think that's clever? Just wait!

MIRACLE: Right! You're set. Off you go. Decide what you are going to do. Surprise me! And be back here in 45 minutes.

(The CHILDREN exchange farewell remarks with MIRACLE ["See you later," "'Bye, Miracle," "Okay."] JONATHAN and ALISON exit upstage right. JENNIFER and BUMPY-BUMPY exit upstage left. As they exit they converse [and continue v.o.].)

ALISON: *(to JONATHAN)* Have you got any idea what you will do?

JENNIFER: *(to BUMPY-BUMPY)*: Are you going to make yourself invisible again?

JONATHAN: *(to ALISON)* Not yet. What about you?

BUMPY-BUMPY: *(to JENNIFER)* Maybe. I need to think it out.

ALISON: There's so little time!

(MIRACLE settles back in his chair, closes his eyes and starts to nap.)

(SAVANNAH gets off her knees, brushes herself off, and tucks one end of her wand into her boot.)

SAVANNAH: *(to the audience)* Now it's my turn.

(SAVANNAH crosses to MIRACLE, who does not hear or see her approach.)

Hi.

(MIRACLE does not respond.)

I said "Hi."

MIRACLE: Oh, hello. *(slight pause)* You live around here?

SAVANNAH: Not exactly.

MIRACLE: What do you mean: "Not exactly?" You either do, or you don't. Live here.

SAVANNAH: You do. I know.

MIRACLE: That didn't answer my question.

(Pause: he looks questioningly at SAVANNAH.*)*

SAVANNAH: You don't recognize me?

MIRACLE: I can't say I do…

SAVANNAH: You should!

MIRACLE: On what grounds?

SAVANNAH: I'm your niece.

MIRACLE: I'm afraid I don't have— *(any recollection of…)*

SAVANNAH: Well, actually, your great-niece.

MIRACLE: With the emphasis on "great?"

SAVANNAH: Of course!

MIRACLE: Ah! I see. Then you must be my sister Marina's grand-daughter: Savannah.

SAVANNAH: Right! You got it in one!

MIRACLE: I haven't seen you since you were… just a baby!

*(*SAVANNAH *shrugs.)*

So, to what do I owe the honor of this visit?

SAVANNAH: Well…it's because—

JONATHAN: *(calls, v.o.)* Miracle! Are you still here?

MIRACLE: Over here, Jonathan.

*(*JONATHAN *runs in from upstage right.)*

JONATHAN: Can I ask you a question?

MIRACLE: Certainly. But first let me—

JONATHAN: I've had a brilliant idea! Absolutely brilliant!

MIRACLE: Whoa! One thing at a time. First let me introduce you to Savannah.

JONATHAN: Oh! I'm sorry. I didn't mean to interrupt.

MIRACLE: No. I know. That's all right.

SAVANNAH: It is?

MIRACLE: Savannah: I'd like you to meet my friend Jonathan.

SAVANNAH: *(to JONATHAN)* Oh, hi! *(to MIRACLE)* Your friend?

MIRACLE: Oh, yes. Definitely. *(to JONATHAN)* And, Jonathan, I'd like you to meet Savannah.

JONATHAN: Hi, Savannah.

MIRACLE: Savannah's my niece.

SAVANNAH: Great-niece, actually.

MIRACLE: With the emphasis on *great!*

(MIRACLE and SAVANNAH laugh.)

JONATHAN: I didn't mean to…. Would you like me to come back? Later?

MIRACLE: No, no. That's fine. All right with you, Savannah?

SAVANNAH: *(shrugs)* As he's your friend.

(Pause.)

MIRACLE: Alright, Jonathan. Out with it. What's this brilliant idea?

JONATHAN: Is it all right to…? *(implies "is it okay to say it in front of Savannah?")*

MIRACLE: Ah! Savannah: can you give us a moment?

SAVANNAH: Uh … Yeah. Sure.

MIRACLE: Thank you my dear. Just sit over there. On the rocks.

(SAVANNAH crosses to stage right, sits, listens. MIRACLE moves to stage left with JONATHAN.)

Now: out with it!

JONATHAN: Yeah. Well, for the competition, is it okay for me to make a thunderstorm?

MIRACLE: A real one? A real thunderstorm?

JONATHAN: Over there. Above the bench.

MIRACLE: I can't see why not. Try it.

JONATHAN: Now?

MIRACLE: Absolutely!

JONATHAN: Alright.

> (JONATHAN *steps toward stage right, raises his wand, and points it to high upstage right.)*

Like this?

MIRACLE: You're doing fine.

JONATHAN: Abracadabra. Make a thunderstorm!

> *(Nothing happens..)*

MIRACLE: A little more emotion, I think.

JONATHAN: Right. **Abracadabra. Make a thunderstorm!**

> *(The lights dim stage right, there is a crash of thunder, lightning, sound of wind and rain. MIRACLE and JONATHAN have to shout to be heard.)*

Wow! Look at that!

MIRACLE: Magnificent, my boy!

> *(MIRACLE peers to upstage right, into the storm.)*

Whoever is that?

> *(ALISON enters upstage right, holding an umbrella over her head. She is bent over as though forcing her way into the wind, which turns the umbrella inside out. She struggles with it and finally gives up. She sees MIRACLE and JONATHAN, starts to walk toward them, and mid-stage steps out of the storm [a lamp makes her clothes look wet.]. She reaches a hand back into the storm.)*

ALISON: Oooh!

(ALISON pulls her hand back, turns, and points to the storm.)

ALISON: *(continuing)* How come?

(MIRACLE cups a hand around his ear. He, ALISON and JONATHAN have to shout at each other.)

Why are you dry, and it's raining over here?

MIRACLE: You'll have to ask Jonathan. *(to JONATHAN)* Can you make Alison dry?

JONATHAN: How do I do that?

MIRACLE: How did you make the thunderstorm?

JONATHAN: Of course!

(JONATHAN points his wand at ALISON.)

Abracadabra. Make Alison dry.

(There is a momentary light flash and the "wet" lamp extinguishes from over ALISON. She pats her clothes.)

ALISON: How did you do that?

JONATHAN: With my wand!

ALISON: That's so cool!

MIRACLE: You can stop the storm now.

JONATHAN: Okay.

(JONATHAN points the wand to high stage right; shouts)

Abracadabra, Stop the storm!

(Nothing happens.)

(SAVANNAH laughs. JONATHAN shouts louder.)

Abracadabra! Make the thunderstorm stop!

(There is no change. MIRACLE waits for JONATHAN to remember how to give an 'undo spell' command.)

(SAVANNAH points her wand at the storm, speaks loudly and authoritatively.)

SAVANNAH: Arba Arbadac. Ekam rednuth pots!

(The storm fades away, with a final grumble. The sun shines on the full stage. SAVANNAH *turns to the audience.)*

SAVANNAH: *(continuing)* There!

*(*SAVANNAH *holds her wand up, waves it about, turns to* JONATHAN.*)*

You see!

JONATHAN: *You* did that?

SAVANNAH: Sure did!

ALISON: Miracle made you a Popsicle-stick wand, too?

SAVANNAH: No way! This is my own wand.

JONATHAN: You're a wizard? A real one?

SAVANNAH: Of course! I am a member of the magician fraternity.

MIRACLE: You really should have let Jonathan do that. He would have worked it out.

SAVANNAH: It was too noisy. And I was bored.

ALISON: *(to* JONATHAN*)* That's what you'll be doing in the competition?

JONATHAN: I guess. I know it works!

SAVANNAH: If he can stop it!

ALISON: He'll work out how. Just you— *(wait and see)*

SAVANNAH: Who do you think you are?

ALISON: I'm Alison.

MIRACLE: One of my four good friends.

SAVANNAH: Armed with a Popsicle-stick wand!

ALISON: It's a good one!

MIRACLE: In fact, it's a very good one. This is my niece, Alison: Savannah.

JONATHAN: Actually she's Miracle's great-niece, with the emphasis on "great"!

MIRACLE: Enough! *(to* SAVANNAH*)* From now on, we'll just say you're my niece.

*(*SAVANNAH *turns away.)*

(to ALISON*)* My intuition tells me you want to ask a question. Right?

ALISON: Y-e-s-s. *(inclines her head toward* SAVANNAH*)*

MIRACLE: In private?

*(*ALISON *nods.* MIRACLE *places a hand on one of* SAVANNAH*'s shoulders, the other on* JONATHAN*'s.)*

Can you give Alison a little space?

JONATHAN: Sure.

*(*JONATHAN *walks toward the rocks.* SAVANNAH *doesn't move.* MIRACLE *gives her a push.)*

SAVANNAH: Oh, if you insist!

*(*SAVANNAH *shrugs and follows* JONATHAN. *They sit on the rocks.)*

ALISON: Would it be all right...? Safe, do you think? For me to freeze someone? So they can't move?

MIRACLE: Like Bumpy-Bumpy did to you, when we first met?

ALISON: Yeah. Sort of.

MIRACLE: You want to get your own back, on Bumpy-Bumpy?

ALISON: Oh, no. Nothing like that.

MIRACLE: You're not planning to do it to me?

ALISON: No, Miracle. Your magic powers are too strong. You'd resist!

MIRACLE: *(points to the rocks)* On one of them?

ALISON: Sure. But not on Savannah. She might...

MIRACLE: Resist?

ALISON: Yeah. Do you think my wand has enough... *(she shrugs)*

MIRACLE: Power?

ALISON: Yeah.

MIRACLE: If you believe it has – really believe – then it will have. You want to give it a try?

(ALISON nods.)

Jonathan!

(JONATHAN crosses to stage left.)

Alison wants to explain something to you. *(to* ALISON*)* I'll keep Savannah occupied.

ALISON: Oh, yes. Please.

(MIRACLE sits on the rocks and moves SAVANNAH *over so* s*he faces away from Alison.)*

Jonathan: will you…? Can I…? Can I try a spell on you?

JONATHAN: What kind of spell?

ALISON: Remember, last year, after we met Miracle—

JONATHAN: Bumpy-Bumpy froze you! With Miracle's wand.

ALISON: D'you think I could do it with my wand?

JONATHAN: On me?

ALISON: I never felt a thing.

(JONATHAN shakes his head.)

Really I didn't.

JONATHAN: This is for the competition?

ALISON: I have to know if it'll work.

JONATHAN: Well… alright.

(JONATHAN stands in front of ALISON.*)*

Go on. Do it.

ALISON: No. Not like that. You've got to be moving.

JONATHAN: You mean like this?

(JONATHAN does an over-emphasized dance, flinging his arms and legs about.)

ALISON: No. Slower.

JONATHAN: Like in slow motion?

ALISON: Sort of.

JONATHAN: Like I'm climbing a ladder?

(JONATHAN acts as though climbing a ladder.)

ALISON: Yeah. That's good.

(ALISON points her wand at JONATHAN.)

Abracadabra. Freeze Jonathan.

(JONATHAN continues climbing).

JONATHAN: You know what Miracle says: "More emotion!"

ALISON: Okay. **Abracadabra. Freeze Jonathan!**

(JONATHAN stops in mid-motion, absolutely still.)

It worked!

(ALISON walks around JONATHAN, looking for movement.)

You're not pretending are you? Are you teasing me?

(She waves her hand in front of his face.)

I did it! I think I did it!

(She circles around JONATHAN, checking on his frozen stillness.)

Now: to bring him back….

(She points her wand at him.)

Abracadabra. Unfreeze Jonathan.

(Nothing happens.)

Hmmm… More emotion: **Abracadabra. Unfreeze Jonathan!**

(Nothing happens.)

Oh, no!

(ALISON stands face to face with JONATHAN.)

ALISON: *(continuing)* Jonathan! Can you hear me? Are you teasing me? Please, Jonathan!

(She looks across at MIRACLE, *speaks in a whisper.)*

Miracle?

*(*MIRACLE does *not hear the call, but* SAVANNAH does*; she steals a glance at* ALISON *and laughs.)*

No! I've got to do this myself. What did that Savannah say when she stopped the thunderstorm? Something like "Rednuth." Rednuth something …

*(*ALISON *walks around* JONATHAN, *muttering.)*

Rednuth… Rednuth... Rednuth. I've got it! Rednuth is Thunder backwards! I remember now: Miracle said, to undo a command, you have to say it backwards! Abracadabra… that's, umm, Arba….Arba Arbadac. Now, Freeze. That's… Zeerf. *(laughs)* Yes! Arba Arbadac, Zeerf. Now, Jonathan… oh, dear, Jonathan's difficult. Jon. That's "Noj." Athan… Umm… "Natha." So, Jonathan is "Nathanoj!" … Arba Arbadac. Zeerf Nathanoj.

*(*ALISON *stands in front and partly to one side of* JONATHAN. *She points her wand at him.)*

Now, let's try it. Arba Arbadac. Zeerf Nathanoj!

*(*JONATHAN *makes a slight movement, then stops.)*

More emotion, I guess. **Arba Arbadac. Zeerf Nathanoj!**

*(*JONATHAN *makes a bigger movement, then stops.)*

*(*SAVANNAH *snickers.)*

*(*ALISON *hears the snicker and glances across at* SAVANNAH *and* MIRACLE. SAVANNAH *gives her an 'I know what you are up to' wave.)*

Ugh! I'm going to need some help. But not from over there! No, *I've* got to do it.

*(*ALISON *faces the audience.)*

Can you help me? Please?

(She waits for, and if necessary encourages, a response.)

ALISON: *(continuing)* Look: I need you to say the unfreeze command with me. Will you do that? ... Oh, thank you.

(ALISON moves to stage left.)

Okay, let's try. On this side, I want you to say "Abracadabra" backwards. That's "Arba Arbadac." Say it with me: Arba Arbadac. Once more, I think. Can you give it more emotion? **Arba Arbadac.** That was great!

(ALISON crosses to stage right, faces the audience.)

Now it's your turn. I want you to say "Freeze Jonathan," but you have to say it backwards. Like this: Zeerf Nathanoj. Can you say it with me? ... Zeerf Nathanoj. Oh, that was good. Just once more, but a little louder this time: Ready? **Zeerf Nathanoj.** Awesome!

(ALISON stands beside JONATHAN, points her wand at him, and addresses the audience.)

Now, let's unfreeze Jonathan. Ready? Say it with me: *(to the audience at stage left)* **Arba Arbadac,** *(to the audience at stage right)* **Zeerf Nathanoj.**

(JONATHAN continues 'climbing the ladder'.)

Jonathan! Jonathan! You can stop now!

JONATHAN: Huh?

ALISON: You can stop. You're unfrozen now!

JONATHAN: I was frozen?

ALISON: You sure were!

JONATHAN: I was waiting for you to freeze me. I didn't feel anything.

ALISON: That's how it was for me, last year. I didn't even know I was frozen. *(points to the audience)* They helped me. *(to each side)* Thank you. Thank you.

JONATHAN: It's so weird. I can hardly believe it. So now you're ready for the competition?

ALISON: We both are! Let's go find Jennifer and Bumpy-Bumpy. See what they're planning.

(JONATHAN and ALISON *exit upstage left.* MIRACLE *is still seated.* SAVANNAH *stands in front of him. She adopts a confrontational stance and speaks strongly.*

[During the following sequence MIRACLE *rises and they continue their confrontation mid-stage.])*

SAVANNAH: You're going to choose the new Miracle from one of those inexperienced, wimpish little kids?

MIRACLE: They're neither wimpish nor little, Savannah.

SAVANNAH: When you've got an experienced magician right in your own family?

MIRACLE: Yes, my sister. Your grandmother.

SAVANNAH: *No*! Anyway, she's retired.

MIRACLE: Then who?

SAVANNAH: You know perfectly well.

MIRACLE: I do?

SAVANNAH: Of course you do. Me!

MIRACLE: Have you ever given me any reason to *want* to choose you? You have never visited me before.

SAVANNAH: Just watch this! I can do *two* tricks at the same time:

(SAVANNAH stands mid-stage facing the audience, with the lamp and seesaw behind her. She points her wand to half way between the lamp and the seesaw. Without looking behind her, she raises the wand slowly.)

Abracadabra. Lamp and seesaw: go up!

(The lamp gets brighter and one end of the seesaw rises while the other drops.)

Now, go down.

(SAVANNAH slowly lowers her wand. The lamp extinguishes and the end of the seesaw drops.)

See! Those precious little brats of yours can hardly do one. And with Popsicle-stick wands! Mine is real!

MIRACLE: Why have you never come to see me before?

SAVANNAH: I've always been there!

MIRACLE: That's not what I asked you.

SAVANNAH: I didn't know you were going to retire.

MIRACLE: So that's the only reason you've chosen—

SAVANNAH: I'm here, aren't I?

MIRACLE: Savannah: I have the absolute right to choose my own successor.

SAVANNAH: I can do much more with this *(she waves her wand)*, and much better than—

MIRACLE: My mind is made up.

(MIRACLE looks into the wings, upstage left.)

SAVANNAH: You think so? I can do three tricks at the same time. Watch this.

(MIRACLE raises his hand.)

MIRACLE: Come: we are about to be interrupted.

(MIRACLE places a hand on SAVANNAH's shoulder. She shrugs it off. They exit downstage right.)

(BUMPY-BUMPY and JENNIFER enter upstage left. Under one arm Jennifer carries a large teddy bear (or a fluffy toy animal) with long arms or paws; in the opposite hand she holds her wand.)

JENNIFER: Good. No one here.

BUMPY-BUMPY: What d'you need the bear for?

JENNIFER: You'll see.

(JENNIFER sits the bear at the base of the lamp-post. As she steps back, the bear topples over backward.)

Oh, no!

(JENNIFER sits the bear again.)

Sit, bear!... Please!

(JENNIFER steps back and again the bear falls backward.)

BUMPY-BUMPY: Wrap the bear's paws around the lamp-post.

JENNIFER: What good will that do?

BUMPY-BUMPY: Like this.

(BUMPY-BUMPY squats in front of the lamp-post. He wraps the bear's paws around the post in a horse-shoe hold. [At the same time, he is hooking a black cord onto the bear's head—or Jennifer takes his place and does it, using her body to shield a view of the bear from the audience]. JENNIFER steps about 2 meters [6 feet] to the side, to stage left.)

JENNIFER: Is this far enough?

BUMPY-BUMPY: About right, I should think. Do you need me to help?

JENNIFER: No. Just watch.

(BUMPY-BUMPY stands back from the lamp-post.)

BUMPY-BUMPY: Okay. Try it.

(JENNIFER points the wand at the top of the lamp-post.)

JENNIFER: Abracadabra. Lamp: get bright!

(The lamp lights up.)

BUMPY-BUMPY: Why d'you need the light on?

JENNIFER: You'll see!

(She points her wand at the bear.)

JENNIFER: Abracadabra. Bear: climb the lamp-post!

(As JENNIFER raises her wand, the bear moves up the post and stops at the top.)

BUMPY-BUMPY: That's cool, Jen!

(SAVANNAH has entered stealthily from downstage right and crouches behind the rocks. She watches.)

JENNIFER: Abracadabra. Bear: blow out the light!

(Nothing happens.)

BUMPY-BUMPY: More emotion, Jen.

JENNIFER: Like Miracle said! I remember. **Abracadabra. Bear: blow out the light!**

70

(There is a whooshing sound and the lamp goes out.)

JENNIFER: *(continuing)* **Abracadabra. Bear: now slide down the lamp-post!**

(The bear slides down the lamp-post.)

BUMPY-BUMPY: That's brilliant, Jen!

JENNIFER: You think so?

BUMPY-BUMPY: Miracle will be so impressed!

SAVANNAH: Hah! *(to the audience)* Not when he sees what I'll do to her precious bear!

BUMPY-BUMPY: You want to do it again?

JENNIFER: No, thanks. I don't want to overstress my wand.

SAVANNAH: That won't take much!

(JENNIFER picks up her bear, tucks it under her arm.)

JENNIFER: So, what are you going to do?

BUMPY-BUMPY: Well, after what I did last year—

JENNIFER: The invisibility trick?

BUMPY-BUMPY: *(waves his wand)* I thought it would be neat to—

JENNIFER: Not on me!

BUMPY-BUMPY: No. Same as before.

JENNIFER: On Alison?

BUMPY-BUMPY: No, no.

JENNIFER: On yourself? You'll be invisible?

BUMPY-BUMPY: Yeah. But I want to do it differently this time. Watch this.

(BUMPY-BUMPY crosses to upstage left and turns to face JENNIFER, who follows him.)

Not too close!

(JENNIFER backs away.)

(BUMPY-BUMPY points the wand at his chest.)

Abracadabra. Make me invisible!

(He twirls, there is a 1.5 second blackout accompanied by a crash of symbols, and he disappears [offstage left].)

JENNIFER: Where are you? Bumpy! Where are you?

(She searches with her hands.)

BUMPY-BUMPY: *(from offstage left)* I'm here, Jen.

JENNIFER: Don't play tricks, Bumpy. Please!

BUMPY-BUMPY: Just stand still. I need to talk to them first.

JENNIFER: Them? Who?

BUMPY-BUMPY: The audience.

JENNIFER: Why?

BUMPY-BUMPY: Just wait.

*(*BUMPY-BUMPY *enters downstage left. He wears an ankle-length hooded cloak, which is wrapped around him. He faces the audience.)*

BUMPY-BUMPY: Can you see me? *(pause)* **Can you see me?**

*(*BUMPY-BUMPY *waits for a response.)*

Say it louder, so Jennifer can hear. Say: "I can see you, Bumpy-Bumpy."

(He waits for a response, then turns to JENNIFER.*)*

Did you hear that, Jen?

JENNIFER: Yes. But *I* can't see you.

BUMPY-BUMPY: That's my new trick. You can't see me, but they can.

JENNIFER: But where are you?

BUMPY-BUMPY: Right in front of you.

*(*JENNIFER *takes a nervous step back.)*

Reach out with your hand. A bit more to the left. No, your right. A bit further.

*(*JENNIFER *touches* BUMPY-BUMPY*'s chest, recoils.)*

It's only me, Jen.

JENNIFER: It's weird.

BUMPY-BUMPY: Stand quite still.

> (BUMPY-BUMPY *holds his hand six inches in front of* JENNIFER*'s eyes.)*

> I'm holding my hand up in front of your face. Can you see it?

JENNIFER: *(takes a step back)* No.

SAVANNAH: Not bad. *(to audience)* But I can do better.

JENNIFER: Who said that?

> (SAVANNAH *ducks her head down.)*

> (BUMPY-BUMPY *looks around, sees no one.)*

> Bumpy? Are you still there?

BUMPY-BUMPY: Yes. I haven't moved.

JENNIFER: Did you say something about you can do it better?

BUMPY-BUMPY: No.

JENNIFER: I heard a voice...

BUMPY-BUMPY: There's no one there, Jen.

JENNIFER: There is. There is! I didn't imagine it, Bumpy.

BUMPY-BUMPY: Wait.

> (BUMPY-BUMPY *turns to the audience.)*

> Did you hear anything?

> *(He waits for a response, which probably will be a muted "Yes".)*

> You did? Did you *see* anyone?

> (SAVANNAH, *faces the audience and holds her hands up negatively in front of her face, palms out.)*

> ALISON *and* JONATHAN *enter from upstage left. They cross to* JENNIFER *without looking downstage right.)*

JONATHAN: So that's where you are!

ALISON: We were looking for you.

JENNIFER: It was *you* I heard! Did you say— *("I can do it better?")*

JONATHAN: Have you seen Bumpy-Bumpy?

JENNIFER: Yeah. He's inv…. He was here a moment ago.

(BUMPY-BUMPY *walks up to* ALISON *and then to* JONATHAN. *He waves a hand in front of each face.)*

ALISON: Are you ready for the competition?

JENNIFER: Sure. I think so.

ALISON: Bumpy-Bumpy, too?

JENNIFER: Oh, yes. Oh, yes!

JONATHAN: What are you doing with that teddy bear?

(BUMPY-BUMPY *grabs one arm of the bear and pulls on it.* JENNIFER *pulls back.)*

JENNIFER: Stop that, bear! It's not time yet!

ALISON: You're making it do that?

JENNIFER: No! It does it on its own!

(JENNIFER *thrusts the bear at* JONATHAN.*)*

Here! You hold it.

(JONATHAN *hesitates.* JENNIFER *lets go of the bear.* BUMPY-BUMPY *grabs it and lowers it to the floor.* JONATHAN *reaches for it and* BUMPY-BUMPY *makes it swoop upward and around* JENNIFER, *and then come back down to the floor. [Some of this has to be improvised].)*

JONATHAN: What have you done to it? Is that what you practiced!

(JENNIFER *laughs.* BUMPY-BUMPY *leaps the bear to* JONATHAN*'s chest and lets go.* JONATHAN *grabs the bear and speaks to it.)*

Did Jennifer teach you to do that?

(BUMPY-BUMPY *reaches in front of* ALISON *and pulls her wand from her hand. He holds it aloft about half a meter in front of her. He turns to the audience.)*

BUMPY-BUMPY: Ssshh!

(ALISON reaches for her wand but BUMPY-BUMPY makes it dance in front of her.)

ALISON: My wand!

JENNIFER: You should control it better! Grab it before it gets away from you.

(ALISON reaches for the wand, but it dances away.)

It's got a mind of its own, Ali!

(ALISON chases after the wand as BUMPY-BUMPY dances it about, until he holds the wand still, in the air above her, for her to retrieve. He picks up Miracle's garden chair, turns to the audience with a 'Ssshh!' motion, then dances across the floor, waving the chair in front of JONATHAN and ALISON. BUMPY-BUMPY places the chair behind JENNIFER, runs around her, and pushes her back into it.)

JONATHAN: It's Bumpy-Bumpy!

ALISON: Of course! Only he would try a trick like that!

(BUMPY-BUMPY runs to upstage left, points the wand at himself.)

BUMPY-BUMPY: Arba Arbadac. Kame eem elbisivni!

(He twirls, there is a cymbal crash, the lights extinguish for 1.5 seconds, and he has vanished [he exits upstage left]. He removes his cloak.)

ALISON: Where's he now?

JENNIFER: Oh, he's … he's coming back, like.

JONATHAN: Trust Bumpy-Bumpy!

(BUMPY-BUMPY enters upstage right.)

BUMPY-BUMPY: Oh, hi. I didn't know you were here.

ALISON: Bumpy! That was you, wasn't it?

JONATHAN: I heard you say "Kame eem… something".

BUMPY-BUMPY: Kame eem elbisivni. Right?

JONATHAN: Yeah, I guess.

BUMPY-BUMPY: That's "Make me invisible," backwards.

JENNIFER: To undo the "Make me invisible" command he used earlier.

(MIRACLE enters upstage left.)

JONATHAN: Hmmm… Kame eem elbisivni … Make me invisible.

MIRACLE: Who said "Make me invisible"?

(Slight pause.)

BUMPY-BUMPY: Uh… that was me.

MIRACLE: Up to your old tricks, eh?

BUMPY-BUMPY: You could say that.

MIRACLE: Well, I'm ready for the contest. Are all of you?

(The four murmur agreement.)

Right, then. Before we start: there are three rules you need to remember.

Rule number one: You will each take a turn, on your own, and you will have exactly five minutes to show me what you can do. Understand?

(There are more murmurs of agreement.)

Rule number two: While one of you is up there, showing what you can do, the other three must sit on the grass and *not* stand up, move about, or interrupt. Agreed?

ALISON: I need Jonathan to help me. Is that all right?

MIRACLE: Yes. Providing he does not speak, or use his wand.

ALISON: Oh, no. He won't need to.

MIRACLE: Rule number three: You may applaud each contestant, but not until they're finished. *(slight pause)* Do you have any questions?

(They shake their heads 'no.' MIRACLE sits.)

MIRACLE: *(continuing)* Right. Then we shall start. But first: sit down, all of you.

(They sit around MIRACLE's *chair.)*

Now, who wants to go first?

(The four look questioningly at each other.)

JONATHAN: All right. I'll be first. Get it over with, then I can watch.

*(*MIRACLE *pulls a stopwatch from his cloak.)*

MIRACLE: All right, Jonathan. Start now.

*(*MIRACLE *clicks the stopwatch.)*

*(*JONATHAN *moves slightly left of center stage, points his wand to high upstage right.)*

JONATHAN: Abracadabra. Make a thunderstorm.

(Nothing happens.)

Uh… More emotion. **Abracadabra. Make a thunderstorm!**

(There is a crash of thunder, and brilliant lights flashing upstage right.)

*(*SAVANNAH, *behind the rocks, raises her wand and points it upstage right.)*

SAVANNAH: *(a stage whisper)* Arba Arbadac. Kame rednuth pots!

(Immediately the thunder and lightning stop. SAVANNAH *points her wand at* JONATHAN.*)*

Arba Arbadac. Elbasid Nathanoj dnaw.

*(*JONATHAN's *wand flies out of his hand. He picks it up, examines it, and raises it again.)*

JONATHAN: Abracadabra. Make a thunderstorm.

(Nothing happens. JONATHAN *shakes his wand, as if trying to give it energy.)*

Abracadabra. Make a thunderstorm!

*(*JONATHAN *examines his wand, shakes his head.)*

(If the audience shouts to JONATHAN *or points to* SAVANNAH, *she turns to the audience and makes a 'No, no!' display with her hands; she may even point her wand at them.)*

ALISON: Miracle! It wasn't like that— *(this afternoon)*

(JENNIFER leans toward ALISON, *a finger to her lips.)*

Oh. Sorry.

JONATHAN: *(to* MIRACLE*)* I'm finished.

MIRACLE: You still have two minutes.

(JONATHAN shakes his head 'no' and sits.)

(JENNIFER opens her hands as though about to applaud, then sees that the others have not done the same and so returns her hands to her lap; awkward pause.)

Well, who wants to be next?

ALISON: I will, I guess.

(ALISON stands, turns to MIRACLE.*)*

I need Jonathan to be my subject.

MIRACLE: That's fine. Tell me when you're ready to start.

(ALISON indicates to JONATHAN *where to stand, roughly center stage. She stands to his stage left.)*

Are you ready?

ALISON: Yes. I want Jonathan to pretend he is climbing a ladder.

(MIRACLE clicks the stopwatch. ALISON *faces* JONATHAN*)*

Start climbing.

(JONATHAN makes motions with his hands and feet as though climbing a ladder. ALISON *raises her wand and points it at him.)*

ALISON: Abracadabra. Freeze Jonathan.

(JONATHAN stops in mid-movement. ALISON *lowers her wand, and waves a hand in front of Jonathan's face.)*

ALISON: *(continuing, to* MIRACLE*)* Jonathan is frozen. Can I have Bumpy-Bumpy up here now?

*(*MIRACLE *nods, signals for* BUMPY-BUMPY *to go.)*

(As BUMPY-BUMPY *stands up,* SAVANNAH *points her wand at* JONATHAN.*)*

SAVANNAH: Arba Arbadac. Zeerf Nathanoj.

*(*JONATHAN *immediately continues 'climbing.')*

ALISON: Oh!

*(*MIRACLE *signals to* BUMPY-BUMPY *to stay where he is.)*

*(*ALISON *raises her wand and points it at* JONATHAN.*)*

Abracadabra. Freeze Jonathan!

*(*JONATHAN *stops in mid-climb.* ALISON *waves a hand in front of his eyes.)*

Whew! *(to* MIRACLE*)* Now can I have Bumpy-Bumpy?

*(*MIRACLE *signals for* BUMPY-BUMPY *to join* ALISON.*)*

*(*SAVANNAH *raises her wand and points it at* BUMPY-BUMPY *when he is half way across to* ALISON.*)*

SAVANNAH: *(stage whisper)* Abracadabra. Freeze Bumpy-Bumpy!

*(*BUMPY-BUMPY *stops in mid-movement; he is completely still.)*

ALISON: Bumpy! I haven't frozen you yet!

*(*SAVANNAH *laughs.)*

Bumpy! Don't pretend! You'll spoil it.

*(*SAVANNAH *laughs again.)*

*(*ALISON *walks around* BUMPY-BUMPY, *waves a hand in front of his face. She turns to* MIRACLE.*)*

I don't understand….

*(*SAVANNAH *points her wand at* BUMPY-BUMPY.*)*

SAVANNAH: Arba Arbadac. Zeerf Ipmub-Ipmub.

(BUMPY-BUMPY continues his move toward center stage. SAVANNAH immediately points her wand at ALISON.)

SAVANNAH: *(continuing)* Arba Arbadac. Elbasid Nosila Dnaw.

(ALISON's wand flies out of her hand and onto the floor.)

BUMPY-BUMPY: *(to ALISON)* How did you get over there? You were over here just now!

ALISON: You were frozen. But I didn't freeze you!

BUMPY-BUMPY: I couldn't have been. *(looks at MIRACLE)* Was I?

(MIRACLE nods.)

You did it, Jen?

JENNIFER: No. Not me!

MIRACLE: No, Jennifer didn't.

ALISON: Then, how....?

(BUMPY-BUMPY looks around the area; he suspects someone is there but does not see anyone.)

(ALISON walks back to the group, is about to sit.)

I've finished, Miracle. That's it for me.

MIRACLE: What about Jonathan?

ALISON: Oh!

(ALISON crosses in front of Jonathan and points her wand at him.)

Arba Arbadac. Zeerf Nathanoj.

(Nothing happens.)

Arba Arbadac. Zeerf Nathanoj!

(Nothing happens.)

My wand doesn't work, Miracle.

MIRACLE: Bring it here.

(MIRACLE examines the wand.)

No. You're right. It has lost its power. And I can't re-enable it. Not until my power builds up.

ALISON: Then I've finished!

(ALISON sits. BUMPY-BUMPY sits on the seesaw. He is constantly looking around.)

MIRACLE: Jennifer: Can you unfreeze Jonathan?

(JENNIFER stands beside JONATHAN.)

JENNIFER: Arba Arbadac. Zeerf Nathanoj!

(JONATHAN resumes climbing. He sees JENNIFER and stops.)

JONATHAN: Why are you...? Where's Alison?

(JONATHAN looks across to the group.)

ALISON: My wand quit on me.

JONATHAN: Oh. Sorry.

MIRACLE: While you're up there, Jennifer, you might as well continue. Is that all right with you, Bumpy-Bumpy?

BUMPY-BUMPY: Sure.

(JONATHAN returns to the group, picks up the teddy bear, and hands it to JENNIFER. He sits.)

JENNIFER: Thank you.

SAVANNAH: A-a-h! *(points her wand at the lamp-post)* Abracadabra. Make lamp-post oily!

(A bright light shines on the lamp-post; it looks shiny.)

Hah! *(to the audience)* That bear sure will have trouble now!

(JENNIFER crosses to the lamp-post, places the bear at its foot, wraps the bear's arms around the post, stands back.)

JENNIFER: I'm ready.

MIRACLE: Right. Start... Now! *(he clicks the stopwatch)*

JENNIFER: Abracadabra. Bear: climb the lamp-post!

(The bear climbs about 12 centimeters (7 inches) up the post, then slides back.)

*(*BUMPY-BUMPY *stands up and stealthily walks downstage left, behind the onlookers, then across the front of the stage.* SAVANNAH *is watching* JENNIFER *and does not notice him.)*

JENNIFER: *(continuing)* Hmmm…more emotion.
Abracadabra. Bear: climb the lamp-post!

(The bear climbs 18 centimeters (10 inches) then slides back.)

*(*SAVANNAH *laughs, points her wand at* JENNIFER.*)*

*(*BUMPY-BUMPY *reaches the rock.)*

BUMPY-BUMPY: *(shouts)* Oh, no, you don't!

*(*SAVANNAH *jumps up.* BUMPY-BUMPY *points his wand at her.).*

Abracadabra: Disable… disable….

JONATHAN: *(stands and shouts)* Her name's Savannah!

BUMPY-BUMPY: Abracadabra. Disable Savannah's wand!

*(*SAVANNAH *leaps behind the rocks, squats down.)*

SAVANNAH: You weren't fast enough!

*(*BUMPY-BUMPY *follows her around the rock, trying to focus his wand on her. She leaps back, runs a zig-zag course and crouches down behind* MIRACLE.*)*

Uncle Miracle! Do something!

MIRACLE: Sorry, Savannah: you're on your own now.

BUMPY-BUMPY: *(to* SAVANNAH, *as they chase)* You spoiled the contest for Jonathan. And Alison. And Jennifer. I'm going to get you for that!

SAVANNAH: With your itsy-bitsy Popsicle-stick wand? Hah!

BUMPY-BUMPY: My wand is much stronger than you think!

(They chase each other around the group.)

MIRACLE: It's up to you, Bumpy-Bumpy. You're on your own, too.

BUMPY-BUMPY: Cool! *(to* SAVANNAH*)* So it's Even-Steven, Savannah. On with the battle!

SAVANNAH: On with the battle!

(During the following sequence, ALISON, JENNIFER and JONATHAN watch, cheer, ad-lib comments to each other. Early in the sequence, JENNIFER fetches her bear and brings it back to the group.)

(MIRACLE watches intently. Privately, he wants Bumpy-Bumpy to win, but he is also interested in seeing how well his great-niece displays her capabilities as a wizard.)

(The exchanges of conversation that follow are built into the chase at appropriate places.)

(Throughout, SAVANNAH and BUMPY-BUMPY move side-to-side and back-and-forth to avoid presenting a stationary target.)

Where did you get that silly name? Bumpy-Bumpy!

(SAVANNAH heads toward the seesaw.)

BUMPY-BUMPY: Too busy now! Tell you later.

(BUMPY-BUMPY trains his wand on SAVANNAH, just as she reaches the seesaw.)

Abracadabra. Savannah…

(Savannah ducks behind the middle part of the seesaw.)

SAVANNAH: You won't get me like that!

(BUMPY-BUMPY runs around the 'down' end of the seesaw. SAVANNAH runs around the 'up' end and uses it to shield herself.)

BUMPY-BUMPY: Why have I never seen you before?

SAVANNAH: Too busy now. Not been here. Tell you later. *(points her wand at BUMPY-BUMPY)* Arba Arbadac. Elbasid…

(BUMPY-BUMPY lifts his end of the seesaw.)

BUMPY-BUMPY: Don't you have anything original to say?

(SAVANNAH leaps onto and sits on the lower end of the seesaw [the stage-left end], then pushes with her feet

83

to make it rise and force BUMPY-BUMPY*'s end down. He in turn jumps on and they push up and down, but have to hang on with both hands so can't use their wands {they try to, but it's too difficult]. Each piece of the following dialogue is linked to an up or down movement.)*

SAVANNAH: Plenty! When I have time.

BUMPY-BUMPY: You ruined the contest!

SAVANNAH: Exactly!

BUMPY-BUMPY: Not fair!

SAVANNAH: In my book it is!

BUMPY-BUMPY: Then you're using the wrong book!

SAVANNAH: No way!

BUMPY-BUMPY: But why? Why are you doing this?

SAVANNAH: I have my reasons.

BUMPY-BUMPY: You didn't give the others a chance!

SAVANNAH: Juvenile stuff!

(As SAVANNAH *comes down she throws herself off the seesaw, runs to the bench, squats behind it, and points her wand at* BUMPY-BUMPY *from around the side of the bench. When* BUMPY-BUMPY's *end of the seesaw drops to the floor, he jumps up and chases after her. As he reaches center stage,* SAVANNAH *levels a command at him.)*

Abracadabra. Freeze Bumpy-Bumpy!

*(*BUMPY-BUMPY *throws himself sideways to the ground by the lamp, levels his wand at her.)*

BUMPY-BUMPY: Abracadabra. Disable Savannah's wand!

*(*SAVANNAH *throws herself offstage right.)*

SAVANNAH: *(v.o.)* You didn't get me!

BUMPY-BUMPY: Oh, I will.

*(*BUMPY-BUMPY *zig-zags to the bench, gingerly looks around, using the bench as a shield.)*

84

BUMPY-BUMPY: *(continuing)* Come out, come out, wherever you are.

*(*SAVANNAH *enters downstage right, creeps stealthily behind [downstage of] the rocks and levels her wand at* BUMPY-BUMPY.*)*

(Ideally, the audience shouts a warning to Bumpy-Bumpy. If there is none, ALISON *shouts to* BUMPY-BUMPY*:* "The Rocks! The Rocks!"*)*

SAVANNAH: Now I've got you! Abracadabra. Freeze Bumpy-Bumpy!

*(*BUMPY-BUMPY *throws himself offstage right.)*

Ugh!

*(*SAVANNAH *turns toward the audience, identifies an empty seat [not next to a small child], and seats herself. She turns to the audience around her and holds a finger to her lips in a 'Sssh!' motion.)*

*(*BUMPY-BUMPY *enters downstage right, looks around, but does not see* SAVANNAH.*)*

(The audience may shout a warning to him. If the audience doesn't, the three CHILDREN *shout and point toward the audience.)*

*(*SAVANNAH *points her wand at* BUMPY-BUMPY. *He dives behind the rocks [upstage of them].)*

You can't zap me here, Bumpy-Bumpy.

BUMPY-BUMPY: Or you me, here!

SAVANNAH: You'll hit the people around me.

BUMPY-BUMPY: You're chicken. Hiding with all those little kids!

SAVANNAH: I can immobilize you easily from here.

BUMPY-BUMPY: That's what you think. Just look behind you! *(slight pause)* **Look!**

*(*SAVANNAH *hesitates.* BUMPY-BUMPY *leaps up, dashes zig-zag to upstage left, swings around, points his wand at his chest.)*

BUMPY-BUMPY: *(continuing)* **Abracadabra. Make me invisible!**

(There is a cymbal crash, the lights extinguish for 1.5 seconds. BUMPY-BUMPY *exits upstage left.)*

(In the following sequence, BUMPY-BUMPY'*s voice comes from an unseen upstage loudspeaker as he counts through the numbers 1 to 20. His voice may be pre-recorded or he may use a lapel mic.)*

All right, Savannah, come out here and finish the battle. I'll give you 20 seconds before I do anything. That's a promise. One…, two…, *(etc)*

(At "5" SAVANNAH *steps onto the stage, looking to left and right.)*

(At "8" BUMPY-BUMPY *enters from upstage left, wearing the grey cloak and mouthing the numbers. To test his invisibility he walks in front of* MIRACLE *and the three seated* CHILDREN, *waves his hand in front of them, then walks up to* SAVANNAH *and waves a hand in front of her face.)*

*(*SAVANNAH *keeps turning, trying to sense where he is. He moves upstage of her, behind her).*

(After "20" is heard from the speaker, BUMPY-BUMPY *speaks in his natural voice.)*

Now, Savannah, it's my turn! Abracadabra—

*(*SAVANNAH *spins around very fast, points her wand in his general direction.)*

SAVANNAH: **Abracadabra! Global command! Make shoes visible!** A-h-h! Now I can see your shoes! I can see where you are!

*(*BUMPY-BUMPY *runs to the rocks, jumps stage right of them, putting them between himself and* SAVANNAH. *He sticks one foot out from behind the rocks.)*

BUMPY-BUMPY: *(calls)* Jennifer! Alison! Can you see my shoe?

JENNIFER: Yes.

JONATHAN: Sure.

ALISON: Yes, I can

> *(BUMPY-BUMPY pulls his foot back. He leans over the rock, keeps his wand trained on SAVANNAH, who has moved upstage and hides behind the bench.)*

BUMPY-BUMPY: *(calls)* Jonathan! Go sit on the seesaw. The bottom end.

> *(JONATHAN looks uncertainly at MIRACLE.)*

Please!

MIRACLE: Alright. *(to JONATHAN)* But you can only sit. Don't say or do anything.

> *(JONATHAN sits on the lower [stage-right] end of the seesaw.)*

BUMPY-BUMPY: Thanks, Jonathan. Watch this, Savannah!

> *(While behind the rock, BUMPY-BUMPY has loosened his shoe laces. He runs swiftly to the seesaw and steps out of his shoes. He places first one on the seesaw in front of JONATHAN, and then the other beside it, as though he has stepped up onto the seesaw, and then "walks" them up to the high end.)*
>
> *(When the shoes are just past the mid-point, BUMPY-BUMPY says:)*

Keep that end firmly on the ground, Jonathan.

> *(JONATHAN looks only to a point about one meter [3 feet} above the shoes.)*
>
> *(When the shoes are at the far end, BUMPY-BUMPY turns them so they are beside each other and face the rocks. He steps away from the seesaw, until he is about one meter downstage of its center.)*

Now, Savannah: I can get you from up here.

> *(SAVANNAH crosses toward the seesaw and points her wand to the high end.)*

SAVANNAH: Oh, no! Now you are an easy target. I can see your shoes! Where you are standing. Abracadabra. Freeze Bumpy-Bumpy!

(BUMPY-BUMPY moves silently stage right. He stops beside the bench, sits on it.)

Bumpy-Bumpy? Are you frozen? ... Is he still there, Jonathan?

MIRACLE: Savannah! You can't talk to Jonathan.

SAVANNAH: Sorry.

(SAVANNAH edges out from behind the rock, walks to the seesaw, looks upward, to above the shoes.)

You are frozen, aren't you?

(BUMPY-BUMPY points the wand at his feet.)

BUMPY-BUMPY: *(stage whisper)* Abracadabra. Make new shoes!

(There is a cymbal crash and a pair of identical shoes slides out from under the bench. BUMPY-BUMPY picks them up and 'steps' them as though he is standing on the bench, facing Savannah. Then he stands to one side and points his wand at SAVANNAH.)

Now it's my turn, Savannah! Abracadabra…

(SAVANNAH, startled, dives behind the seesaw. JONATHAN is now between her and BUMPY-BUMPY.)

No, I can't. I might hit Jonathan.

(BUMPY-BUMPY moves downstage and stands behind the rock.)

(SAVANNAH reaches around the seesaw, points her wand at the bench.)

SAVANNAH: Abracadabra. Freeze Bumpy-Bumpy! **Freeze Bumpy-Bumpy**

(Pause; SAVANNAH walks to mid-stage.)

I think I got him this time!

(BUMPY-BUMPY *steps into a pair of shoes hidden from the audience, beside but upstage of the rock.*)

BUMPY-BUMPY: 'Fraid not, Savannah! *(points his wand toward his feet)* Abracadabra...

(SAVANNAH *thinks the wand is pointed at her. She steps behind the lamp-post.*)

Make me new shoes.

(*There is a cymbal crash and* BUMPY-BUMPY *steps in front [downstage] of the rock, where Savannah cannot train her wand on him. He points to his shoes and addresses the audience.*).

See?

(BUMPY-BUMPY *steps out of the shoes and makes them 'climb' onto the upper rock, where they face inward toward stage center. He walks to downstage left.*)

Now you will have to decide where I am, Savannah.

(BUMPY-BUMPY *points his wand at the bench.*)

Abracadabra. Shoes dance!

(*The shoes on the bench do a small dance.*)

See, Savannah! Which shoes am I standing in?

(SAVANNAH *looks around, edges toward stage center, sees all shoes are pointing at her, then backs toward downstage left.*)

(BUMPY-BUMPY *crosses toward* SAVANNAH. *When he is about 1.5 meters (4 feet) from her, he points his wand and speaks very fast.*)

Abracadabra! Freeze Savannah!

(*As she turns,* SAVANNAH *freezes facing the audience, her wand outstretched in front of her.*)

(JENNIFER *and* ALISON *applaud.*)

(BUMPY-BUMPY *walks around* SAVANNAH, *waves his hand in front of her face, and takes her wand.*)

BUMPY-BUMPY: *(continuing)* You won't need this for a while. Will you, Savannah?

JONATHAN: Can I get up now?

BUMPY-BUMPY: Sure.

JENNIFER: Shall I put her in a cage? Like I did with you, last year?

BUMPY-BUMPY: Oh, yes! Good idea.

JENNIFER: *(to MIRACLE)* Is it okay to do that?

MIRACLE: Yes, my dear.

> *(JENNIFER steps forward and points her wand at SAVANNAH.)*

JENNIFER: Abracadabra. Stay Savannah!

> *(Immediately a glow surrounds SAVANNAH.)*

> *(BUMPY-BUMPY reaches out, tests that the invisible shield is there; the other CHILDREN join him and with their hands test the 'cage.')*

> *(BUMPY-BUMPY lays Savannah's wand just outside the cage, in front of her. He steps back, points his wand at himself.)*

BUMPY-BUMPY: Arba Arbadac. Kame eem elbisivni

> *(There is a cymbal role and BUMPY-BUMPY's robe drops to his feet. He bends down, rolls up the robe, and hands it to MIRACLE.)*

I won't need this anymore!

MIRACLE: I agree.

> *(MIRACLE places the robe under his chair.)*

> *(BUMPY-BUMPY levels his wand at SAVANNAH.)*

BUMPY-BUMPY: Okay, Savannah, now it's your turn. Abracadabra—

ALISON: Are you unfreezing her?

BUMPY-BUMPY: Yes.

ALISON: Then you have to say it backwards: Arba Arbadac.

JENNIFER: Freeze is Zeerf. I can remember that.

JONATHAN: And Savannah is…. um… Hanna… um … Hannavas.

ALISON: She's not going to like that!

(They laugh, echo "Hannavas" several times.)

BUMPY-BUMPY: Sssh! *(points his wand at* SAVANNAH*)* Arba Arbadac. Zeerf Hannavas!

*(*SAVANNAH *continues the turn she was making and points her hand at* BUMPY-BUMPY.*)*

SAVANNAH: Abracadabra, Freeze… Where's my wand?

BUMPY-BUMPY: *(points to it)* Right there, Savannah.

*(*SAVANNAH *lunges for it, crashes her hand against the invisible wall, feels along it.* MIRACLE *stands and walks toward her.)*

MIRACLE: I'm sorry, my dear. You're the victim of your own willfulness.

SAVANNAH: Let me out of here!

MIRACLE: I didn't put you in there.

SAVANNAH: But you can let me out.

MIRACLE: You'll have to ask Jennifer about that.

SAVANNAH: Not me!

MIRACLE: Your choice. *(to the others)* I think this would be a good moment to hold the competition again. Alison, Jonathan: bring me your wands and I'll re-enable them.

JONATHAN: Do it all over again?

MIRACLE: Yes, now there won't be any interference.

ALISON: *(to* JONATHAN *and* JENNIFER*)* Wait! *(to* MIRACLE*)* Can we – Jonathan and Jennifer and me – can we talk to each other? Just for a minute?

MIRACLE: I suppose… if you wish.

(ALISON beckons to JONATHAN and JENNIFER and leads them to the rock, where they huddle.)

(BUMPY-BUMPY looks at them, as though questioning whether he should join them, but ALISON signals him not to.)

SAVANNAH: Ha! They don't want you!

(BUMPY-BUMPY shrugs and sits on the floor outside the invisible cage, directly in front of SAVANNAH. There is a pause, then she sits.)

(hesitantly) I… I'm sorry for what I did.

BUMPY-BUMPY: You are?

SAVANNAH: Yeah, I guess…. Hey: it was good. The battle. You're good. And with a Popsicle-stick wand!

(BUMPY-BUMPY holds up his wand, which is now broken.)

BUMPY-BUMPY: Not any more!

(SAVANNAH laughs. BUMPY-BUMPY reaches as though to pick up her wand.)

I could always use yours.

SAVANNAH: I guess you've earned it.

BUMPY-BUMPY: No. I wouldn't. Ever. *(pause)* You really made me work, you know.

SAVANNAH: And you, me.

(They grin; a complicit grin.)

(The huddle breaks up. JONATHAN, JENNIFER and ALISON gather around MIRACLE.)

ALISON: Miracle: We – Jonathan, Jennifer and I – we don't want another contest.

MIRACLE: You don't?

JENNIFER: We think, after seeing Bumpy-Bumpy—

JONATHAN: What he did—

ALISON: It should be Bumpy-Bumpy—

JENNIFER: He should be the new Miracle.

JONATHAN: If that's all right with you?

MIRACLE: You mean, you three are withdrawing from the contest?

JENNIFER: Oh, yes.

ALISON: Definitely.

JONATHAN: Sure.

MIRACLE: So, you're suggesting I should choose Bumpy-Bumpy to be the new Miracle the Magician?

(THEY nod; murmur agreement.)

SAVANNAH: *(quietly; almost humbly)* Yes, Uncle Miracle. He is good.

MIRACLE: From you, Savannah, that *is* a recommendation! Then, I couldn't agree more.

(With a sense of ceremony, MIRACLE stands, walks over to BUMPY-BUMPY, indicates he should stand.)

Bumpy-Bumpy: here is my wand. I am very pleased to appoint you as "Miracle the Magician Two."

(MIRACLE hands his wand to BUMPY-BUMPY, to the sound of a cymbal roll. JENNIFER, JONATHAN and ALISON crowd around BUMPY-BUMPY, pat him on the back.)

(MIRACLE sits in his chair.)

(BUMPY-BUMPY raises his hands to silence them; he strokes the wand.)

BUMPY-BUMPY: Miracle. I am so honored. You have shown all of us what it is to be an honorable magician. I promise you to do the very best I can, in your image.

MIRACLE: Well said! Now, before I go home this evening I want to see you perform your very first miracle.

(MIRACLE gestures toward SAVANNAH.)

BUMPY-BUMPY: Oh! Oh, of course. *(to ALISON, JENNIFER and JONATHAN)* You think I should?

JENNIFER: Sure.

JONATHAN: Yeah, why not?

ALISON: It's time.

BUMPY-BUMPY: Then I want all of you to help.

> (BUMPY-BUMPY *makes a sweeping gesture to the audience.*)

> Are you ready, Savannah?

SAVANNAH: I'm to be the subject of your first performance?

BUMPY-BUMPY: Yes. And I want you to feel, from now on, you are one of our friends. *(to the other three)* Am I right?

> *(Murmurs of agreement.)*

MIRACLE: Great idea!

> (BUMPY-BUMPY *picks up* SAVANNAH*'s wand. He turns to the audience.*)

BUMPY-BUMPY: To release Savannah from the spell that's holding her in the cage, we have to say "Abracadabra. Stay Savannah," but say it backwards. *(to* JENNIFER*)* The first words are?

JENNIFER: Arba Arbadac. *(to the audience)* I think you all know that by now!

BUMPY-BUMPY: *(to* ALISON*)* And then?

ALISON: Yats. *(pronounced "Yates")* That's backwards for Stay.

> (BUMPY-BUMPY *extends a hand toward* JONATHAN.*)*

JONATHAN: Hannavas.

> *(*SAVANNAH *grimaces.*)*

BUMPY-BUMPY: *(to the audience)* Is everyone ready?

> *(He listens, accepts response.)*

SAVANNAH: Especially me!

> (BUMPY-BUMPY *points his new wand at Savannah.*)

BUMPY-BUMPY: Right. Come and join us, Savannah!
Everyone: **Arba Arbadac. Yates Hannavas!**

(There is a cymbal crash, the cage light goes out, and SAVANNAH steps forward, toward BUMPY-BUMPY.)

(MIRACLE and the three CHILDREN applaud.)

(BUMPY-BUMPY hands SAVANNAH her wand and they, facing each other, raise their wands in a traditional X, then turn to the audience and wave.)

BUMPY-BUMPY and SAVANNAH: *(in chorus, to the audience)* Thank you, everyone!

LIGHTS FADE TO BLACKOUT

Character Sketches

Jennifer

Jennifer is an outgoing, happy young woman, always ready with a smile and a genuinely cheerful greeting. As a student she shines, and particularly in debating and drama. Yet normally she does not push herself forward, preferring to be an active member of the debating team and drama group rather than be the leader.

Jennifer is quietly adventurous, always ready to try new approaches when making presentations; generally, she prefers to be around or with people rather than on her own. Occasionally she tends to act and speak spontaneously without thinking too closely about the possible outcome, sometimes with an unexpected result that surprises her.

Alison

Alison also is a cheerful young woman, but in a much more reserved way. At first newcomers think she is shy; yet, once she gets to know and accept a new friend, she becomes a very true companion. She enjoys life, but inwardly more than outwardly.

She is a B+ student, but she has to work hard to achieve it. She tends to think a problem or a situation through very carefully before making a decision or voicing her opinion. She does not like, even inadvertently, to do or say anything that might hurt someone's feelings. She is admired (and liked) for her sensibility and sensitivity.

Jonathan

Jonathan is a soccer player and an ardent supporter of the local soccer team. He is outgoing, adventurous, and definitely not a "stay at home and read a book" person. This does not imply he does not like reading; it just means he is very particular in his choice: he especially likes books that focus on computer games.

He loves fishing, but not on his own: he prefers to share the adventure with his special friends. He is loyal, open-minded, trusting, and fairly outspoken – sort of midway between Jennifer and Alison. He is particularly friendly with Alison, whom he trusts and respects for her stability and fairness. Jonathan is easy-going and takes life as it comes.

Bumpy-Bumpy

His real name is Bertrand Bermandson, which several years ago his friends shortened to the nickname "Bumpy-Bumpy." The name has stuck ever since, and he does not mind.

Bumpy-Bumpy is mischievous, but in a nice way. Adults who do not know him tend to think he is a bit of a truant, which is not so, although Bumpy-Bumpy tends to promote the image. He is not a particularly good student, not because he is incompetent but because he is *bored* with the dull way that interesting subjects are sometimes taught at their school. He loves to question and to conduct experiments (he does better in Science than most other subjects), and often he pushes himself into apparently extravagant or unnecessary situations because his mind keeps questioning why and how.

He likes his three friends because they accept him the way he is, whereas many other children—and particularly their parents—think he is a bit of a ragamuffin. (His nickname does not help!) In some ways he is quite shy, but intentionally acts boisterously so as not to let it show.

Savannah

Savannah is age 15, nearly 16, and is generally taller than Alison, Jonathan and Jennifer, and about the same height as Bumpy-Bumpy. She tends to be annoyingly precocious, and when people react to her in what she feels is a "negative way," she takes it as a personal challenge; in turn, this makes her feel she is a "loner" and that no one seems to like her.

Savannah's only sibling is a brother called Charleston, who is six years older and was (and still is) a brilliant student. Although Savannah is no dummy, she has continually been faced by relatives, friends and teachers who *expect* her to be a carbon copy of her brother. Consequently, for as long as she can remember, Savannah feels she has been living in Charleston's shadow and not measuring up to the standards he has established.

Savannah has strong opinions and is not afraid to voice them. Because she can be dogmatically defensive when challenged, people tend to think she has "an attitude." This convinces Savannah they "just don't like her," resulting in her sometimes feeling (wrongly) that the world seems to be against her.

Miracle the Magician

Miracle is an unusual magician/wizard, because he has always maintained a low profile. He is very skilled, and proud of his skills. Even though he is over 60, he has not until this year felt that his age is depriving him of some of his capabilities as a wizard.

He is well-educated and has a strong control of the language: he speaks carefully and thoughtfully, and rarely lets himself become flustered. He is particularly fond of children and his lack of pretentiousness means he relates well with them; he has taken a particular liking to the four friends he has known for the past year. He is charmed by Jennifer's smile and openness, by Alison's reserve and genuine friendliness, by Jonathan's outgoing personality, and even by Bumpy-Bumpy's mischievousness.

He has known for a long time that he wants one of the four friends to become his successor—for he trusts all of them. Yet, and he has thought seriously about this, if he were to make an arbitrary choice, it would most likely be Bumpy-Bumpy: Miracle senses that he has the innate capability to become a truly strong magician/wizard. But Miracle wants to be objective and so decides he will set up a competition among the four, so he can judge them equally.

How much does Miracle know about Savannah? Very little. He knows his sister Marina had a daughter, who is not a magician, and that she in turn had two children, one of which has exhibited magician tendencies. He has since heard that it is the girl, Savannah, who is his great-niece. Yet, apart from being present at her Christening nearly 16 years ago, since then Miracle has neither seen nor heard much about her.

Production Notes

The idea to have a second play about Miracle the Magician and his four young friends was generated immediately after the final performance of *The Popsicle-Stick Wand* at the 2006 Winnipeg Fringe Festival. Alysha Barrie, Lexi Carvey, Scott Austin and Kevin Carruthers—who played the four children—simply did not want the characters they had been playing (Alison, Jennifer, Jonathan and Bumpy-Bumpy) to "stop having fun and experiencing unique adventures." Their enthusiasm for a new script to perform at the next (2007) Fringe prompted me to consider what happened during the intervening 12 months. I supposed that Miracle, now in his early 60's, might consider it was time he retired, yet he would like "Miracle the Magician" to continue to exist.

The idea to hold a competition among his four young friends, to identify a potential "Miracle the Magician 2," evolved from that initial thought. Then a second idea crept in: to have a young relative from his family suddenly appear and challenge his decision by asserting what she considers is her right to become the new "Miracle." At that point I knew I had a unique conflict to insert into the story.

That conflict erupted into a battle between the challenger and one of the four children who, as the plot evolved, became the precocious Bumpy-Bumpy. The word "Battle" also became a key word in the play's title.

The same five actors were determined to play the same roles they played in the first play, so all I had to do was find an actor to take on the role of Savannah, the intruder. I was very fortunate in finding Megan Wilson, who was a couple of years older than the original four children and had a strong capability to portray a "nice but nasty" young woman. The audience disliked her intensely, yet found they felt sorry for her. A neat mix!

Creating the magic effects was simple in some cases and more difficult in others. For example, commanding the wand to dim and then bring up the streetlamp was achieved by having the stage manager operate a dimmer control. But making the seesaw (teeter-totter) rise up and down on its own required a more innovative approach.

99

The seesaw was constructed so that one end was slightly lighter than the other; consequently, when the seesaw was at rest that end would always be elevated. To that end we attached a black piece of fine fishing line, which hung straight down to a ring set in a black-painted piece of wood that protruded out from the black curtain at the back of the stage. The fishing line was then fed to a second ring, offstage, behind the curtain, where the stage manager could pull on it to make the seesaw fall and then rise again. (The seesaw had to be positioned well upstage to achieve this, but still needed space behind it for actors to walk between it and the back curtain.) To help create the illusion of magic, and distract the audience from thinking the seesaw's axle was cranked from behind the stage, early in the play we had two of the actors walk right around the seesaw. Later, the seesaw became an integral part of the action.

Having the bear climb the lamp-post was achieved by having a very fine string start at the foot of the lamp-post, run to a loop at the top, through the top of the post to another loop, and then down the back to the foot of the lamp-post, and then along the floor to off-stage back, where it was pulled by the stagehand. That the bear had long arms was important, so they could be wrapped around the post and prevent the bear from swinging outward.

For the pair of shoes that dance on the bench, we inserted a stick through a hole at the back of each shoe, to the inside toe, and then extended it about half a meter (20 inches) beyond the back of the shoe. The stage hand crept behind the bench (where it was essential that the towels Bumpy-Bumpy placed on the bench early in the play fully covered its back) and waggled the sticks up and down to create a dancing effect. We deviated slightly from the script, bringing the shoes directly onto the bench rather than the floor, because the sticks prevented Bumpy-Bumpy from moving the shoes from the floor to the bench seat.

As with the first play, after the final scene children from the audience would crowd onto the stage and ask the actors if they were correctly saying their own names backwards. Cool!

Play No. 3

Puss in Boots

Synopsis

In this new version of the famous fairy tale, Puss overcomes the King's resistance to his daughter's wish to marry Darren, who is Puss's penniless owner/master.

Darren's brother and sister are their usual miserable selves, with the sister being the least likeable. The King is a well-meaning but bumbling man who really does want his daughter to be happy, and the Princess is the sweet person the audience expects her to be. There is the Ogre, of course, but he falls for Puss's sneaky plan and changes himself into a rodent, a role from which he cannot recover. Darren then acquires the Ogre's castle and riches.

Young members of the audience are invited to participate in the action on stage.

The Set

There are three main areas where the story takes place, with most of the action occurring in the central area. Upstage center there is a porch with the front of a house behind it (on a backdrop, since no entrances or exits are required from the house). On or adjacent to the backdrop, middle stage right, is a windmill with, if possible, sails turning. Beside the porch, also stage right, is a somewhat decrepit but usable handcart. To stage left, lit separately, is a small section of the King's palace, with a throne on a dais and drapes behind it. To stage right, also lit separately, is the entrance to the Ogre's castle. (If there are limited resources, the production can be achieved without the windmill and handcart, which are simply referred to during the play.)

Special Effects

If facilities exist, special effects can comprise a handcart in which the wheel becomes damaged and then repairs itself, a windmill that has revolving sails (one of which falls off), and a sack that self-inflates. Alternatively, the effects can be simple with, in the case of the sack, an empty sack being replaced with a full one. Some 15 to 20 cushions are required for the final scene, to form a bed for Puss.

Before each performance, four children in the audience need to be prepared to carry a prop onto the stage as part of the action during the play. This means the stage manager, or an appointee, has to be at the front of the house to identify children of a suitable age, and to approach them to see if they are willing to take part. Those who do are given one of the following props to carry with them when they take their seats:

- Two children each carry one of Puss's long boots.
- One child carries Puss's sombrero-like hat.
- One child carries Puss's sack (empty).

Ideally, selecting the children is done without other audience members noticing. Similarly, it's wise to have each of the four props concealed in a bag, so that neighboring audience members do not notice them and ask questions.

There are more suggestion in the Production Notes, page 132.

Length of Play: Approximately 50 minutes.

The Characters

The play can be performed with as few as 5 or as many as 7 actors. The characters are:

> Puss, *(ageless)*
> Darren, *18*
> Phoebe *(Darren's sister), 28*
> Karl *(Darren's brother), 30*
> The King, *50*
> Princess Marina, *17*
> The Ogre, *(ageless)*

Ideally, Puss, Darren and Marina are played by teen-age actors, and Phoebe, Karl, the King, and the Ogre by adults. (It's feasible to have Karl, the King, and the Ogre played by the same actor, thus reducing the cast to 5.) Alternatively, the cast can be composed entirely of young actors with age ranges between 9 and 16.

The actor playing Puss needs to be agile and able to cavort and tumble comfortably, even able to be acrobatic. The Ogre should be very tall, if necessary wearing platform boots.

The characters are so well known there is no need to provide histories or biographies for them.

Production History

The first production of this version of *Puss in Boots* was by Fantasy Theatre for Children, in the Forrest Nickerson Theatre, Winnipeg, Canada, from October 13th to 19th, 2008. The cast comprised:

Puss	*Ryan McMahon*
Darren	*Jordon Macklin*
Marina	*Meagan Cloutier*
Phoebe	*Samantha Arnold*
Karl	*Jeff Wahl*
The King	*Gordon Sangster*
The Ogre	*Jeff Wahl*
Director	*Tony Frost*

Some Script Guidelines

Throughout the script, two symbols are used occasionally at the end of a piece of dialogue to indicate how the sentence ends:

- ... An ellipsis at the end of a statement means the speaker just trails off and leaves his or her thought hanging in the air (possibly accompanied by a shrug).

- — A dash at the end of a statement means the speaker is interrupted by the next speaker and the first speaker's statement is incomplete. Sometimes there is an italicized continuation of the statement *(within brackets)* immediately following the dash, to help the actor sense where the sentence was going.

v.o. means "voice over"

Script: *Puss in Boots*

© 2006, Ron Blicq

(At curtain up, lights are up center stage. PHOEBE *is sweeping the porch, on which* PUSS *is sleeping.* PHOEBE *roughly pushes* PUSS *away with her broom and gives him a kick on the rump.)*

Scene One

PHOEBE: Out of my way, cat!

*(*PUSS *jumps away, moves to another spot, starts licking his paws.* PHOEBE *shakes her broom at* PUSS.*)*

Worthless, that's you! Sleep all day. Eat our food, what there is of it.

KARL: *(calls v.o.)* Phoebe! Phoebe! Where are you?

PHOEBE: Out here, Karl. On the porch.

KARL: *(v.o.)* Right.

*(*KARL *enters bearing an envelope held aloft.)*

Look! It's here! I've got it!

PHOEBE: You've got what?

KARL: The letter! The letter from the lawyer.

PHOEBE: So?

KARL: With our father's Will.

PHOEBE: Ah-ha!

*(*PHOEBE *throws the broom at* PUSS, *crosses to* KARL.*)*

About time, too! Well, what does it say?

KARL: I don't know.

PHOEBE: How much do I get?

KARL: I don't know!

PHOEBE: How can you *not know*?

KARL: It says not to open it.

PHOEBE: Karl!

KARL: Well, it does!

PHOEBE: Oh, give it here!

(She snatches the envelope from him.)

KARL: It says it's to be read only by—

PHOEBE: I can read! *(reads)* "To whom it may concern—"

KARL: That's us!

PHOEBE: Of course it's us. *(reads)* "To be opened only in the joint presence of Karl, Phoebe and Darren—"

KARL: There! You see.

PHOEBE: Where *is* Darren?

KARL: Went to see Shrek.

PHOEBE: The Ogre?

KARL: The new movie!

PHOEBE: Well, I'm not waiting for Darren. If he's not here— *(then he's not entitled...)*

KARL: We don't have a choice. Legally, we don't.

PHOEBE: Oh, yes we do!

(PHOEBE tears the envelope open.)

KARL: Give it back!

PHOEBE: No, Karl!

(They chase; PHOEBE opens the envelope as they chase.)

KARL: We have to wait.

PHOEBE: You can wait; I'm not.

(DARREN enters from stage left, scratches PUSS's ears. He watches KARL and PHOEBE [who have not noticed him]. PUSS stands on all fours, arches his back, rubs himself against DARREN's legs, purrs.)

(KARL grabs the envelope, but PHOEBE has already pulled the letter out and holds it up.)

KARL: We shouldn't be doing this!

PHOEBE: Hah! *(reads)* "My dear children: I am sad to have to tell you that I have died penniless, so I have no money to leave you."

KARL: No money!

PHOEBE: There's *got* to be money!

KARL: Of course there's money.

PHOEBE: *(reads)* "I have only three possessions to pass on to you: the mill, which in good times produces an income—"

KARL: As I am the eldest, that'll be mine.

PHOEBE: Oh, no!

KARL: It's traditional.

PHOEBE: Not in this family! *(reads)* "My second possession is the handcart, which can provide you with an income because you can haul goods for local merchants."

KARL: That can be yours.

PHOEBE: Oh, no. The mill is for me.

KARL: That's what you think!

PHOEBE: *(reads)* "My third possession is my cat who, although he will not provide you with an income, will provide you with much affection." Hah! Who'd want that mangy, useless animal?

DARREN: I would.

(KARL and PHOEBE *jump.)*

KARL: How long have you been standing there?

DARREN: Long enough.

PHOEBE: How much did you hear?

DARREN: Quite enough.

PHOEBE: Everything?

DARREN: Enough to know that, although I am penniless like father, I don't want the mill.

KARL: *Not* the mill?

DARREN: Nor the handcart.

PHOEBE: You don't want the handcart?

DARREN: I'm tired of listening to your squabbles. I will be glad just to have Puss.

KARL: If that's what you want. *(turns toward exit)*

PHOEBE: Well, good riddance then. *(to KARL, shouts)* Hey, Karl. Stop! You know Dad would want me to have the mill.

KARL: No! *(exits)*

PHOEBE: It's my right, as his daughter.

(PHOEBE grabs the handcart and exits with it.)

KARL: *(shouts, v.o.)* You wouldn't know how to run a go-cart—

PHOEBE: *(shouts, v.o.)* You couldn't manage opening a book!

KARL: *(shouts, v.o.)* Much less a mill!

PHOEBE: *(shouts, fading v.o.)* Wait! Stop! Stop!

(DARREN strokes PUSS behind the ears.)

DARREN: You see, Puss? Come on. We're on our own now. Let's see if we can find Marina.

PUSS: The Princess?

DARREN: Of course.

PUSS: Oh! *(stands on two feet)* The Princess Marina!

DARREN: Yes. *(looks around)* Who said that?

PUSS: I did.

DARREN: *You* did? Oh, don't be silly. Cats can't talk.

PUSS: This one can.

DARREN: Am I going mad?

PUSS: No. Not at all.

(PUSS addresses the audience.)

Did you hear me speak?

(PUSS waits for, and may have to encourage, audience response. He turns back to DARREN.)

PUSS: *(continuing)* You see? They heard!

DARREN: *(to the audience)* You heard him?

(DARREN *awaits audience response.*)

Oh, my! I've inherited a cat who can speak!

PUSS: I am your servant, sire. *(bows)* And you have inherited far more than you think. Far more than you would with a mill or a handcart.

(Fade lights center stage.)

Scene Two

(Lights up stage left: the KING *is on his throne, with Princess* MARINA *standing in front of him. We hear the King's first two "No's" before the lights come up.)*

KING: No! No! No! No! Out of the question!

MARINA: But, father, I love him.

KING: As my daughter, Marina, you are to marry a prince. Nothing less will do.

MARINA: But I have yet to find a prince who I would want to marry.

KING: Then we must look farther afield. I will arrange for you to— *(have a great dance, a reception...)*

MARINA: Oh, father, you don't want me to be unhappy, do you?

KING: Of course I don't. *(relents slightly)* Who is this young man?

MARINA: His name is Darren.

KING: Does he have an estate? A castle?

MARINA: I don't think so.

KING: Does he have money?

MARINA: No. No, he is penniless.

KING: Does he have any possessions?

MARINA: Well, he does have a cat.

KING: A cat! Oh, Marina. He certainly will not do.

(Fade lights stage left.)

Scene Three

(Lights up center stage. DARREN *and* PUSS *enter from upstage.)*

PUSS: So, when am I going to meet the Princess?

DARREN: Soon. She will bring us good news I hope.

PUSS: You don't really expect the King to approve of you, do you?

DARREN: The Princess can be very persuasive.

PUSS: You're dreaming, master.

(Enter MARINA *stage left.)*

MARINA: Oh, Darren! The king does not approve of you. He says you must have property, money, and possessions—and be a prince—before he could possibly say "yes."

DARREN: Oh, I had so hoped…

MARINA: What are we to do?

PUSS: Talk to your cat!

MARINA: *(to* DARREN*)* I beg your pardon?

DARREN: That was Puss.

MARINA: Darren! Cats can't speak!

PUSS: This one can.

MARINA: *(to* DARREN*)* He can **talk**?

DARREN: So I have discovered!

PUSS: *(bows)* Princess: it would give me great pleasure to help my Master meet His Majesty's demands.

MARINA: You mean, you can help Darren have property?

PUSS: I believe it would be possible.

DARREN: Be wealthy?

PUSS: More difficult, but it could be done.

MARINA: Oh, my! But how is he to have possessions?

PUSS: You will have to trust me.

DARREN: But, Puss, how can I possibly be a prince?

PUSS: Just give me time.

> (DARREN *shakes his head, scratches* PUSS*'s ears;*
> MARINA *joins in.* PUSS *lies on his back while they*
> *scratch his stomach; he paws the air and purrs.)*

MARINA: Puss, if you really can help, I will love you forever.

DARREN: And you shall have anything you want.

> (PUSS *jumps up onto two feet.)*

PUSS: Enough! Enough! We are wasting time. If I am to help
you, Master, then first you must find me three things.

DARREN: Of course! Of course! Just tell me what.

PUSS: I will need a pair of large boots.

MARINA: Boots?

PUSS: Spectacular boots. To give me added height.

DARREN: I have no money to buy boots. And I don't own any.

PUSS: Well, then, can the princess help?

MARINA: Oh, no. I am not supposed to be here. Or see Darren.
If I were to ask for boots, the King would know right away—

PUSS: That you are seeing my Master?

MARINA: Yes.

PUSS: His Majesty would make life difficult for you?

MARINA: Impossibly difficult.

PUSS: Then I will have to look elsewhere.

> (PUSS *walks downstage, addresses the audience.)*

Can you help me?

DARREN: *(faces audience; calls)* Can we have the house lights
up, please? So we can see who is out there.

> (*Nothing happens;* DARREN *turns to* PUSS*, shrugs.)*

PUSS: Let me try.

(PUSS faces the audience, holds his upper paws forward and down, and then slowly raises them. As he does so the house lights come up.)

DARREN: How did you do that?

MARINA: Are you a wizard?

PUSS: In a mild way, I suppose you could say I am.

MARINA: And that's why you can speak?

(PUSS nods.)

Do you have a wizard's name?

PUSS: Most certainly. Have you never heard of Hairy Mouser?

MARINA: No, but I am glad to meet you, Hairy Mouser.

PUSS: And am I to call you Princess Marina?

MARINA: Yes. Please.

DARREN: So the Princess is to call you 'Hairy Mouser?'

PUSS: Oh, no. I think 'Puss' would be better; like you do. *(suddenly brisk)* But enough. Let's get back to the business in hand. *(to the audience)* Is there a true friend sitting out there who might have a boot with them? A splendid boot?

(Audience response – there should be calls from two children, each with a boot.)

Oh, wonderful! Wonderful!

(PUSS walks to steps leading from stage to audience.)

Would you mind bringing your boot up here?

(Ad-libbed sequence. PUSS greets the children, introduces them to DARREN and MARINA, has them help him pull on the boots, and returns them to the audience. PUSS struts toward DARREN.)

DARREN: Cool boots, Puss!

MARINA: They make you look so much taller.

PUSS: Yes, I think they do.

(PUSS turns back to the audience.)

PUSS: *(continuing)* Now for another question: Does someone out there happen to have a big, sombrero-like hat with them? … You do? Oh, good, good. Would you mind bringing it up here?

(A second ad-libbed sequence. PUSS greets and introduces the child, has the child place the hat on his [Puss's] head, asks the child—and the audience—if he looks good, then returns the child to the audience.)

There! *(to DARREN)* What do you think?

DARREN: Impressive!

PUSS: Thank you, Master. *(bows to MARINA)* I take my hat off to you, Princess Marina!

MARINA: Magnificent, Puss!

PUSS: *(to the audience)* Now: there is one more thing I need. Would anyone have a sack, like a big brown bag, with them? One in which I can put things? … Oh, marvelous. Can you bring it to me?

(A third ad-libbed sequence. PUSS greets and introduces the child with the sack.)

That's exactly what I need. You are so clever.

(PUSS escorts the child to the edge of the stage, then walks up to DARREN and MARINA.)

There! Now I am ready.

DARREN: Fine. But what will you do with them?

PUSS: Ah! That is something I plan to do on my own.

MARINA: Will it take long?

PUSS: Oh, Princess, turning my Master into a prince will take time. You will just have to be patient. *(slight pause)* But first: a word of warning: if you see me in the presence of the King, you must pretend you do not know me. You have never seen me before.

MARINA: If you so wish.

PUSS: I do. *(to DARREN)* You too, Master.

(DARREN nods agreement.)

PUSS: *(continuing)* Now! Please depart, so I may start.

MARINA: Good-bye, Puss. And thank you.

PUSS: My pleasure.

(MARINA and DARREN exit stage right. PUSS turns to the audience, raises his front paws and then lowers them slowly: the house lights dim.)

Now: to work.

(He lays the sack on the ground, then stands back and points both front paws at it.)

Alright, bag: Fill.

(The sack fills [compressed air].)

Good.

(PUSS shoulders the sack and exits upstage center.)

(Fade lights center stage.)

Scene Four

(Lights come up stage left, with the KING sitting on his thrown. MARINA approaches.)

KING: Ah! 'Tis My Marina.

MARINA: Hello, father. *(she kisses him)*

KING: You have taken heed of my advice?

MARINA: Oh, yes, father.

KING: That you and I will go in search of a prince to become your consort?

MARINA: Yes, father. I understand. I will start soon to— *(entertain visiting princes)*

PAGE: *(v.o., loud)* Announcing Count Hairy Mouser!

KING: Who?

MARINA: *(conceals a smile)* I have no idea.

(PUSS enters from stage right, bearing a now well-filled

sack over his shoulder. He halts in front of the KING, *places the sack on the floor, and makes two grand bows, first to the* KING *and then to* MARINA.)

PUSS: Your Majesty. Your Royal Highness.

(The KING *preens;* MARINA *curtsies.)*

Your Majesty: I am the bearer of greetings and gifts to you, from my much-honored employer, the Marquis de Montmorency. The Marquis has great respect for the manner in which you rule the kingdom in which he is your respectful servant.

KING: Methinks you speak well, young man.

MARINA: Oh, yes. Oh, yes.

KING: Did I say young man? *(to* MARINA*)* Is this not a cat I see before me?

MARINA: I do believe it is, Your Majesty.

KING: But...but a cat who can speak? Methinks this is strange...

MARINA: *(conceals a smile)* Very strange, Your Majesty.

KING: But one cannot deny that he speaks with a gentle tongue, and says words of great wisdom.

MARINA: I do so agree, Your Majesty.

KING: *(to* PUSS*)* May I enquire again, the name of your Master?

PUSS: *(with a sweeping bow)* The Marquis de Montmorency, Your Majesty.

KING: *(to Marina)* Have you, my dear, have you heard of this Marquis de... de...?

MARINA: Montmorency, father... uh, Your Majesty.

PUSS: The Marquis will present himself to you as soon as he can, Your Majesty. In the meantime, he has sent gifts as an indication of his great respect for you.

*(*PUSS *lifts a large, gold-colored box from the sack and hands it to the* KING.)

KING: Oh, Princess Marina! Chocolate-covered ginger bon-bons. *(he opens the box and pops one into his mouth)* Umm!

KING: *(continuing)* Oh, superb. *(offers one to* MARINA*)* Try one, my dear. Only one, mind! *(to* PUSS*)* How did the Marquis know they are my favorite?

PUSS: The Marquis tries to satisfy Your Majesty's every need.

(The KING *offers the box to* PUSS*, who backs away.)*

Oh, no, Your Majesty. Such delicacies are only for Royalty.

KING: Ah, of course. Tell me, young man…uh…courtier, where does the Marquis dwell?

PUSS: Your Majesty: the Marquis has lived along the north Mediterranean coast for several years, where he has accumulated considerable wealth.

KING: A-h-h. Considerable wealth, you say?

PUSS: Oh, yes, Your Majesty.

KING: Are you listening, Marina?

MARINA: *(feigns boredom)* Yes, your majesty.

(PUSS reaches into the sack and pulls out an ermine cloak with red and gold trim. He holds it out to the KING. *MARINA shakes her head at* PUSS *[implying 'a commoner cannot help the King dress'], takes the robe, and holds it while the* KING *puts it on.)*

KING: Oh… It is magnificent!

MARINA: You have never looked so royal, father.

KING: My, oh my! Such a beautiful cloak. The Marquis has such good taste! And your master has a castle in…?

PUSS: At this very moment the Marquis is in the process of acquiring one of the best castles in the land, Your Majesty.

KING: Oh? And which one, may I ask?

PUSS: That, Your Majesty, I am not at liberty to say until the transaction is complete. The Marquis assures me you will understand.

KING: Of course, of course. Such undertakings are confidential. *(to* MARINA*)* You would do well, I think, Princess, to learn more about the Marquis.

MARINA: I have heard others speak highly of him, Your Majesty, and— *(I will make a point of...)*

KING: You have not met him personally?

MARINA: No, but I am told he is uncommonly handsome.

KING: *(to* PUSS*)* Then we must take steps to meet your Master.

*(*PUSS *reaches into the sack and pulls out a violet jewelry box, holds it before the* KING.*)*

PUSS: The Marquis has sent this for her highness, the Princess Marina, as an indication of his admiration for her.

(The KING *takes it, opens it, holds up a gold necklace.)*

KING: Oh, my! Oh, my! Come, my dear.

(The KING *places the necklace around* MARINA's *neck.)*

Oh, such eminent taste!

*(*PUSS *bows to the* KING, *backs toward center stage.)*

PUSS: I bid you farewell, Your Majesty.

*(*PUSS *turns and strides toward center stage. Lights fade on the King and Marina.)*

Scene Five

(Lights come up on DARREN *sitting on a bench at center stage. He leaps up as* PUSS *approaches.)*

DARREN: Have you had success?

PUSS: Oh, yes, Master. Yes! The King wants to meet you.

DARREN: *(points to his poor clothes)* How can I ever present myself to the King?

PUSS: All in good time, Master. One step at a time.

*(*MARINA *runs in from stage left; she and* DARREN *hug, then stand with an arm around each other.)*

MARINA: Oh, Darren! Puss was wonderful! *(to* PUSS*)* Or should I call your Master "Marquis" now?

*(*PUSS *and* MARINA *laugh)*

PUSS: Now the King knows who you are—

MARINA: As the Marquis de Montmorency.

PUSS: He wishes to meet you in your castle.

DARREN: What castle? I have no castle!

MARINA: The one you are buying!

DARREN: Oh, please! Do not tease me! Tell me what is happening.

PUSS: Today, I will find a castle for you.

DARREN: You do not just *find* a castle!

PUSS: I have a plan. This afternoon I will visit the Ogre—

DARREN: Not the Ogre!

MARINA: Not Humpa-Rumpa?

PUSS: Of course. Humpa-Rumpa. He is the Ogre.

MARINA: Oh, no, Puss. That's much too dangerous.

PUSS: Ah, but I have a strategy!

DARREN: He will eat you. For his lunch.

PUSS: The Ogre lives quite alone.

MARINA: No, Puss, no!

PUSS: He has no servants. There is no one else in the castle.

DARREN: Please, Puss, don't.

PUSS: If I can make Humpa-Rumpa go away, then the castle will be yours!

(*PUSS ushers* DARREN *and* MARINA *toward the exit upstage center.*)

Just you wait and see.

(*As* DARREN *and* MARINA *exit,* PUSS *turns toward stage right.*)

Scene Six

OGRE: *(v.o., deep and rasping)* Fee, fi, fo, fum,

I smell someone,

Who is a stranger here

117

OGRE: *(continuing)* And whom I do not fear.

Indeed, my lunch he will make

For he has made a big mistake.

(Lights come up on the castle entrance, stage right. The OGRE is standing at the entrance or leaning over a balcony. Only his face is seen. The clothing beneath him is a prop that collapses.)

PUSS: *(entering from stage center)* Fee, fi, fo fum,

Sounds so humdrum!

So today, I am after blood

To make someone fall with a thud.

OGRE: *(looking into the distance)* I hear a voice,

Not of my choice,

But I cannot see

Where that fellow be.

PUSS: Humpa-Rumpa may be big,

Humpa-Rumpa may be tall,

But that to us, one and all,

Means he has farther to fall!

I see you, Humpa-Rumpa

You with your large bumper!

(PUSS puts his hands to his mouth, like a megaphone.)

Hello, up there! Look down toward your feet.

OGRE: Ho, ho, ho! And who may you be, little one?

PUSS: My name is Count Hairy Mouser. And you, my friend, are Humpa-Rumpa.

OGRE: And what right have you to call me "friend?"

PUSS: Oh, your name, sir. Your name. It does so warm my heart.

OGRE: My name does *what*?

PUSS: It inspires me with confidence. To want to be your friend.

OGRE: I need no friend! I think I shall step on you. Erase you.

PUSS: Ah, yes. But then you would erase… oh, such an opportunity.

OGRE: Opportunity? What opportunity?

PUSS: To demonstrate how clever you are. Your skill as a magician.

OGRE: How do you know I can do magic?

PUSS: Your cleverness is well known, sire.

OGRE: It is? It is?

PUSS: I have never seen you perform myself, but I understand you can transform yourself into any animal you choose.

OGRE: True. True.

PUSS: Such as a hyena.

(The OGRE *gives a loud hyena-like laugh.)*

PUSS: Oh, clever. Clever! But a lion, that would be far beyond your means.

OGRE: You think wrongly, little one. Just watch me.

(The OGRE *gives a very loud lion roar and leans forward, as though about to leap like a lion.)*

Abracadabra—

PUSS: No, no! Stop! You need not go all the way. I believe you!

OGRE: *(resumes vertical stance)* Thank you.

PUSS: I have seldom met an Ogre with such wisdom.

OGRE: Quite. Quite.

PUSS: I have seen how you transform yourself into a large animal. But would you ever be able to shrink yourself into something small?

OGRE: Not a problem.

PUSS: I mean, really, really tiny.

OGRE: Still not a problem.

PUSS: Such as… umm… let me think… No, that would be out of your range.

OGRE: Nothing is out of my range!

PUSS: You mean, you could even transform yourself into a mouse?

OGRE: Of course! Of course I could.

PUSS: But you would prefer not to show me?

OGRE: Just watch me! Abracadabra. A mouse I shall be!

(There is a flash, a puff of smoke, and the OGRE disappears. His clothing collapses onto the floor.)

PUSS: Oh, so clever!

(PUSS pounces and we hear squeaks. PUSS chases after the [invisible] mouse. He finally stops and holds a dead mouse aloft by the tail, which he shows to the audience.)

Ah, ha! Now I have you!

(PUSS throws the mouse into a wooden box, snaps it shut.)

There! You may be dead already, but I'm not taking any chances.

(PUSS places the box in a prominent position. [It is a magician's box, which will conceal the mouse]. He stands back, holds his hands out toward the box.)

Abracadabra. Mouse: disappear for ever.

Scene Seven

(Lights up center stage. PUSS strides downstage and addresses the audience.)

PUSS: Keep an eye on that box, will you?

(He walks back and forth, deep in thought.)

Now, we have a castle for Darren, but I still have to convince the King that the Marquis de Montmorency is well respected. To do that I will need your help. First I need two woodcutters and two apple-pickers. Who would like to help me?

(PUSS raises his hands and the house lights come up.)

Ah, good. Just four will do. I'll take you, and you, and you, and you.

(PUSS adlibs the following sequence. He brings [ideally] two boys and two girls on stage, introduces them to the audience, and then divides them into two groups. At an appropriate moment, DARREN enters.)

DARREN: What have we here, Puss? Who are these people?

PUSS: Ah, Master. These are some of your tenants.

DARREN: My *tenants*? I have tenants?

PUSS: Yes, Master. Now that you are Marquis de Montmorency, you have— *(a large property)*

DARREN: Marquis of *what*?

PUSS: Montmorency, sire.

DARREN: Next you're going to tell me I have a castle!

PUSS: Oh, yes! You do, you do!

DARREN: I do?

PUSS: *(to the children)* Darren does have a castle, doesn't he?

(The children respond.)

Behind you, Master.

(DARREN turns and faces the castle entrance.)

DARREN: That castle belongs to the Ogre.

PUSS: Not now. *(He pulls the Ogre's clothing toward him)* You know who these belonged to, don't you?

DARREN: They're the Ogre's clothes!

PUSS: Not any more. Help me, will you?

(PUSS and DARREN bundle the clothes and throw them offstage.)

The castle is now yours, Master.

DARREN: But where is the Ogre?

PUSS: *(to the children)* Where is the Ogre? You saw where I put him.

(He waits for a response then picks up the box with the mouse in it.)

PUSS: *(continuing)* In here: right?

(PUSS hands the box to one of the children.)

Tell the Marquis what is in the box.

(The child describes, probably with a prompt from PUSS, that it's a mouse who once was the Ogre.)

DARREN: The Ogre? Oh, Puss, the Ogre can't be in there!

PUSS: *(to the child)* Show him. Open the box.

(The child opens the box: there is nothing in it. PUSS takes the box and shows it to the audience, who can see right through it. He turns to the children.)

Can you see the mouse? Of course you can't. I used my magic on it. You will never see the mouse—or the Ogre—again! *(to Darren)* And that is why you are now the Marquis de Montmorency.

DARREN: *(pats his clothes)* But I don't look like— *(a marquis)*

PUSS: Not a problem!

(PUSS faces his bag, which is lying upstage.)

Watch this, master.

(PUSS waves his hand toward the bag and calls out.)

Abracadabra. Make new clothes for the Marquis!

(PUSS pulls the bag to center stage; addresses the children.)

Will you help me find some clothes suitable for the Marquis?

(Ad lib as PUSS helps the children pull out a finely embroidered jacket, long gilt pants, boots, a crested hat.)

DARREN: Those are all for me?

PUSS: Yes, Marquis, and there are many more fine clothes to come. May I suggest you repair to your castle and come back to us in your new clothes?

DARREN: *My* castle?

PUSS: Absolutely, Master.

(DARREN *shakes his head and exits into the castle.* PUSS *turns back to the children.*)

PUSS: *(continuing)* Now, two of you are woodcutters. *(he takes two children aside)* This is how you chop down a tree.

(PUSS *demonstrates as though swinging an axe. When the axe reaches the extremity of its swing, there is the sound of an axe hitting wood. He repeats the motion, with the same accompanying sound.*)

Now you do it.

(*The children try, in turn, ideally with the sound of an axe hitting wood.*)

Fine! Fine!

(PUSS *turns to the two other children.*)

Now for my apple pickers.

(*He digs into the brown bag and pulls out two carrier bags. He opens them and gives one to each child*).

This is how you pick apples.

(*He reaches up and picks invisible apples and mimes dropping them into the bags.*)

Ah! Of course, you are not tall enough to reach into the tree. So I will put my arms around the tree and shake it. Like this.

(PUSS *wraps his arms around an invisible tree and shakes it. There is the pop-pop-pop sound of apples dropping onto the ground and bouncing.*)

Now, go pick up the apples. Like this.

(PUSS *scrambles around the floor, picking up imaginary apples and dropping them into the bags.*)

Come on, you do it!

(*The children reach down and "pick up" apples, dropping them into the bags.*)

Good. That's so good!

(PUSS *turns to all four children.*)

PUSS: *(continuing)* Now, that is what you will be doing when the King comes in. But when he arrives, I want you to stop and greet him. Like this. *(he executes an exaggerated bow)* Now you try.

(PUSS *coaches the children's bows.*)

(DARREN *enters, dressed as the Marquis.*)

Oh, look, my friends: the Marquis de Montmorency. Bow!

(They all bow, including PUSS.*)*

DARREN: Thank you my friends. It is indeed strange to be so honored. But not unpleasant.

(They all bow again.)

I think there is something wrong here: girls don't bow, they curtsy. *(to the girls)* Is that not so? Show the girls how to curtsy, Puss.

PUSS: Oh, Master! Me?

DARREN: Yes, you.

PUSS: But Master....

DARREN: Puss! That is an order!

PUSS: Yes, Master.

(PUSS *gives a bad curtsy.*)

DARREN: No, no, Puss. Like this.

(DARREN *gives an even-worse curtsy. Both he and* PUSS *try again.*)

Stop! Stop! *(walks downstage, faces the audience)* Is there, by some chance, a young lady out there who knows how to curtsy? Oh, good. Would you mind coming up here to show my friends how to do it?

(Ad lib: DARREN *introduces the girl [or possibly more than one] to the audience. She demonstrates and the children copy.* DARREN *and* PUSS *are terrible at first, then gradually improve. The girls on stage are now doing it correctly.)*

DARREN: *(continuing)* That's fine. Thank you *(name)*. Would you like to join the apple pickers?

(If she says "yes," DARREN escorts her there. If "no," he escorts her off the stage.)

PUSS: *(to the wood-cutters)* Now! If the King asks who your Master is, you are to say "The Marquis de Montmorency." Okay? Then let's try it. Tell me: who is your Master?

(Ad lib responses and coaching. PUSS turns to the apple-pickers.)

Now for you: if the King asks if the Marquis is a good Master, I want you to say "He is the very best." Let's try that. Do you have a good Master?

(Ad lib responses and coaching. PUSS turns to the audience.)

I want you to help, too. If I go like this *(gestures with a sweep of his hat)* I want you to shout "Hooray for the King." Ready?

(PUSS gestures with the hat; the audience responds.)

Again, please. But louder this time.

(PUSS again gestures and the audience responds.)

DARREN: You are just in time, Puss. I hear the King approaching.

PUSS: Oh, Master! Please! Don't call me Puss in front of the King. Call me Count Hairy Mouser.

DARREN: Who?

PUSS: Count Hairy Mouser.

DARREN: Count Hairy Mouser?

PUSS: Right. *(to the audience)* Am I not Count Hairy Mouser?

(PUSS encourages their response; turns to DARREN.)

You see!

DARREN: Yes, now I do see. 'Tis strange, but I agree.

PUSS: Oh, Master: you are a poet, and I doubt you know it!

DARREN: You, too, my jester friend.

PUSS: But, shush. The King is nearly here. *(to woodcutters and apple pickers)* Are you ready? You're on your own now. Swing those axes! Pick up those apples!

(The woodcutters swing their axes, the apple pickers search for apples. PUSS partly conceals himself and draws DARREN with him.)

(The KING and Princess MARINA enter from stage left. PUSS makes a flourishing gesture with his hat and the audience responds. The KING stops and beams. PUSS does it again and the audience responds.)

KING: Oh, it is so grand to be popular. My people do like their King.

MARINA: Of that there is no doubt, Your Majesty.

KING: Oh, yes. Yes. *(to the woodcutters)* What industrious people we do have here. Tell me, who is your Master?

(The children respond. PUSS may have to coach them.)

Ah! The Marquis de Montmorency!

(The KING turns to the apple pickers.)

Tell me, do you have a good Master?

(The children respond. PUSS may have to coach them.)

(PUSS gives DARREN a shove. He steps up to the KING.)

And who, may I ask, do we have here?

DARREN: Your Majesty: I am one of your most loyal subjects.

KING: That I am glad to hear. But it would be even better if I knew who you are.

DARREN: Your Majesty: I am the Marquis de Montmorency.

KING: The Marquis de Montmorency! *(to MARINA)* Did you hear that, my dear? *(pushes MARINA forward.)* Marquis: may I introduce my daughter to you. I speak of the beautiful Princess Marina, heir to my thrown.

DARREN: *(bows)* Princess Marina: I am honored to meet you. Word of your beauty is well known indeed.

(MARINA curtsies, invites DARREN to take her hand.)

MARINA: Oh, Marquis: news of your work in the world, it too is well known.

(The KING rubs his hands, almost prances with delight.)

DARREN: Your Majesty! Your Highness! May I have the honor of showing you my simple castle?

KING: That would indeed be a pleasure. I shall lead the way. *(to the PRINCESS)* Take his arm, Marina, as a lady should when accompanied by a Marquis.

(The KING, DARREN and MARINA exit into the castle. PUSS cavorts and rubs his hands.)

PUSS: Aha! It worked!

(PUSS turns to the woodcutters and apple pickers.)

You were wonderful! Just wonderful! Now that your job is done, let me help you return to your seats.

(House lights up. The children are re-seated. PUSS returns to the stage and addresses the audience.)

You were marvelous too! The King loved to hear your voices, your praise.

(PUSS raises and then lowers his arms: the house lights dim. DARREN enters.)

DARREN: The King and Princess seem well pleased with the castle, Puss... er... Count. I have left them to tour on their own. Now, I suggest we—

(PHOEBE enters, bumpily trying to roll a damaged wheel from the cart. She stands it upright against a post.)

PHOEBE: Oh, woe is me! Woe is me. How am I to earn money if my cart is broken. *(to DARREN and PUSS)* Just look at this wheel.

DARREN: I can see it, Miss Phoebe!

PHOEBE: You know my name?

DARREN: I certainly do.

PUSS: And I can say the same

*(*PUSS *rubs his rump.)*

PHOEBE: But who are you to—

(Enter KARL*, holding his head.)*

KARL: Oh, my head! A sail fell off my windmill and laid me out, right on the ground!

PHOEBE: It did what?

KARL: I cannot earn money if the mill does not work.

PHOEBE: I told you, *I* should have the mill.

KARL: And be holding your head in great pain, as I am now.

PHOEBE: If I ran the mill, the sails wouldn't dare fall off!

KARL: If I had the cart, I would never allow the wheels to get out of shape!

DARREN: Enough, you two. We no longer want to hear your complaints.

PHOEBE: And who do you think you are?

PUSS: This is the Marquis de Montmorency.

PHOEBE: So?

DARREN: And this is Count Hairy Mouser.

KARL: Having a rank like that means nothing to me.

PHOEBE: Get real!

DARREN: Oh, I am real all right. I am Darren, your brother.

PHOEBE: You? Darren? A Marquis?

KARL: How could you be?

PHOEBE: And dressed in expensive clothes!

KARL: You inherited only a mangy old cat.

DARREN: That is not correct. I inherited Puss—Count Hairy Mouser—because neither of you wanted him.

PHOEBE: Well, if you are a Marquis, you will be able to help me.

KARL: And me.

DARREN: You want some of my money, I suppose?

PUSS: Of course!

KARL: Now that you seem to be wealthy, can you not share some of it with your loving brother?

PUSS: Loving?

PHOEBE: And your dear sister, who cares so much for you.

PUSS: Cares for you? Ha!

DARREN: Did you share any of our father's inheritance with me?

PHOEBE: Well, that was different.

PUSS: Different? *(to* DARREN*)* Master: a word if I may.

*(*PUSS *draws* DARREN *downstage and speaks so that the audience hears but Karl and Phoebe do not.)*

Master, we must hurry. I have little time left as a magician.

DARREN: You mean, you will no longer— *(be able to be my...)*

PUSS: Hush! Listen carefully. I am left with only four more wishes. Two I am willing to use for your sister and brother. One each. Then I will use one for you and the Princess. And the very last one I will save for myself.

DARREN: You will share your wishes?

PUSS: Watch, Master!

*(*PUSS *faces the handcart wheel and holds his hands out toward it.)*

Abracadabra. Make the wheel round.

(The handcart wheel falls to the ground with a clatter.)

Miss Phoebe! The Marquis has arranged for your cart wheel to be repaired.

*(*PHOEBE *runs to the [now round] wheel, lifts it, and rolls it toward the upstage exit.)*

PHOEBE: See, Karl. Darren did it just for me. Not for you.

(PHOEBE exits)

PUSS: *(to DARREN)* Huh! I don't think a "thank you" would have been out of place!

(PUSS turns to face upstage.)

Now for the windmill. Abracadabra. Repair the windmill.

(If facilities permit, the windmill on the backdrop turns. PUSS turns to DARREN.)

Tell him.

DARREN: You may go, Karl. I have arranged for someone to repair your windmill. Indeed, it has already been done.

KARL: Well, well. Little brother does have his uses!

PUSS: Don't expect it to happen again. Ever!

KARL: *(uncertainly)* No. No. *(exits)*

DARREN: Puss! How am I to thank you?

PUSS: That is my third wish, master: for you and the Princess to marry and live happily ever after.

DARREN: How can you possibly arrange that?

PUSS: Ah! The King is already planning it. Be patient.

DARREN: Oh, thank you, Puss. You have done so much for me.

PUSS: With good reason, Master.

DARREN: But what about your wish? The fourth one.

PUSS: Oh, that is the easy one.

(PUSS turns to DARREN, bows with a flourish of his hat, and then throws the hat into the wings. Then he removes his boots and, one by one, throws them into the wings. As he does so, he says:)

My wish will be for a comfortable place to sleep within your castle, which you and the Princess Marina will share.

(Princess MARINA runs in, hugs DARREN. She is dressed regally.)

MARINA: Oh, Darren…Marquis! *(she curtsies) My* Father, his Majesty, has given his blessing—

KING: *(entering)* Has given his blessing for you and the Princess Marina to marry! Already I have sent a messenger to my castle, to announce the forthcoming wedding!

MARINA: Oh, father! You are just wonderful!

DARREN: *(bows)* You do, indeed, do me an honor, Your Majesty.

KING: Welcome to my family...son!

(During the above, PUSS has reverted to walking on all fours. He crosses to MARINA, rubs against her legs; she scratches his ears. Then he goes to DARREN, who does the same.)

DARREN: Now, what about you, Puss? You haven't had your own wish.

(PUSS rises to a kneeling position.)

PUSS: You are correct, Master. But, remember, once I have made my wish I will no longer be able to speak like you and my friends out there *(points to the audience)*.

(DARREN and MARINA both go to speak, but PUSS silences them with a raised paw.)

Abracadabra. I wish for a lovely cushion to sleep on.

(There is a humming noise, lights flash, and cushions of all shapes and sizes and colors fly in from the wings and above. The KING, MARINA and DARREN run around excitedly, clapping and shouting, and pile the cushions in the middle of the stage.)

DARREN: There you are, Puss. Your personal castle.

(PUSS climbs up the pile to the top, where he stretches out.)

PUSS: A-a-a-h!

(The KING, MARINA and DARREN applaud.)

LIGHTS DIM TO BLACKOUT

Production Notes

The production is generally straightforward, with three areas to be lit:

- The porch of the family home and a general area, center stage.
- The King's throne, stage left.
- The castle entrance, stage right.

The throne and castle entrance require only a small space each. The positioning of actors at the end of each scene permits the lights on one area to fade at the same time as lights on the next scene are brought up.

The extent to which three of the magic tricks are achieved will depend on local capability. Principally, these will be the ability for:

- The windmill to turn.
- The handcart wheel to repair itself.
- Puss's sack to inflate.

In each case, a slight amendment may be required to the script and accompanying dialogue.

Before the first production, we wondered how the children coming into the theatre would react to our approach to some of them as they arrived, with a request to be the bearer of a boot, hat or sack. We need not have worried: the children not only welcomed the idea but were excited by it: they all willingly accepted. (It's interesting that young audiences *like* to be included in the action, whereas many adults, if faced with a similar request to take part in an adult play, tend to step back and say "No, no thank you.")

Whether a boy or girl plays Puss is immaterial. However, having a young actor who is agile and has acrobatic prowess is a bonus that adds vitality and a sense of warmth to the character.

Play No. 4

Adventures with a Psammead

Synopsis

While digging in a sandpit near their holiday home in the summer of 1911, the five de Havilland children discover, and make friends with, a furry animal about the size of a nine-year-old boy. The animal walks on two legs, is something like a monkey, speaks perfect English, and identifies himself as a Psammead (pronounced *Sammy-ad*). He is a sand wizard and he grants the children a limited number of wishes. Their wish-making, however, leads them into a series of unusual adventures and unexpected predicaments.

A well-to-do neighbor discovers her jewelry has been stolen and engages the local policeman to apprehend the culprit. Because the children's actions seem strange, and because he thinks they are concealing something, the policeman suspects they committed the robbery. To prove they did not, the children decide to find the real thief and recover the jewels.

The Psammead invites them to use his wish-granting powers to help them find the culprit, but some of their wishes turn out to have hidden twists that create an exciting and often humorous adventure, which in turn increases the policeman's suspicions.

Robert, Cyril and Jane outside the Sweet Shop.

Photo: John Fitzgerald

133

A unique final wish, combined with help from the audience, sets the wheels in motion for the children to find the jewelry and identify the culprit.

The Cast

Primary Characters

The de Havilland Children:
    Cyril (14)
    Anthea (12)
    Robert (10)
    Jane (8)
    Hilary (6 months & 20) *
The Psammead (527) *

Secondary Characters

The Baker's Boy (17)
The Policeman (50)
Lady Chittenden (55)
The Pirates:
    Captain Hook (45)
    Smee (35)
A Housekeeper (40)

* ***The Psammead*** *is a sand wizard who is invested with the capacity to grant magic wishes to the children. Although he is 527 years old, he appears to be youthful and very lively.*

Hilary *is a six-month-old baby girl who is in a pram (baby-carriage) throughout the play, except for the last scene. At this point one of the children makes a 'magic wish' that turns Hilary temporarily into a 20-year-old young woman who discovers the person who committed a robbery. Ideally, Hilary is short and slight in build.*

*The Psammead
(James le Lacheur)
in a typical pose on
top of the sandpit.*

Photo: John Fitzgerald

Character sketches for all the roles start on page 201.

Background

Edith Nesbit's book *Five Children and It*—on which *Adventures with a Psammead* is based—was first published in 1902 by T. Fisher Unwin. I have used the same primary characters, and some of the events, but have introduced other events and associated characters to give the play a more dramatic focus that leads to a unique climax.

There are references in the play to J. M. Barrie's story *Peter Pan,* as both a book and a play. The play *Peter Pan* was first produced in London in 1904 and was revived annually for many years thereafter (and still appears frequently on stages worldwide). Because his play became so popular, Barrie subsequently converted the playscript into a novel, also called *Peter Pan*, which was published seven years later, in 1911. The eldest boy reads excerpts from the book in Act 1 of *Adventures with a Psammead*. Consequently, I have assumed the play takes place in 1911, so that the date coincides with the year that Barrie's book was published.

Captain Hook and Smee tie 'Wendy' (Anthea) to the mast and prepare to make 'Peter Pan' (Cyril) walk the plank. From the GADOC 2009 production.
Photo: John Fitzgerald

An unusual twist is the introduction of a sequence involving Captain Hook and Smee from *Peter Pan*, who capture the two eldest children because they think they are Peter Pan and Wendy.

There is no copyright infringement when drawing information from either Nesbit's or Barrie's books, since copyright has expired for both. I have also corresponded with Great Ormond Street Hospital in London, holder of the rights for the Barrie playscript, and have received approval from the registrar that excerpts from the book can be read aloud in *Adventures with a Psammead*.

Length of Play   Approximately 70 minutes:
(Act 1: 34 minutes; Act 2: 36 minutes)

Production History

The first production of *Adventures with a Psammead* was by the Guernsey Amateur Dramatic and Operatic Club (GADOC) in the UK, from July 20th to 24th, 2009. (For that production the title was changed to *Five Children and a Psammead.*) The cast:

Cyril	*Alex Crossan*
Anthea	*Sydney Henley-Roussel*
Robert	*Jean-Luc Parker*
Jane	*Emily Andrijasevic*
Hilary	*Natalie Wrigley*
The Psammead	*James Le Lacheur*
The Baker's Boy	*Jamie Reid*
The Policeman	*Mack Tachon*
Lady Chittenden	*Lorna Burns*
Captain Hook	*John Gaisford*
Smee	*Steve Ozanne*
Housekeeper	*Sybil Roberts*

The play was directed by Jane Blower, with Emma Hodge as Stage Manager.

Some notes describing the set and techniques used for the first production start on page 204.

The Set

Act 1: *At Stage Left* there is a sandpit, shaped rather like a doughnut, from which the Psammead appears.

At Stage Right there is the front of a Sweet Shop (candy store), with an entry door used by the children.

Act 2: *At Stage Center,* a simple platform is set approximately 36 inches (1 meter) high, on which the children stand when they are 'flying.' The platform later becomes the flat roof of a church with, beside it, a backdrop of the church roof and steeple. Still later it becomes the deck of a pirate ship.

At Stage Left, a window set moderately high in a wall. There is a deep shelf containing a prepared meal.

At Stage Right and Center, part of a pirate ship, with a section of deck, with a gangway visible from the audience; there also is the front of the Sweet Shop. (These two parts are used at different times in Act 2.)

Some Script Guidelines

Throughout the script, two symbols are used occasionally at the end of a piece of dialogue to indicate how the sentence ends:

- **...** An ellipsis at the end of a statement means the speaker just trails off and leaves his or her thought hanging in the air (possibly accompanied by a shrug).

- — a dash at the end of a statement means the speaker is interrupted by the next speaker and the first speaker's statement is incomplete. Sometimes there is an italicized continuation of the statement *(within brackets)* immediately following the dash, to help the actor sense where the sentence was going.

v.o. means 'voice over' (the speaker is off stage)

Script: *Adventures with a Psammead*

© 2007, Ron Blicq

Act 1

(At midstage left: a sandpit with a pile of sand shaped like a doughnut, protruding some 3 ft (0.9 m) above the stage surface. There is room for two or three children to be inside the sandpit. Upstage right: the front of a shop with a door in it and a bench to one side. When the lights come up they are primarily on the sandpit.)

Curtain Up

(CYRIL, ROBERT and JANE are sitting near the sandpit they started digging yesterday. A short distance from them is the pram (baby carriage) with the baby (Hilary) supposedly in it. CYRIL has the book Peter Pan *on his knees and is reading from it to the other two. He reads evocatively, imitating the voices of the characters. ANTHEA is inside the hole, with only her head and upper torso visible when she stands. She is digging energetically and throwing sand over the edge.)*

CYRIL: *(reads)* Peter said he was crying because he couldn't get his shadow to stick on.

'It has come off?' asked Wendy.

'Yes,' he said.

Then Wendy saw the shadow on the floor, looking so bedraggled. 'How awful,' she said— *(but when she saw that Peter had been trying to stick it on with soap...)*

(ANTHEA throws a spadeful of sand in the other children's direction.)

Hey, Anthea! Watch where you're throwing that sand!

(ANTHEA pokes her head over the edge of the sandpit.)

ANTHEA: Sorry! I wish you'd all help.

ROBERT: I've still got blisters.

ANTHEA: I'll never get finished, digging on my own.

JANE: Bor..ing.

ANTHEA: You helped yesterday.

JANE: But Cyril's reading to us.

ROBERT: About a dog who's a nanny, and looks after three children—

ANTHEA: How can a dog be a nanny?

ROBERT: And there's a boy called Peter.

CYRIL: Actually, the book's named after him. *(holds the book up)* Peter Pan.

ROBERT: And he can fly!

ANTHEA: Yes, Robert. Like I'm going to dig down to Australia today.

(ANTHEA *throws two or three spades of sand as* CYRIL *continues reading.*)

CYRIL: *(reads)* 'Wendy,' Peter said, 'do come with me and tell stories to the other boys.'

Wendy was very pleased to be asked. 'But I can't fly.'

'I'll teach you,' said Peter, grabbing her arm…

PSAMMEAD: *(v.o.)* Let me alone!

CYRIL: *(reads)* 'I'll teach you to jump on the wind's back, and then away we go.'

JANE: Oooh!

PSAMMEAD: *(v.o.)* Stop! Oh, please stop!

(The seated CHILDREN *lift their heads and listen.)*

ANTHEA: Oh, my! Oh, my! Cyril! Come here! Quickly!

*(*CYRIL, ROBERT *and* JANE *scramble up and peer over the sandpit edge.)*

It's alive! Oh, it'll get away.

ROBERT: What is it?

PSAMMEAD: *(v.o.)* Let me alone! Oh, please! Let me alone.

CYRIL: *(reaches for a spade)* Here, let's dig it out.

ANTHEA: No, Cyril! You'll hurt it! Dig with your hands.

JANE: Maybe Anthea did dig down to Australia.

ROBERT: Not deep enough.

PSAMMEAD: *(v.o.)* Oh, do you have to do that?

JANE: It's someone's head, I think.

ROBERT: Couldn't be. Unless he's walking upside down.

JANE: Upside down?

ROBERT: They walk upside down in Australia. We'd see their feet first.

PSAMMEAD: *(v.o.)* Please let me alone!

ROBERT: But we want to see you.

JANE: I wish you'd come out.

PSAMMEAD: *(v.o.)* Oh, well. If that's your wish.

> *(The* PSAMMEAD *climbs out of the hole, runs downstage, and shakes sand from his body like a dog shaking off water.)*

I believe I must've fallen asleep.

> *(The* PSAMMEAD *is about Robert's size, with much of his body covered with hair. He has an ugly but strangely likeable face. As he wakens he becomes more and more lively, gamboling around and making leaps or backflips when pleased or excited.)*

> *(*CYRIL *and* ANTHEA *climb out of the sandpit during the following conversation.)*

JANE: What on earth is it?

PSAMMEAD: *(to* ANTHEA*)* Does she always talk nonsense? *(scornfully, echoing Jane)* What on earth is it?

ANTHEA: Jane doesn't mean to be rude.

CYRIL: None of us do.

ANTHEA: You don't have to be frightened. We don't want to hurt you.

(The PSAMMEAD *'humphs.')*

And we don't want to make you cross.

(The PSAMMEAD *'humphs' again.)*

Can you tell us who you are?

PSAMMEAD: I'm a Psammead. You should know that.

ROBERT: Well, we don't.

PSAMMEAD: *(to the audience)* Is he always rude like that?

ROBERT: Who're you talking to?

PSAMMEAD: All those young people sitting out there.

*(*ROBERT *and* OTHERS *peer out, hands above their eyes.)*

ROBERT: I can't see anybody.

JANE: Nor me.

PSAMMEAD: *(to audience)* Tell them you're out there.

(Slight response from audience.)

Oh, come on! You can do better than that! Shout it out: 'We're out here!' Like that!

(Audience response. The PSAMMEAD *looks at the* CHILDREN.*)*

CYRIL: I didn't hear anything.

JANE: Or see anyone.

PSAMMEAD: A-a-a-h.

(The PSAMMEAD *leans forward, arms outstretched toward the audience, raises his arms slowly; the house lights brighten in time with his movement.)*

Now can you see them?

ANTHEA: Yes, I can!

CYRIL: Well, I'll be…

ROBERT: How did you do that?

JANE: Who are you?

PSAMMEAD: Well, if you must know, I'm a sand-wizard.

JANE: Of course! It's quite plain, now I look at you.

PSAMMEAD: If all you want is to look at me...

(The PSAMMEAD *leaps toward the sandpit and starts to climb in.)*

JANE: Oh, don't go away. Please talk some more.

PSAMMEAD: Well, if you insist.

ANTHEA: How long have you lived here?

(The PSAMMEAD *cavorts center stage.)*

PSAMMEAD: Oh, hundreds of years. Hundreds and hundreds.

ROBERT: Then you must be very old.

(The PSAMMEAD *faces the audience, stretches hands forward, lowers them; the house lights dim.)*

JANE: Oooh!

CYRIL: Has no one found you before?

PSAMMEAD: Oh, no. I take care to keep myself hidden. It was only when you *(to* ANTHEA*)* kept digging. I couldn't get away fast enough. *(to* JANE*)* And then you made a wish.

JANE: I did?

PSAMMEAD: Correct me if I am wrong, but didn't you say: 'I wish you'd come out'?

JANE: Something like that.

PSAMMEAD: Well, I granted your wish: I came out.

JANE: You .. granted .. my.. wish?

PSAMMEAD: That's what a Psammead does.

CYRIL: You mean, if I make a wish, you'll make it come true?

PSAMMEAD: Within reason. But there are limitations.

CYRIL: Such as?

PSAMMEAD: No frivolous wishes.

JANE: Friv..o..lous?

ANTHEA: He means silly, thoughtless wishes.

PSAMMEAD: And only two wishes each. *(to* JANE*)* You have already used one, Miss Jane.

JANE: I have?

PSAMMEAD: When you wished for me to come out.

JANE: Oh. But couldn't that be a friv..o..lous wish?

PSAMMEAD: If you consider wanting to see me is a frivolous request, then there is no point in my staying.

(The PSAMMEAD *starts climbing into the sandpit.)*

ROBERT: Oh, no! Don't go!

ANTHEA: Oh, please stay!

PSAMMEAD: Why should I?

CYRIL: Could you, perhaps, show us— *(how to make a wish)*

ROBERT: If I were to wish for the sun to shine!

ANTHEA: Oh, yes. It's been so cloudy lately.

ROBERT: Would that be frivolous?

PSAMMEAD: I suppose not.

ANTHEA: I think Robert just wants to see—

JANE: How it's done!

ROBERT: Just a test wish.

PSAMMEAD: Humph! All right. Just for once.

(Pause.)

CYRIL: Go on! Make your wish!

ROBERT: I wish…. I wish the sun would shine.

(Nothing happens.)

I wish—

PSAMMEAD: No, no! Never make a wish twice. It cancels everything and you lose your wish.

ROBERT: Oh, sorry.

PSAMMEAD: Just learn to be patient. A wish doesn't always happen immediately.

(The PSAMMEAD *looks upward; the* CHILDREN *follow suit. A brilliant spot shines on their faces, and broadens across the stage.)*

JANE: Oh, it worked.

ROBERT: Wonderful!

ANTHEA: You *are* clever!

(The PSAMMEAD *preens. Sound of baby crying.)*

Oh, the sun's shining in her eyes.

*(*ANTHEA *turns the pram around, looks in at the baby.)*

PSAMMEAD: What's in that box?

ROBERT: Box?

PSAMMEAD: That one, with those round things underneath.

JANE: Oh, that's a pram.

CYRIL: Perambulator.

JANE: For our baby sister.

ROBERT: We take her everywhere with us. Unfortunately.

ANTHEA: Only when mother has to go out.

JANE: Or she's too busy to look after the baby.

PSAMMEAD: Can I look?

(The PSAMMEAD *gambols over to the pram.)*

She's not very pretty.

ANTHEA: Oh, but she is. She's lovely.

PSAMMEAD: Not where I come from. Oh, no!

CYRIL: *(looks up at the sky)* Umm... is each wish permanent?

PSAMMEAD: Only until sunset. Every wish ends at sunset.

ROBERT: Can you turn it off?

ANTHEA: Oh, no. It's too nice.

PSAMMEAD: No. Once I have created a wish, I cannot un-create it; cancel it.

JANE: You really are a wizard, aren't you?

PSAMMEAD: One tries one's best.

(He swings his legs over the edge of the sandpit.)

Then I will say good night to you.

CYRIL: But how are we to make wishes, if you're not here?

PSAMMEAD: Don't worry about that. Wherever you are, I will be listening. Waiting for your commands.

(The PSAMMEAD *drops out of sight; the* CHILDREN *peer over the edge.)*

ANTHEA: There he goes, digging into the sand.

JANE: Bye-bye, Psammy… Psammy…

ROBERT: Psammead. Thank you for granting my extra wish.

(The CHILDREN *turn away from the sandpit.)*

CYRIL: Well, who wants to have the first wish?

JANE: We don't have to wish right away, do we?

ANTHEA: No. No, I don't think so. Anyway, there's more fun if we think about it first. Anticipate. You know?

CYRIL: Let's go into the village then, while we think.

ROBERT: Could we buy some sweets?

CYRIL: *(feels in his pocket)* Perhaps. I do have some change.

ANTHEA: Who's going to push the pram, then?

JANE: Not my turn. I pushed her down here.

CYRIL: I'll be buying the sweets.

ROBERT: I've still got blisters on my hands.

ANTHEA: Me again, I suppose…

(Lights dim on the sandpit, come up on the Sweet Shop. CYRIL, ROBERT *and* JANE *enter.)*

ANTHEA: *(calls after them)* See if they have raspberry drops, Cy. They're my favorite.

CYRIL: Right. *(exits)*

(ANTHEA sits on the bench, rocking the pram. Lady Chittenden [LADY C] enters from stage right.)

LADY C: Oh, hello!

ANTHEA: Oh, hello, Lady Chittenden.

LADY C: You're one of the de Havilland children, aren't you?

ANTHEA: Yes. Anthea.

(ANTHEA looks in awe at LADY C.)

LADY C: And your brothers and sister? In the Sweet Shop?

ANTHEA: Yes, ma'am.

LADY C: *(peers into the pram)* And who is this?

ANTHEA: That's our baby sister.

LADY C: Does she have a name?

ANTHEA: Hilary, ma'am. Hilary Joan.

LADY C: Oh, she is lovely. Lovely. Aren't you, my little chickadee?

(The baby gurgles.)

I see you often. Just like a little mother.

ANTHEA: Yes, ma'am.

LADY C: Please give my good wishes to your mother. Tell her I will call in to see her… umm… next week, I should think.

(LADY C exits stage left; ANTHEA gazes after her.)

ANTHEA: Oh, isn't she just beautiful? I do so wish I was beautiful.

(The baby cries slightly, ANTHEA leans over the pram. [She is putting on a Psammead-like mask.] CYRIL, ROBERT and JANE enter from the shop, each carrying bags of sweets.)

146

JANE: *(to* CYRIL*)* Can you read some more? About Peter Pan?

CYRIL: Yes, let's. More about Peter Pan. *(calls)* I've got your raspberry drops, Anthea.

ANTHEA: *(from inside the pram)* I'll be right there.

> *(The three* CHILDREN *settle on the ground stage right. As* CYRIL *reads, a light comes up on the sandpit; the* PSAMMEAD *climbs out, listens.)*

CYRIL: *(reads)* Peter had fairy dust on his hands and he blew some of it on Wendy, John and Michael. 'Now, just wiggle your shoulders this way,' he said, 'and let go'.

> They were all on their beds and gallant Michael let go first and rose from his bed. 'I flewed!' he screamed while still in mid-air.

> *(While he reads,* ANTHEA *sits beside them, closest to* JANE. *Her face now looks very much like the* Psammead's. *When the* PSAMMEAD *sees her, he does a little dance of joy.* ROBERT *looks up.)*

ROBERT: Oh, look at… at… Anthea?

> *(*JANE *shrieks, backs away from* ANTHEA.*)*

JANE: It's the Psammy….!

CYRIL: *(holding a bag of sweets out to her)* No, it's Anthea. Where did you get the mask?

> *(*ANTHEA *takes the sweets.)*

ANTHEA: Thanks. What mask?

ROBERT: You look awful!

JANE: What have you done?

ANTHEA: Done? Me? Nothing!

ROBERT: But your face… *(reaches toward it)*

> *(*ANTHEA *backs away, reaches up, feels the whiskers.)*

ANTHEA: I've got **hair**!

JANE: Just like the Psammy…Psammead.

ANTHEA: Has anyone got a mirror?

> *(The* CHILDREN *shake their heads 'no.')*

But why? Why me?

CYRIL: Did you… did you make a wish?

ANTHEA: No. I don't think so. All I said was… oh! "I do wish I was beautiful." But I wasn't making a wish!

ROBERT: The Psammead must have thought you were.

JANE: The wish must have gone wrong.

ROBERT: He didn't make you beautiful at all!

> *(*ROBERT *and* JANE *start to laugh;* CYRIL *joins in, reluctant, but can't help it.)*

ANTHEA: Oh, no! This is terrible. I can't stay like this all day. No one must see me.

CYRIL: It will end at sunset.

ANTHEA: At sunset!

CYRIL: That's what the Psammead said.

ANTHEA: That's hours away. I can't stay like this! *(jumps up)* I've got to find the Psammead. Ask him to undo it.

> *(The* PSAMMEAD *retreats into the sandpit.)*

Read to them, Cyril!

> *(*ANTHEA *runs stage left. Lights dim slightly stage right. Lights come up brighter on the sandpit.* ANTHEA *leans over the edge.)*

ANTHEA: Psammead! Psammead! I need to talk to you.

PSAMMEAD: *(v.o.)* Sufficiently to disturb my sleep?

ANTHEA: Oh, yes. Yes!

PSAMMEAD: *(v.o.)* Then please have the good manners to explain.

ANTHEA: It's me, Anthea, and—

PSAMMEAD: *(v.o.)* I know who you are.

ANTHEA: I must see you!

PSAMMEAD: *(v.o.)* Humph!

ANTHEA: Oh, Please!

PSAMMEAD: *(peers over the edge)* Ah, I know. You want to show me how beautiful you are.

ANTHEA: Beautiful?

(The PSAMMEAD *climbs out, shakes sand from his hair, and walks around* ANTHEA, *inspecting her.)*

Oh, yes. You are. Truly beautiful.

ANTHEA: *(fingers the hair on her face)* This isn't beautiful. It's a hairy mess!

PSAMMEAD: Oh, no, my dear. In the land of the Psammeads, you are just beautiful.

ANTHEA: But I didn't ask—I didn't wish—to look like a Psammead!

PSAMMEAD: You didn't specify, my dear. You didn't say—

ANTHEA: Oh, yes, I did. I—

PSAMMEAD: Correct me if I am wrong, but I believe you said: *(adopting the tone Anthea used when she made the wish)* 'I do so wish I was beautiful.' So... I made you beautiful, as I know beauty to be.

ANTHEA: My brothers laughed at me! So did my sister!

PSAMMEAD: Oh, what a pity they cannot see you as I see you. They would not laugh then. *(to the audience)* Don't you agree that Anthea is beautiful?

(Muffled replies from the audience.)

ANTHEA: *(to the audience)* Oh, please, *please,* tell the Psammead I'm not beautiful!

PSAMMEAD: Louder, please. I can't hear you.

ANTHEA: Tell him!

(The shouts from the audience are probably mixed.)

ANTHEA: There! You see. So, please, can you undo my wish?

PSAMMEAD: I'm sorry, that is not possible.

ANTHEA: Just for once? For me?

(The PSAMMEAD *shakes his head.)*

I have to stay like this all day?

PSAMMEAD: Until sunset.

ANTHEA: Oh, that's much too long!

PSAMMEAD: I'm sorry: there is nothing— *(I can do.)*

ANTHEA: I have to hide! I must. No one must see me like this.

PSAMMEAD: Ah! There, perhaps I can help you.

(The PSAMMEAD *reaches into the sandpit and pulls out a furled black umbrella.)*

Although it pains me to see you hide a face of such beauty!

ANTHEA: Oh, thank you.

*(ANTHEA *unfurls the umbrella and ducks behind it.)*

Thank you.

*(ANTHEA *walks stage right, holding the umbrella between her and the* CHILDREN. *Lights fade stage left, come up on* CYRIL, JANE *and* ROBERT.)*

CYRIL: *(reads)* Peter called out to Wendy: 'Fly second to the right, and straight on till morning. That's the way to Neverland.'

ROBERT: Just like that?

*(ANTHEA *sits with them,* CYRIL *pauses, looks at her around the umbrella. She shakes her head, indicates for him to go on reading.)*

CYRIL: Right. *(reads)* They flew all through the night and past the dawn.

JANE: Oooh!

CYRIL: *(reads)* On and on they flew, toward the rising sun, until Peter suddenly announced: 'There it is: Neverland.'

(The POLICEMAN *has entered stage right. He looks at the* CHILDREN *as he passes. When he is just past center*

stage, LADY C *enters stage left. She is distraught, doesn't immediately see the policeman.*

LADY C: Oh, help. Help! I've been robbed! Robbed! *(sees the* POLICEMAN*)* Oh, thank goodness you are here. When I went home, the side door was open. I never leave it open. Oh, they've stolen my jewelry, and...and...

(The POLICEMAN *takes out a notebook and pencil.)*

POLICEMAN: Steady now, madam. Let me take down the details.

LADY C: There's no time to be wasted.

POLICEMAN: When did you say this happened?

LADY C: I went out at two o'clock. The candlesticks were there then.

POLICEMAN: Candlesticks?

LADY C: On the hall table. My silver candlesticks. A family heirloom, and worth, oh, hundreds of pounds.

POLICEMAN: Yes, I'm sure they were. Now, when did you discover the burglary?

(The BAKER'S BOY *enters stage right, carrying a large wicker basket with loaves poking out of it. On seeing Lady C and the Policeman, he withdraws toward the* CHILDREN*.)*

LADY C: Oh, it was no more than half an hour ago. I could see the side door was open as I walked up the drive.

POLICEMAN: Right, madam. I think we should go down to the police station, so I can file a report.

LADY C: Yes. Oh, yes. We must not waste time if you are to apprehend the culprit.

(The POLICEMAN *and* LADY C *exit stage left. The* BAKER'S BOY *turns to the* CHILDREN*.)*

BAKER'S BOY: Oh, ho, ho...the little de Havilland children.

JANE: We're reading Peter Pan.

BAKER'S BOY: Peter what?

JANE: Peter *Pan*. The boy from Neverland.

BAKER'S BOY: Neverland? Never heard of it.

ANTHEA: *(whispers from behind the umbrella)* Cyril! Cyril!

CYRIL: What?

ANTHEA: Buy some bread.

CYRIL: Bread?

ANTHEA: Two loaves. We promised mother.

CYRIL: Ooops! *(puts hand in pocket, pulls out coins)* Three-halfpence *(pronounced 'hayp'nce')* That's all I have.

ANTHEA: That's not enough. What did you do with the money mother gave you?

CYRIL: Spent it on the sweets. I forgot.

ANTHEA: O-h-h....

BAKER'S BOY: Well? Are you or aren't you buying bread? Can't stand round here all day!

CYRIL: *(to* ROBERT *and* JANE*)* Have you got any money?

JANE: Girls don't have pockets.

ROBERT: *(pulls out pocket linings; shakes head)* Must've fallen out while we were flying.

(Laughter from ROBERT *and* JANE*. The* BAKER'S BOY *looks strangely at them.)*

With Peter Pan!

BAKER'S BOY: Well?

ANTHEA: *(to* CYRIL*)* Ask him if we can take the bread today and pay him tomorrow.

(The BAKER'S BOY *edges toward* ANTHEA, *tries to peer behind the umbrella.* ROBERT *jumps up, stands in his way.)*

ROBERT: Oh, no, you don't!

BAKER'S BOY: I just want to see—

CYRIL: Tell you what: we'll take two loaves today, pay you tomorrow.

(The BAKER'S BOY *still tries to edge past* ROBERT.*)*

BAKER'S BOY: Cash on the nail. That's what my Dad says. *(to* ROBERT*)* Get out of my way!

ROBERT: No! You get back!

JANE: S-s-s-h. You'll wake the baby.

BAKER'S BOY: Time for his tea, anyway, I should think.

(The POLICEMAN *enters stage left, stops and listens.* CYRIL *jumps up, stands beside* ROBERT*; together they push the* BAKER'S BOY *back.)*

What're you hiding back there?

(The POLICEMAN *nods knowingly.)*

ROBERT: Nothing!

CYRIL: You're not to go back there.

BAKER'S BOY: Why ever not?

ROBERT: It's private.

CYRIL: A family matter.

BAKER'S BOY: G'arn!

(The BAKER'S BOY *tries to run around* CYRIL *and* ROBERT. *They push him away.)*

(The PSAMMEAD *jumps down from the sandpit. He shows concern.)*

(Very slowly, the brightness in the sky has been fading as sunset approaches.)

I just want to see—

ROBERT: No!

CYRIL: You keep away!

JANE: Please, Baker's Boy.

(The BAKER'S BOY *puts his basket down, then suddenly runs to one side, trying to outflank* CYRIL

and ROBERT. *A chase ensues.)*

(The PSAMMEAD *jumps up and down with excitement.)*

(JANE sidles over to the basket, tries to lift it, finds it's heavy, lifts it only an inch off the ground.)

BAKER'S BOY: *(shouts)* Put that down! Now!

(JANE lets go and the basket drops. There's a clink [optional]. The BAKER'S BOY *runs to the basket and picks it up.)*

Nobody! Nobody… touches my basket! Ever!

JANE: *(backing away from him)* Alright. Alright.

BAKER'S BOY: It's agin the law. Only *I* must touch the bread. My Dad says so.

CYRIL: You didn't need to shout at her like that!

BAKER'S BOY: She was going to steal my bread.

ROBERT: Rubbish! Jane would never do that!

CYRIL: None of us would.

BAKER'S BOY: Looked like it to me! *(slight pause)* Alright. Suppose I do let you have two loaves on tick? Until tomorrow.

CYRIL: You've changed your mind?

BAKER'S BOY: That's what you wanted, isn't it?

CYRIL: Yes, but you said— *(you wouldn't.)*

BAKER'S BOY: *(to ROBERT)* You choose one.

(ROBERT reaches toward the basket.)

Don't touch it! Just point to it.

ROBERT: That was what I was going to do. That one.

(The BAKER'S BOY *hands ROBERT a loaf.)*

Thank you.

BAKER'S BOY: *(to Cyril)* Now you.

(CYRIL points to a loaf; the BAKER'S BOY *hands it to him.)*

CYRIL: Yes, thanks.

BAKER'S BOY: That'll be eightpence-halfpenny *(pronounced "hayp'ny").* By lunchtime tomorrow.

CYRIL: Right.

(The BAKER'S BOY *steps toward* JANE.*)*

BAKER'S BOY: And you keep away from my basket!

(The BAKER'S BOY *dives toward the umbrella and lifts it away.* CYRIL *and* ROBERT *try to stop him but are hampered by the loaf each carries.)*

Ah, ha!

*(*ANTHEA *is revealed squatting on the ground, knees drawn up, her elbows resting on her knees and her hands trying to cover her face. She is turned away, trying to hide from the* BAKER'S BOY.*)*

(The PSAMMEAD *looks at the sky, leaps with joy.)*

BAKER'S BOY: Why're you doing that? You afraid of me?

*(*CYRIL *throws bread into the pram. The* BAKER'S BOY *tries to pull* ANTHEA's *hands away from her face.)*

ANTHEA: Get him away! Get him away from me!

*(*ROBERT *grabs the* BAKER'S BOY's *arm, but he roughly pushes* ROBERT *away and backs away slightly from the group.)*

BAKER'S BOY: What's the matter with her?

CYRIL: Nothing.

*(*CYRIL *kneels in front of* ANTHEA *and prizes her hands away from her face.)*

Anthea! Anthea! It's all right! It's past sunset. You're back to being you!

ANTHEA: *(feels her face)* No hair! It's me again!

*(*ANTHEA *laughs almost hysterically, then subsides into intermittent giggles.)*

JANE: It worked! At sunset. It really worked!

CYRIL: Just like the Psammead said it would.

(The PSAMMEAD *gives a joyous leap.)*

BAKER'S BOY: What are you all talking about?

JANE: It was a sand wizard. He made Anthea—

CYRIL: No, Jane. Keep it in the family.

ROBERT: *(to* BAKER'S BOY*)* You wouldn't understand.

BAKER'S BOY: What d'you mean, I wouldn't—

CYRIL: It's private.

BAKER'S BOY: You lot are crazy!

(The BAKER'S BOY *backs toward stage right.)*

ANTHEA: *(to* CYRIL) Can we go home now?

JANE: Oh, yes. I'm so hungry.

CYRIL: Why not?

(The CHILDREN *cross to stage left, passing the* POLICEMAN. ANTHEA *pushes the pram. The* PSAMMEAD *watches from the sandpit.)*

ROBERT: How're we going to explain…?

ANTHEA: To mother?

CYRIL: We're not. She wouldn't understand.

ANTHEA: Would anybody?

CYRIL: Hardly!

(The CHILDREN *exit. The* POLICEMAN *beckons to the* BAKER'S BOY.*)*

POLICEMAN: Come here, lad.

BAKER'S BOY: Me?

POLICEMAN: Do you see anyone else?

BAKER'S BOY: No.

(The POLICEMAN *paces slowly toward the* BAKER'S BOY, *who puts down the basket and walks quickly to the* POLICEMAN. *They meet center stage.)*

POLICEMAN: Tell me, lad, did you see anything unusual about....? *(points to exit where the children departed)* Did you think they were trying to conceal something?

BAKER'S BOY: Conceal...?

POLICEMAN: Were they trying to hide something from you?

BAKER'S BOY: Oh! Yes. Oh, yes.

POLICEMAN: Did you *see* anything? Anything suspicious?

BAKER'S BOY: Nah. Though they were acting a bit strange.

POLICEMAN: In the pram, perhaps?

BAKER'S BOY: They wouldn't let me.

POLICEMAN: H-h-h-m-m...

(The POLICEMAN turns stage left, then turns back.)

If you do see anything unusual, you will tell me?

BAKER'S BOY: *(picks up basket)* I'll keep me eye open.

POLICEMAN: Good lad.

(They exit in different directions. Lights fade to 10%, accompanied by brief music.)

(The lights come up on the sandpit and bench. The PSAMMEAD and ANTHEA are sitting on the bench. It's the next day. ANTHEA gently rocks the pram. The PSAMMEAD touches her cheek.)

PSAMMEAD: Such a pity. Such a pity. You were so beautiful.

ANTHEA: Among your people, perhaps.

PSAMMEAD: No 'perhaps' about it.

ANTHEA: Then I'm sorry I couldn't keep it, just for you.

PSAMMEAD: I know. I know. But I can still console myself that, among people of your kind, you do have nice features.

(Enter CYRIL, ROBERT and JANE from stage left.)

ANTHEA: Oh, Psammead! But my brothers don't think so.

PSAMMEAD: Then we shall ask them. *(to CYRIL and ROBERT)* Why don't you think your sister is pretty?

CYRIL: Who said?

JANE: All the de Havilland girls are pretty!

ROBERT: She's only a girl!

PSAMMEAD: You're only a boy.

CYRIL: Well, she's all right, I suppose.

PSAMMEAD: You only suppose? *(to* ANTHEA*)* Do you think he's good looking?

ANTHEA: He's all right, I suppose.

(Laughter.)

PSAMMEAD: So! What is your wish for today? Better be quick. It's mid-afternoon already.

CYRIL: Well, we were thinking—

JANE: We didn't have enough money yesterday, for both bread *and* sweets.

ROBERT: We want to be rich.

JANE: Have lots of money.

ANTHEA: But just for one day.

JANE: Half a day, really.

CYRIL: Would that be asking too much?

PSAMMEAD: You're *asking* me? You can't ask me. You can only make a wish.

CYRIL: Then... I wish... I wish we could have lots of money.

(There is a growing whining sound. The PSAMMEAD *concentrates. The sound becomes louder until it is accompanied, from inside the sandpit, by a clinking sound like coins being ejected from a slot machine. The* PSAMMEAD *relaxes. The* CHILDREN *lean over the edge and look in.)*

JANE: Oooh, look at all that money!

ROBERT: Tons of it!

ANTHEA: The coins look awfully big.

CYRIL: *(reaches in, holds one up)* They're gold I think.

ROBERT: Are they real?

CYRIL: Of course they're real! *(to* PSAMMEAD*)* Aren't they?

PSAMMEAD: That's what you asked for.

CYRIL: They're sovereigns.

JANE: Golden sovereigns.

ANTHEA: Worth...?

CYRIL: One pound. Each.

JANE: Oooh, we can buy lots for that!

ROBERT: Come on, then!

*(*ROBERT *leans into the sandpit and stuffs his pockets.* CYRIL *follows suit.* JANE *hold her apron in front of her, to form a hollow.)*

JANE: Fill mine, too!

*(*ANTHEA *and* ROBERT *each scoop a handful into* JANE's *apron.)*

Oooh, they're heavy.

(The boys' pockets in their jackets and trousers are sagging. They and JANE stagger around. Only ANTHEA remains steady, as she puts all she can into her satchel.)

*(*JANE *stumbles to the pram and pours her coins into it. The baby yells.)*

ANTHEA: Jane, be careful!

CYRIL: Don't squash the sandwiches.

PSAMMEAD: Or the baby! *(does a backflip)*

ANTHEA: *(to the boys)* You can't walk into the village like that. You'll have to put some back.

ROBERT: Put them back?

*(*CYRIL *throws some coins back into the sandpit.)*

CYRIL: We'll spend what we have, then come back for more.

ROBERT: *(to the* PSAMMEAD*)* Will it still be here?

PSAMMEAD: Of course. Until sunset.

ANTHEA: Then *all* the money disappears?

PSAMMEAD: Right.

ANTHEA: What about the money we've given to others, in payment?

PSAMMEAD: Oh, that stays with them. You've got to be honest.

ROBERT: Let's go, then!

JANE: Oh, yes.

PSAMMEAD: *(climbs onto the sandpit)* Good-bye, my friends. Spend wisely.

(The CHILDREN *wave, say good-bye.* JANE *grasps the pram handle and they cross to stage right, stop outside the Sweet Shop. Lights dim on the sandpit.)*

JANE: Think of all the sweets we can buy! Sherbet dabs, lollipops…

ROBERT: Gum drops.

ANTHEA: No. Raspberry drops. They last longer.

CYRIL: If you don't bite them. Toffees are better.

ROBERT: Doesn't matter. Now we've got so much money!

(The BAKER'S BOY *steps out of the Sweet Shop, his basket beside him. He hears Robert's last line.)*

BAKER'S BOY: You're late.

CYRIL: We've got your money.

BAKER'S BOY: Tenpence-halfpenny. *(hayp'ny)*

CYRIL: It was eightpence-halfpenny yesterday!

BAKER'S BOY: Penalty. For being late.

ROBERT: That's cheating.

BAKER'S BOY: I never cheat. Just good business. My dad says—

ROBERT: I don't care what your dad says.

CYRIL: We've got the money.

ROBERT: More than your dad'll ever have.

JANE: Or you.

CYRIL: Here.

(CYRIL *hands a sovereign to the* BAKER'S BOY.)

BAKER'S BOY: What's this?

CYRIL: A sovereign.

BAKER'S BOY: Never seen... *(bites it)* Is it real?

ROBERT: It'll buy everything in your basket.

JANE: If we wanted to.

ANTHEA: But we don't.

CYRIL: You need to give me change.

BAKER'S BOY: I can't take this.

CYRIL: It's legal; it's real money.

ANTHEA: Take it to your father. He'll know.

JANE: *(holding up coins from the pram)* We've got lots more!

CYRIL: *(pushing* JANE*'s hand down)* Keep it covered, Jane!

(*The* BAKER'S BOY *shakes his head, crosses toward stage-left, but the* POLICEMAN *enters and stands in front of him. They converse silently, with the* BAKER'S BOY *holding up the coin and pointing to the children.*)

(CYRIL *turns to* JANE, *who is still holding the pram handle, and inclines his head toward the Sweet Shop.*)

CYRIL: What do you want?

JANE: Can't I come? *(points to pram)* Anthea?

ANTHEA: I stayed out here yesterday.

JANE: *(to Robert)* What about you, then?

ROBERT: Still got blisters.

JANE: Don't believe you!

(ROBERT *holds his hands palms-out toward* JANE.)

JANE: *(continuing)* Not fair! *(to* CYRIL*)* Sherbet dabs. Two.

CYRIL: Right.

> *(*CYRIL, ANTHEA *and* ROBERT *enter the Sweet Shop. The* BAKER'S BOY *exits. The* POLICEMAN *approaches* JANE.*)*

POLICEMAN: Hello, young miss.

JANE: Oh, hello, sir.

POLICEMAN: On your own today?

JANE: No. They're in the shop.

POLICEMAN: Buying sweets for you, I hope.

JANE: Yes, sir.

POLICEMAN: Baby still asleep?

JANE: Yes.

POLICEMAN: Boy or girl?

JANE: Girl. Six months.

POLICEMAN: Can I see her?

JANE: Uh … you'll have to ask my sister.

> *(The* POLICEMAN *bends* over *the pram.* JANE *pulls the blanket over the baby and coins.)*

POLICEMAN: Surely, you can— *(let me see her)*

JANE: No, sir. Mother says not to let strangers—

POLICEMAN: Oh, come now! I'm hardly a stranger. Are you trying to hide something from me?

JANE: *(shrieks)* Anthea! Cyril! Come quick!

> *(The* POLICEMAN *backs off.* ANTHEA *runs out of the shop, closely followed by* CYRIL. *The coins clink in his pocket.)*

ANTHEA: What's the matter?

JANE: He wants to wake the baby.

ANTHEA: *(to the* POLICEMAN*)* Why would you do that?

POLICEMAN: A misunderstanding. I just wanted to see her.

CYRIL: But why?

POLICEMAN: I like babies.

JANE: He said I was trying to hide something.

(CYRIL *jumps between the* POLICEMAN *and* JANE.)

CYRIL: What would Jane be hiding?

POLICEMAN: Same as what rattles in your pocket, I should think.

CYRIL: In my pocket?

(*The* POLICEMAN *nods, waits expectantly.*)

POLICEMAN: Well?

CYRIL: Just…bits of metal.

(JANE *smoothes the blanket over the coins in the pram, tucking the edges in.* ANTHEA *places a hand on her arm.*)

ANTHEA: *(whispers)* Easy.

(ROBERT *enters from the Sweet Shop, carrying several bags of sweets. His pockets clink as he walks. He hands a sweet bag each to* CYRIL *and* ANTHEA.)

ROBERT: *(to Jane)* Yours are in my pocket. *(to Cyril and Anthea)* What's going on?

(ROBERT *pulls two sherbet dabs from his pocket and hands them to* JANE. *A sovereign is pulled out, falls to the ground, and rolls toward the* POLICEMAN. CYRIL *jumps forward but the* POLICEMAN *gets there first, holds it up, inspects it.*)

CYRIL: That's my change!

POLICEMAN: Pretty big for change, isn't it?

(*The* POLICEMAN *bites the coin, slips it into his tunic pocket.*)

It's real! I'll just hang onto it, for the time being.

CYRIL: But it's ours.

POLICEMAN: Don't worry. You'll get it back. *(slight pause)* Now, yesterday you were short of money, weren't you?

CYRIL: We had money.

POLICEMAN: Enough to buy a loaf of bread?

CYRIL: Uh… no.

POLICEMAN: But today, you seem to be quite… what shall I say? Wealthy?

CYRIL: Well, hardly.

POLICEMAN: So, where did you get a coin like this?

JANE: We wished for it.

POLICEMAN: Young lady: this is *not* the time for jokes.

ANTHEA: Excuse me, but why are you questioning us like this?

(The PSAMMEAD *jumps down from the sandpit, listens.)*

POLICEMAN: You need to know I am investigating a robbery—a very serious robbery.

ANTHEA: And you suspect *us*?

POLICEMAN: I must follow every possible avenue—

ANTHEA: You think we *stole* the money?

POLICEMAN: As I said, I— *(must follow…)*

ANTHEA: That's horrible!

POLICEMAN: How else can you explain where the money came from?

(Pause. The CHILDREN *look at one another. The* POLICEMAN *steps in front of* ROBERT.*)*

So, young man, if you could just empty out your pockets.

ROBERT: Me?

JANE: Oooh, Robert!

ROBERT: *(to* CYRIL*)* Do I have to?

CYRIL: No. I don't think so.

POLICEMAN: As I am an officer of the law, you are required to do as I say.

ANTHEA: Not without reasonable cause, I think. *(to* CYRIL*)* I read that in a book, once.

POLICEMAN: Are you going to empty your pockets?

(LADY C enters stage left. She pauses and listens.)

(ROBERT shakes his head 'no.')

POLICEMAN: *(continuing)* Then I am going to have to do it for you. Raise your arms. Raise them!

(CYRIL jumps between ROBERT and the POLICEMAN.)

CYRIL: No!

POLICEMAN: Out of my way!

ANTHEA: *(jumps to CYRIL's side)* No. This isn't right—

(LADY C pulls a piece of paper from her bag)

LADY C: *(calls)* Constable! Constable! I have made a list for you. Everything that's missing. You weren't at the police station, so I hurried into the village.

POLICEMAN: *(backs away from the children)* Ah! Lady Chittenden. Thank you. So kind. That's just what I need.

(The POLICEMAN takes the list from LADY C.).

LADY C: What was happening? Just now?

POLICEMAN: The actions of these children are consistent with those of someone who has acquired stolen goods and sold them.

LADY C: You think *they* stole my jewelry?

POLICEMAN: And the candlesticks. Which could be hidden in that perambulator.

LADY C: My dear man! I know these children. I applaud your zeal, but really...

POLICEMAN: They have money with them. Big money.

LADY C: How do you know that?

POLICEMAN: Madam: I have seen it! *(shows coin from his pocket)* And I have reason to believe they have more—much more—in the boys' pockets and the pram.

LADY C: Is it a crime to be carrying money?

POLICEMAN: They have been trying to conceal it.

LADY C: *(to* the CHILDREN*)* Do you have money with you?

> *(The* CHILDREN *nod.)*

> A lot of money?

CYRIL: Some money.

JANE: But it's ours!

LADY C: I'm sure it is.

ROBERT: He wanted to search in my pockets.

JANE: And to look in the pram.

LADY C: As the Constable is investigating a robbery—on my behalf—he does have a right to ask you questions.

ANTHEA: But not to search us, surely?

LADY C: Hmm! *(to the* POLICEMAN*)* Do you have sufficient evidence—cause—to search them?

POLICEMAN: Money. Big money. And I heard metal clinking.

ROBERT: Meccano pieces. I always carry them.

POLICEMAN: In the pram, too?

ANTHEA: *(to* LADY C *and the* POLICEMAN*)* Can I talk to my brother for a moment? *(points to* CYRIL*)* Privately?

> *(*LACY C *exchanges a questioning glance with the* POLICEMAN*; he nods and turns to* ANTHEA.*)*

POLICEMAN: Providing you both remain in my sight.

> *(*ANTHEA *and* CYRIL *walk upstage and huddle. In mime, Anthea confides an idea. They look up at the sky [the stage light has grown slightly dimmer]. CYRIL laughs;* ANTHEA *giggles. They approach the others.)*

ANTHEA: *(to* LADY C*)* We realize the Constable has a job to do, so we are willing to turn out our pockets.

> *(*ROBERT *gasps.* ANTHEA *turns to the* POLICEMAN.*)*

> And let you look in the pram.

> *(*JANE *gasps.)*

CYRIL: But not quite yet.

(CYRIL *takes* ROBERT *aside; whispers*)

CYRIL: *(continuing)* Slap your pocket.

ROBERT: What?

CYRIL: Just do it.

ROBERT: Like this? *(he slaps his pocket; there is no metal clinking)*

CYRIL: Right! Good.

ANTHEA: *(to JANE)* Rock the pram. Hard!

JANE: But it'll—

ANTHEA: No it won't.

(JANE rocks the pram. There is no sound.)

(ANTHEA turns to CYRIL.)

It's all right, Cy!

CYRIL: Ah! Good!

(The PSAMMEAD leaps off the sandpit and advances toward stage center; he stops and listens.)

JANE: Shall I check inside the pram?

ANTHEA: Yes, but don't make it obvious.

JANE: *(acting)* Oh-oh. I think the baby's awake.

(JANE leans over the pram with her back to the POLICEMAN; she feels inside the pram.)

No, she's all right now.

CYRIL: *(to JANE)* Call him.

(JANE skips across to the POLICEMAN, pats his lower jacket pocket.)

JANE: Sir! Sir!

POLICEMAN: Oh! You're ready?

JANE: Yes.

POLICEMAN: To show me your money?

JANE: Yes!

POLICEMAN: Right. Right. Now, who wants to be first?

CYRIL: You can start with me if you—

ROBERT: No! Me! You were asking me before.

POLICEMAN: Right. Well, I think you can empty your own
pockets.

*(ROBERT pulls out a handful of gold coins and holds
them out to the POLICEMAN.)*

ROBERT: Here you are, sir. Just like you said.

POLICEMAN: Ah! I thought as much.

*(The POLICEMAN takes a coin, holds it to his mouth,
and bites hard.)*

POLICEMAN: Ugh… it's soft.

*(The PSAMMEAD makes a gleeful leap. The
POLICEMAN peels the gold cover back.)*

It's chocolate!

JANE: Chocolate?

ROBERT: Yes, chocolate! Have one.

*(ROBERT hands a coin to each child and LADY C.
They unwrap and start munching. JANE runs to the
pram, pulls out a handful.)*

JANE: Mine are the same.

ANTHEA: That Psammead!

PSAMMEAD: *(to the audience)* I did that! Cool, eh?

JANE: *(to the POLICEMAN)* Please have another.

POLICEMAN: Thank you, miss.

(He takes another coin, holds it up, turns to LADY C.)

It's…. It's unbelievable. They were hard metal before.

LADY C: So that's all right, then?

(The POLICEMAN shakes his head)

POLICEMAN: I… I don't understand…

LADY C: Hmmm. Then I suggest you search elsewhere. *(exits stage right)*

ROBERT: *(to the* POLICEMAN*)* Oh, I do have some metal in here. You may feel in my pocket if you wish....Go on. It won't bite.

(The POLICEMAN *lowers his hand into* ROBERT*'s pocket and pulls out two short pieces of Meccano.)*

Sorry they're so sticky. My toffees were in there, too.

POLICEMAN: Ugh.

(He hands the Meccano pieces back to ROBERT*.)*

Well, young people, I'll bid you good night, then.

CYRIL: And we'll head for home.

POLICEMAN: Right, you just do that. Before it gets dark.

ROBERT: Good-night, sir.

JANE: Night-night.

CYRIL: Au revoir.

ROBERT: Enjoy the chocolate.

PSAMMEAD: *(gleefully, echoes Robert)* Enjoy the chocolate!

ANTHEA: That Psammead! Such a sense of humor.

(The CHILDREN, *relieved, double up with laughter. The* PSAMMEAD *echoes them with a leap.)*

(The POLICEMAN *turns stage right and crosses toward the exit. Then he pauses and pulls out the original coin, compares it with the chocolate one.* CYRIL *watches.)*

POLICEMAN: This one is real. I'll get them yet, I know I will. *(exits)*

CYRIL: *(to* ANTHEA) The Constable. He's still suspicious. We've *got* to find the jewels.

ANTHEA: But how?

ROBERT: If we could fly. Look down from above.

CYRIL: Like Peter Pan?

JANE: And Wendy.

ROBERT: And Michael and John.

ANTHEA: Yes, but…

JANE: Nobody'd notice us.

ROBERT: Grown-ups just don't think to look up.

ANTHEA: Yes, but….

CYRIL: Oh, Anthea! Don't be such a downer!

ANTHEA: Yes, but … *how*?

CYRIL: We could ask the Psammead.

PSAMMEAD: O-o-h-h?

ROBERT: Ask for wings!

PSAMMEAD: Wings!

CYRIL: Tomorrow. Just for one day.

JANE: Oooh!

　　(The CHILDREN *exit stage left.)*

PSAMMEAD: *(to the audience)* Well, what do you think? Will I be able to give them wings? Hmmm?

CURTAIN

INTERMISSION

Act 2

(Above stage center is a sturdy platform lit by four spotlights, one for each child. On it the children are standing, raising their arms as though they are flying. Ideally, the platform has several levels—small platforms—one for each child, so they are not necessarily flying in a horizontal row. Behind them there is a projection of passing clouds, which move opposite to the direction the children are flying. When they come to rest on the flat segment of the church roof, a backdrop of the church spire and sloping roofs rises from a roller at floor level, so the children appear to be descending toward and alighting on the roof. Their platform is broad enough for them to sit. Light on it should be so arranged that the presence of the platform is not easily seen).

(Each child has—at the director's discretion—a set of wings or a simple extension on each hand, like a glove with white feathers on it that extend by about 18 centimeters (7 inches). The wings or finger extensions should be sufficiently obvious that the children cannot risk being seen in public.)

Curtain Up

(Only the PSAMMEAD is visible. He faces upstage, raising his arms in time with the background music, as he strives to make the children's wish come true. He then cavorts downstage and addresses the audience.)

PSAMMEAD: It took some doing, but I did it! You should've seen little Jane: light as a feather. Just held her hands out horizontally beside her, bent her knees, fluttered her fingers, and gave a smart little kick with her feet. And there she was, sailing over the rooftops!

JANE: *(v.o. above stage)* Oh, Sammy! Look at me!

PSAMMEAD: Where? Where are you, Miss Jane?

JANE: *(v.o.)* Up here!

PSAMMEAD: Ah! Is that you, circling around planet Jupiter?

JANE: *(spotlight on her)* No, silly! Just above the trees.

PSAMMEAD: Now I see you! Very nice.

ANTHEA: *(spotlight on her)* I'm here, too!

PSAMMEAD: Ah, yes, Miss Anthea. Looking very graceful, too!

ANTHEA: Oh, you!

ROBERT: *(spotlight on him)* It makes you feel funny, like you want to reach down, touch the ground, just to be sure you can!

PSAMMEAD: That's normal. You'll get used to it.

CYRIL: *(spotlight on him)* I flew down, to check I could. Didn't gauge it right. Bumped onto the gravel.

PSAMMEAD: You have to approach s-l-o-w-l-y.

CYRIL: So I discovered!

(The CHILDREN *laugh.)*

PSAMMEAD: All right, then. Now you've got your wings, how are you going to use them?

JANE: We're going on a search.

ROBERT: All over the town.

ANTHEA: See if we can find Lady Chittenden's jewels.

PSAMMEAD: Well, get on with it! You've only got so much time.

CYRIL: *(swiveling to his right)* Right! *(looking back, to the others)* Follow me!

*(*THEY *swivel toward stage right, waving their arms. The* PSAMMEAD *backs toward the left exit, as though they are flying away from him.)*

PSAMMEAD: *(calling after them)* Watch the time, Master Cyril.

CYRIL: I will.

PSAMMEAD: Make sure you're on the ground before sunset. If you're in the air, you'll just fall.

JANE: Oooh!

CYRIL: I've got my watch. 'Bye.

(The others call goodbye. The PSAMMEAD *exits stage left. Pause, while the children fly.* LADY C *enters stage right, backing in, bending over and scraping a hoe along the earth, as though tending her garden.)*

ROBERT: How fast d'you think we're going?

ANTHEA: About ten miles an hour, I should think.

ROBERT: Oh, more than that, surely.

ANTHEA: Look! There's Lady Chittenden.

JANE: Hello, Lady Chittenden. We're looking for—

*(LADY C *looks around for the voice.)*

CYRIL: No, Jane! No one must know we're up here.

ROBERT: Because they'd hide things.

JANE: Oh, sorry.

*(LADY C *exits backwards, still raking, stage left.)*

CYRIL: Keep your eyes peeled, for anything suspicious.

(The CHILDREN *look from side to side. The* POLICEMAN *enters stage right, swinging his truncheon, moving across the stage.)*

ANTHEA: Look who's here!

ROBERT: Let's follow him.

CYRIL: Good idea.

(The CHILDREN *swing around to face stage left. The* POLICEMAN *reaches mid-stage and then seems to be stepping but is staying center.* LADY C *backs in from stage left, hoeing the ground. The* POLICEMAN *clears his throat.* LADY C *looks around. The* CHILDREN *stop waving their arms/wings and just flutter them gently to stay airborne.)*

LADY C: Ah! Constable. Any news yet?

POLICEMAN: I regret not, Lady Chittenden. But I do have my suspicions. Those children…

LADY C: The de Havilland children?

POLICEMAN: They have been acting very strangely.

ROBERT: He should see how strangely we're acting now!

(The CHILDREN *giggle.)*

JANE: Just don't look up, Mister Policeman.

CYRIL: Come, we can't waste any more time.

(The CHILDREN *swing around and fly toward stage right. The* POLICEMAN *and* LADY C *exit stage left.)*

POLICEMAN: *(as they exit, to* LADY C*)* I have to follow every lead.

ANTHEA: We really must find the culprit.

CYRIL: Definitely.

ANTHEA: Look who's coming now!

(The BAKER'S BOY *enters stage right, swinging his basket.)*

JANE: It's the Baker's Boy!

CYRIL: Ssssh!

ROBERT: I've got something for him.

*(*ROBERT *throws a chocolate coin at the* BAKER'S BOY*. It bounces on the ground. The* BAKER'S BOY *looks around, picks it up.)*

BAKER'S BOY: Another one! Now where did that come from?

*(*ROBERT *throws a second coin. The* BAKER'S BOY *picks it up.)*

CYRIL: That's enough, Robert!

ROBERT: But it's so much fun.

JANE: Don't waste them on him.

ANTHEA: Too true.

(As the BAKER'S BOY *moves to exit stage left, the* POLICEMAN *enters and faces him. The* CHILDREN *turn to watch, hovering.)*

POLICEMAN: Ah! Just the young man I want to see.

BAKER'S BOY: Uh... *(holds his basket behind him)* Sir?

POLICEMAN: Do you, by any chance, happen to have one of those coins?

BAKER'S BOY: Yes. I just found one. *(holds out chocolate coin)*

POLICEMAN: No, no. Not the chocolate ones. A real one. Like this. *(he holds up a golden sovereign)* Did the de Havilland children use one to pay you for bread?

BAKER'S BOY: Yes. They did.

POLICEMAN: Do you still have it?

BAKER'S BOY: Yes.

POLICEMAN: Well, can I have it?

BAKER'S BOY: Oh, I don't know about that. My father—

POLICEMAN: Oh, come now! I only want to borrow it. Take me to your father. I'll ask him.

(The BAKER'S BOY *and* POLICEMAN *exit stage left.)*

ANTHEA: The Constable still thinks we did it!

JANE: Oooh!

ROBERT: Now he'll have three golden sovereigns.

CYRIL: Come on then. We can't waste any time.

(The CHILDREN *fly toward stage right. Fade to blackout, then fade in with the children facing downstage, flying toward the audience.)*

JANE: Oh, I'm so tired.

ANTHEA: We all are, Jane.

JANE: I think my arms want to fall off.

ANTHEA: *(to* CYRIL*)* We really should take a rest.

ROBERT: But we haven't found anything yet.

ANTHEA: Just for a short while. We don't want Jane to fall.

CYRIL: All right, then. But it must be somewhere where we can't be seen.

(The CHILDREN *look around.)*

JANE: Oh, do be quick. Please!

ROBERT: What about that flat roof, beside the church?

CYRIL: Yes. That'll do. Come on.

(The CHILDREN *lean forward. A backdrop of a church spire rises from the floor behind them.)*

Easy! Not too fast, or you'll land too hard. Hurt yourself.

JANE: Oooh!

(The backdrop stops and the CHILDREN *sprawl then sit up. They rub their shoulders and upper arms.)*

Just in time.

ROBERT: Anthea: did you bring anything to eat?

ANTHEA: No.

ROBERT: No sandwiches?

ANTHEA: We were going home for lunch. Remember?

JANE: Oh, I'm so hungry. I think I shall die if I don't eat.

CYRIL: Oh, don't be silly, Jane.

JANE: It's like there's a knot tied in my— *(tummy.)*

*(*ROBERT *is peering over the edge of the roof, looking down toward stage left.)*

ROBERT: Look in that larder window down there: Bread and butter! Cakes! Scones! All laid out.

JANE: Ready to eat! Oooh!

*(*ROBERT *sits on the upstage edge of the roof.)*

ROBERT: I'm going down. Borrow some.

ANTHEA: No, Robert. You can't. That'd be stealing.

(Pause. They eye the food.)

JANE: If only we still had some golden sovereigns. Then we could pay for it.

CYRIL: Has anyone got some money? Small coins? We could leave some in payment. *(feels in his pocket)* I've got a florin.

ROBERT: *(counting)* I've got ninepence.

ANTHEA: *(searches in satchel)* Ummm…. Two sixpences and a threepenny bit. *(pronounced threp'ny)*

(They look at JANE.*)*

JANE: Girls don't have pockets. You know that.

CYRIL: That's four shillings even. Give it to me. I'll fly down.

ROBERT: No. It was my idea. I'll do it.

ANTHEA: Here: take my satchel.

*(*ROBERT *slings the satchel over his shoulder, leans toward upstage, spreads his arms, dives off the platform [he is now out of sight of the audience]. The others watch him and then swing around to face downstage left.)*

JANE: Do be careful, Robert.

ANTHEA: Mind those trees.

CYRIL: As you come down, flap your wings fast so you drop slowly.

(Lights up on a window stage left, at face level. In the window there are plates of small cakes, sandwiches, and a pitcher of lemonade. Enter ROBERT. *He leans into the window and stuffs sandwiches into the satchel.)*

JANE: *(calling)* Bring a jam roll for me.

CYRIL: *(calling)* And me!

ANTHEA: *(calling)* Drinks, too.

JANE: Yes, I am *so* thirsty.

*(*ROBERT *exits stage left.)*

CYRIL: Not so fast, Robert! You won't be able to stop in time.

JANE: Oh, do be careful.

(ROBERT's head and shoulders appear at the upstage edge of the platform.)

ROBERT: Take these!

CYRIL: Right.

(ROBERT passes the satchel to CYRIL, who empties it and hands it back.)

ANTHEA: Cucumber sandwiches!

JANE: Jam roll too!

ROBERT: There's some lemonade. I'm going back for it.

(ROBERT dives away and appears at the window.)

JANE: *(calling)* Oh, you are clever, Robert.

CYRIL: *(calling)* Bring four cups. And don't forget to leave the money.

ANTHEA: *(calling)* Take your time, Robert, or you'll bump into the wall.

(ROBERT places money on the window ledge, picks up cups, shoves them into the satchel, grabs the pitcher [thermos], and exits.)

JANE: Here he comes.

(ROBERT's head appears behind the platform. ANTHEA grabs the pitcher, CYRIL the satchel. ROBERT pulls himself onto the platform. ANTHEA pours out drinks.)

JANE: We saved the biggest piece of cake for you.

ROBERT: Thanks.

CYRIL: Nice work, Rob.

ANTHEA: *(passing cup to ROBERT)* Here. You can be first.

ROBERT: *(takes a drink)* Lovely!

(There are murmurs of appreciation: 'That's good;' 'Nice sandwich;' 'I needed that!)

JANE: My tummy feels so much happier!

ANTHEA: Mine, too!

CYRIL: Which way shall we search next?

ROBERT: *(munches, points upstage)* We haven't been that way.

JANE: Oh, Cy, not yet. I'm still tired.

ANTHEA: We could all do with a bit of a rest.

ROBERT: How long have we got until…? *(holds up his wings)*

CYRIL: Sunset?

(ROBERT *nods.*)

A couple of hours.

ROBERT: Then we could.

CYRIL: Well… just fifteen minutes.

ANTHEA: *(to JANE, points to her own lap)* Rest your head here.

(The CHILDREN lean back, eyes closed, as the lights dim slowly to a blackout.)

(Sound of screams. Lights up on the window stage left. There is no light stage center.)

HOUSEKEEPER: *(v.o.)* Oh, no! I've been robbed! *(her head appears at the window)* Help! Help! Call the police! All the tea things have been stolen. The lemonade, too. And I just made it!

(The POLICEMAN enters stage left.)

Oh, thank you for coming so quickly.

POLICEMAN: Yes, madam, I heard you call.

HOUSEKEEPER: Everything's gone. All the things I made for the vicar's tea.

POLICEMAN: Now, can you tell me—

HOUSEKEEPER: Oh, he will be so upset.

POLICEMAN: Did you see anyone?

HOUSEKEEPER: He does so like his cucumber sandwiches.

POLICEMAN: Yes, madam. Did you see anyone?

HOUSEKEEPER: No. No one.

POLICEMAN: Hear anyone?

HOUSEKEEPER: No. I was out in the scullery. At the back of the vicarage.

POLICEMAN: *(pulls out his notebook)* Now, what exactly has been stolen?

(The HOUSEKEEPER *and* POLICEMAN *mime conversation; he makes notes.)*

(Lights up on the CHILDREN, *who are asleep. Their wings have gone.* CYRIL *wakens and looks at his watch, then at the sky.)*

CYRIL: Oh, my goodness. *(looks at his hands)* Oh, no! *(shakes the others)* Wake up, wake up! We've slept too long.

(The CHILDREN *waken sleepily.* ROBERT, *more alert, grabs the pitcher and satchel, stuffs the cups into it.)*

ROBERT: I must take these back.

*(*ROBERT *stands on the upstage edge of the platform, spreads his arms, is about to dive down.)*

CYRIL: No, Robert! Stop! You can't fly any more. It's past sunset.

ROBERT: What?

(They inspect their arms and fingers.)

JANE: No more wings!

ROBERT: *(holds up satchel and pitcher)* How am I going to…?

ANTHEA: How are we going to get down?

JANE: Oooh, and it'll be dark soon.

CYRIL: *(points offstage left)* There's a door over there. I'll check.

*(*CYRIL *scrambles offstage; sound of door being rattled.)*

(v.o.) No. It's locked. *(he re-enters)*

ROBERT: There's no other way?

CYRIL: No. I looked.

ANTHEA: We can't stay here all night.

CYRIL: We'll have to shout for help; hope someone hears us.

(They lean over the roof edge and shout: 'Help,' 'Help us,' 'We're up here,' etc. The POLICEMAN *and* HOUSEKEEPER *look around and eventually up.)*

POLICEMAN: What are you young people doing up there?

CYRIL: We're trapped.

ROBERT: The door's locked.

JANE: We can't get down.

POLICEMAN: How did you get up there?

JANE: We were flying and—

*(*ROBERT *claps a hand over* JANE*'s mouth.)*

POLICEMAN: This is no time for levity, young lady.

ANTHEA: Do you think you could get a key, sir? Open the door?

POLICEMAN: *(to the* HOUSEKEEPER*)* Do you have a key?

HOUSEKEEPER: *(takes a bunch of keys from her pocket)* One of these, I should think.

(The POLICEMAN *exits stage right. Sound of steps on stairs, keys in lock, then squeaky door opening. The* POLICEMAN *enters stage right, on the roof.)*

POLICEMAN: Ah! I might have known: the de Havilland children! Come on!

(All exit stage right, scrambling one after another, and re-enter at floor level stage right.)

Now: How did you get up there, in the first place?

(The CHILDREN *look at each other.)*

ROBERT: Well, it's a little difficult— *(to explain)*

CYRIL: By the stairs.

POLICEMAN: But the door was locked.

CYRIL: Uh... It wasn't when we climbed up.

ROBERT: Someone must have locked it while we were up there.

ANTHEA: We fell asleep, you see.

POLICEMAN: You children! This is most suspicious.

(The HOUSEKEEPER *angrily pulls the cups and flask from ROBERT's satchel.)*

(Fade stage left, then bring spotlight up on the PSAMMEAD *downstage right.)*

PSAMMEAD: *(to the audience)* They really did fly, didn't they? Wish I could fly like that. Trouble is, as a sand wizard I can grant wishes for other people—special people—but never for myself. It's not allowed. *(does a little leap)* I wish I could help the de Havilland children more. That constable is so suspicious of them. You don't think they stole Lady Chittenden's jewels, do you? *(listens)* No. Of course not. *(hand to lips, to silence audience)* Ah! Here they come now!

(Enter CHILDREN *stage left,* CYRIL *pushes the pram.* ROBERT *and* JANE *run up to the* PSAMMEAD.)*

ROBERT: We've got such a good idea!

PSAMMEAD: *(irony)* Another one?

JANE: We're going to wish for pirates.

PSAMMEAD: Pirates?

ROBERT: Pirates know how to find hidden treasure.

CYRIL: Like in Treasure Island.

JANE: And in Peter Pan.

PSAMMEAD: Ah. I see. *(to* ANTHEA*)* Good morning, Miss Anthea. You are looking nice today.

ANTHEA: Thank you. Do you think pirates can help us?

PSAMMEAD: I cannot give you advice. Only grant your wishes.

CYRIL: *(takes a decisive stance)* Alright. Alright. Then, I wish for pirates to help us find the jewelry.

ROBERT: Pirates just like Captain Hook and his mate Smee.

JANE: Oooh!

(The PSAMMEAD *goes into a trance. The lights come up on a pirate ship [the deck and base of a mast, center stage], with a gangplank facing downstage and a plank*

jutting out left from the ship's side. HOOK *and* SMEE *are offstage. The* PSAMMEAD *gestures to the audience as though saying: 'See: I did it!' He exits left.)*

HOOK and SMEE: *(chanting, v.o. until on the deck)*
>Ho, ho, ho, and a bottle of rum,
>We sail the seas in the burning sun
>In hope of finding buried treasure;
>That, my hearties, is our pleasure.
>Ho, ho, ho, and it's land ahoy.
>And we're not afraid of that pesky boy
>Who cut off Captain Hook's right hand,
>The boy from Never Never Land.
>Ho, ho, ho, of whom do we speak?
>By now you'll know the one we seek
>The boy who acts like he's a man.
>Who else, but Master Peter Pan!

ROBERT: *(to* CYRIL*)* You got your wish!

CYRIL: More than I expected!

ANTHEA: A boat, too!

HOOK: Did I hear someone call?

ROBERT: Look! The Captain's got a hook instead of a hand!

CYRIL: It really is Captain Hook!

JANE: Oooh!

ROBERT: And the other one must be Smee.

HOOK: Did I hear someone say Smee?

SMEE: Oh, you did. Of that I'm sure.

HOOK: Come then. We must investigate.

*(*HOOK *and* SMEE *walk down the gangplank, approach the* CHILDREN.*)*

Ah-ha, me hearties: who do we have here?

CYRIL: Good morning, sir. I am Cyril de Havilland.

HOOK: *(whispers to* SMEE*)* Cyril? I think not.

CYRIL: And this is my sister Anthea.

SMEE: *(to* HOOK, *whispers)* Anthea? I think not.

CYRIL: And these are Robert and Jane.

HOOK: Oh, ho, ho! How do you do?

> *(*HOOK *holds forward his hook, as though to shake hands.* ROBERT *reaches forward, hesitates, partly withdraws, then reaches forward again, grasps the metal, and wraps his fingers around it.)*

JANE: Oooh!

HOOK: Ah! You are a brave one!

SMEE: Few men, even, like to shake hands with Captain Hook!

ANTHEA: *(to Smee)* Then may I shake hands with you?

SMEE: Ah, my dear! That would be a pleasure.

> *(*HOOK *places his left hand over* ROBERT's. *Robert cannot let go.* SMEE *grasps* ANTHEA's *hand firmly.)*

You have such a small, gentle hand.

> *(*ROBERT *struggles to let go.* CYRIL *offers his hand to* HOOK.*)*

CYRIL: May I say good morning to you, too, sir?

HOOK: Oh, most certainly.

> *(*HOOK *releases* ROBERT's *hand, takes* CYRIL's.*)*

Good morning to you.

CYRIL: Good morning, sir.

HOOK: *(to* SMEE*)* You know who I have here, Smee, don't you?

SMEE: I could make a guess, sir.

HOOK: And you know who you have a-hold of?

SMEE: She says her name is Anthea. But I think not.

*(*ANTHEA *struggles to pull her hand free.)*

HOOK: You cannot fool Captain Hook, my friends.

> *(to* CYRIL*)* You are Peter Pan!

CYRIL: Peter Pan?

HOOK: At long last I have captured you. *(to* ANTHEA*)* And you, my dear, are Wendy. The 'mother.' Right, Smee?

SMEE: Oh, Wendy, sir. Without doubt. You can see the likeness.

ANTHEA: I'm Anthea. Anthea!

HOOK: And those over there: they're Michael and Tinker Bell.

CYRIL: This is ridiculous!

HOOK: Ridiculous? I think not.

(HOOK *is pulling* CYRIL *up the gangplank.)*

Pull her on board, Smee! Tie her to the mast.

SMEE: Exactly what I intend to do, Cap'n.

(ROBERT *and* JANE *run up to the gangplank, try to dislodge the pirates' hands from* CYRIL *and* ANTHEA. *Grunts and groans, shouts of 'Stop that,' etc.)*

Oh, no you don't!

(SMEE *pulls a coil of rope from the deck and swings it.* ROBERT *and* JANE *back off.* SMEE *holds* ANTHEA *against the mast, ties a rope around her.)*

HOOK: Time I got my own back, Peter Pan. Fix your impetuousness! Hand me a rope, Smee.

ROBERT: *(shouts)* Leave them alone, you great bullies!

JANE: *(runs stage left, shouts to offstage)* Help! Help! Someone please come.

CYRIL: Do what you want with me. But please let Anthea go!

HOOK: She's Wendy, and you know that! You can't fool me.

CYRIL: Oh, please!

SMEE: Not likely. Right, Cap'n?

HOOK: Right.

ANTHEA: *(shouts)* Robert! Jane! Go and get help! Run!

SMEE: You just stop that.

(SMEE *ties a handkerchief around* ANTHEA*'s mouth.)*

CYRIL: *(shouts)* Get the Constable! He'll know what to do.

ROBERT: *(shouts back)* He wouldn't believe us. Not now.

HOOK: Ha, ha! Is anyone going to believe you?

SMEE: No one! Ho, ho, ho.

> *(The pirates tie up Cyril. JANE beckons to ROBERT to join her at stage left.)*

JANE: Robert! I've got an idea… *(whispers in ROBERT's ear)*

ROBERT: Do you think he will?

JANE: We can but try.

ROBERT: You sound just like mother!

JANE: *(shouts to offstage left)* Psammy! Oh, Psammy. Please come! We need you.

ROBERT: Oh, please, Mister Psammead. Jane does need you.

PSAMMEAD: *(v.o.)* I hear you, Miss Jane; Master Robert.

> *(The PSAMMEAD enters stage left.)*

Now, what is there that's so urgent?

JANE: Look! Do you see what the pirates have done?

> *(The three look toward the pirate ship.)*

HOOK: You, Peter Pan, are going to walk the plank!

JANE: Oh, no!

SMEE: It's ever so deep. You'll make quite a splash.

HOOK: And then it will be Wendy's turn.

> *(SMEE picks up a rock from the deck, throws the rock overboard. There is the sound of a tremendous splash.)*

SMEE: See?

JANE: Oooh! *(to the PSAMMEAD)* Do you think I could have just one more wish? A very special one?

PSAMMEAD: Under the circumstances, I think it might be granted.

JANE: Captain Hook thinks I'm Tinker Bell. Could you really turn me into Tinker Bell? Just for fifteen minutes?

PSAMMEAD: Most unusual. But innovative, I must say.

JANE: Please?

PSAMMEAD: What will you do, though?

JANE: I'll be able to fly. Annoy Captain Hook and his Mate. Get in their way.

ROBERT: And I'll scoot home and get help.

PSAMMEAD: Ah!

JANE: But we must hurry!

PSAMMEAD: Right, then. Make your wish!

JANE: Oh, you are sweet, Sammy.

(JANE takes a wishing stance close to the stage left exit.)

I wish… I wish I was Tinker Bell. For just 15 minutes.

(The PSAMMEAD concentrates. There is a musical wishing sound accompanied by little bells, a puff of smoke, and JANE disappears. In her place a bright blue light is projected from stage front, which will 'fly' across the backdrop and harass HOOK and SMEE. We hear JANE's voice, accompanied by the tinkle of a bell.)

Oh, look at me! I'm flying! Oh, thank you, Psammy. Run, Robert, as quick as you can.

ROBERT: Right. I'm off. *(exits stage left)*

PSAMMEAD: *(to audience)* This should be interesting!

(The TINKER BELL light 'flies' across the back of the stage, hovers over HOOK and SMEE, then dives down and buzzes around SMEE's head. SMEE tries catching her, and then waves her away, arms flung around him.)

JANE: *(v.o. stage right)* He, he, he! You can't catch me!

SMEE: Get away! Get away!

HOOK: Stop fooling around, Smee. Help me push Peter out onto the plank.

(TINKER BELL swoops around HOOK's head. SMEE crosses to help HOOK.)

Get away! Get away from me!

187

JANE: *(v.o.)* You leave Cyril alone. Peter alone.

(TINKER BELL 'flies' to ANTHEA and hovers over and around her [trying to untie the rope].)

HOOK: Stop her, Smee!

SMEE: Yes, Cap'n.

(TINKER BELL 'flies' straight at SMEE, harasses him. The PSAMMEAD gives a leap of pleasure.)

PSAMMEAD: Go on, Miss Jane. You're doing marvelously. But watch the time.

(TINKER BELL harasses HOOK; he waves his hook in annoyance. CYRIL is now far out on the plank.)

HOOK: Get away, drat it! Get away.

(ROBERT enters stage left, bearing a leafy branch in front of him. He is carrying a very large alarm clock.)

PSAMMEAD: Ah! You're back. What's *that* for?

(ROBERT turns so Hook and Smee can't see the clock. He winds it up.)

ROBERT: It's an alarm clock. In the book of Peter Pan, Captain Hook is terrified of alarm clocks.

PSAMMEAD: Of alarm clocks?

ROBERT: The crocodile that ate his arm swallowed an alarm clock. When he hears the ticking he thinks the croc is after him again.

PSAMMEAD: Oh, ho.

ROBERT: You sound like Captain Hook!

(ROBERT stops winding. We hear ticking.)

Now, I'll hide behind the bush.

(ROBERT buries the alarm clock among the leaves of the branch. Holding the branch in front of him, he advances slowly toward the pirate ship, The sound of the ticking grows louder and louder as ROBERT nears the ship.)

HOOK: Get away, drat it!

SMEE: Do you hear that, Cap'n?

HOOK: Hear what?

SMEE: Listen.

(They listen, look around. HOOK registers horror. TINKER BELL crosses to ANTHEA, starts 'working' on her ropes. We hear JANE's merry laugh.)

HOOK: It can't be the crocodile?

SMEE: Methinks it is.

(They look in all directions. ROBERT stops near the ship's side, abandons the bush, and hides. The ticking of the clock is now very loud.)

HOOK: It's that dratted crocodile.*(looks out into the water)* It's no good, Smee, I can't stay.

SMEE: Run then, Cap'n!

(ANTHEA, now untied, removes the gag from her mouth.)

ANTHEA: Thanks, Tinker Bell!

(TINKER BELL attacks HOOK and SMEE who, screeching and waving their arms, run down the gangplank, SMEE in front. ROBERT pushes his foot forward, trips up SMEE, who sprawls onto the ground with HOOK on top of him.)

HOOK: Get up, you fool.

(HOOK and SMEE make a galloping exit stage right. ANTHEA pulls CYRIL to safety, unties his ropes. TINKER BELL hovers around them, 'helping.')

CYRIL: Oh, thank you. You are clever, Tinker Bell... Jane!

(ROBERT climbs on the deck, throws the clock over the side. There is a splash and the ticking stops.)

PSAMMEAD: *(shouts)* Miss Jane! Tinker Bell!

(TINKER BELL hovers and 'listens.')

You have used up fourteen minutes. Get onto the ground! Please! Or you will fall.

JANE: *(v.o.)* Oh, Sammy! Thank you.

(The TINKER BELL *light 'flies' across the stage and into the wings stage left.* CYRIL, ANTHEA *and* ROBERT *cross to the left, stand beside the* PSAMMEAD, *and look into the wings. There is a tinkling sound and a light flash off stage left. We hear* JANE *laugh. The lights fade quickly over the boat.* JANE *enters.* ANTHEA *and* CYRIL *hug her and* ROBERT *claps her on the back. The* PSAMMEAD *turns to the audience, claps his hands, and they respond.*

Oh, thank you, Sammy. You saved the day!

PSAMMEAD: *(equivalent of a blush)* Oh, Miss Jane. *(he does a backflip)* But it was your idea. *(turns to the others)* Now, if you don't mind, I will return to my sandpit for a short nap. *(exits stage left)*

ANTHEA: That was a narrow escape for Peter – I mean Cyril!

(The POLICEMAN *enters stage right, watches. listens.)*

CYRIL: You were brilliant, Robert.

ANTHEA: I expected you to snap your jaws at any minute!

(ANTHEA makes crocodile jaws with her arms, and snaps them together.)

ROBERT: So: what's next?

CYRIL: *(indicates* POLICEMAN*)* Go on searching.

(The BAKER'S BOY *enters stage right, stands beside the Policeman. As the children talk, the* POLICEMAN *inclines his head toward them and nods to the* BAKER'S BOY, *who nods in return. The* POLICEMAN *exits.)*

JANE: *(to* CYRIL*)* Couldn't we read a bit more, about Peter Pan?

CYRIL: I think I've had enough of Peter Pan for the moment.

JANE: All that flying has made me tired.

CYRIL: *(searches in the pram)* I'm not sure I brought the book.

BAKER'S BOY: *(approaches)* So, what are the de Havilland children up to today?

ROBERT: None of your business.

BAKER'S BOY: And who do you think you're talking to?

ROBERT: You, you ignoramus.

(The BAKER'S BOY *lifts* ROBERT *up by the front of his shirt, speaks directly into his face. [Note: the pram is facing them, so the baby 'sees' what happens.])*

BAKER'S BOY: Any more cheek from you, and I'll smash you to pulp!

(The BAKER'S BOY *throws* ROBERT *down, who falls onto his back. The* BAKER'S BOY *brandishes his fist.)*

And that goes for the lot of you!

(He picks up his basket and exits stage right. CYRIL *and* ANTHEA *help* ROBERT *get back on his feet.)*

ROBERT: One day, when I'm bigger, I'll beat the—

ANTHEA: Robert!

ROBERT: You know what I mean.

CYRIL: We do. Come on, let's go.

ANTHEA: Whoa! Whose turn is it to push the baby?

JANE: Robert's.

ROBERT: Can't. Still got blisters.

ANTHEA: Show me. Come on, show me!

ROBERT: Oh, all right!

*(*ROBERT *grasps the pram handle and pushes toward stage right. Close to the exit he leans forward and speaks to the baby in the pram.)*

I wish you were grown up!

(The baby cries. The pram shakes and bounces.)

What's going on ….?

(The CHILDREN *crowd around the pram. The crying is replaced with a young woman's voice.)*

HILARY: *(v.o.)* Good lord! Well I'll be damned!

*(A young woman of 20, wearing fashionable clothes and
a boater hat, rises from 'inside' the pram.)*

HILARY: *(continuing)* It's only me!

ANTHEA: Who are you?

HILARY: I'm Hilary. Your sister. Hilary Joan.

JANE: The baby?

ANTHEA: How can you be? *(looks in the pram)* She's not there!

ROBERT: I… um…. I wished she was grown up.

CYRIL, ANTHEA, JANE: *(in chorus)* You did what!

ROBERT: *(shrugs, points)* There she is.

HILARY: It's true. But now I'm grown up, I am going to help
you find Lady Chittenden's jewels.

CYRIL: How do you know about that?

HILARY: I may be—I may have been—little, but I could see and
hear what was going on. Now, what's the plan?

CYRIL: We're walking around the village—

ANTHEA: To see what we can find.

HILARY: Walking?

ROBERT: How else are we to get there?

HILARY: But I'm not used to walking. I wish I had a bicycle.

(There is a whooshing sound and the PSAMMEAD
*enters stage right, somewhat erratically riding a bike. He
dismounts in front of the children.)*

JANE: Oh, Sammy!

PSAMMEAD: Special delivery for Miss Hilary de Havilland.

HILARY: You brought that for me?

CYRIL: You mean the *baby* gets a wish?

PSAMMEAD: Does she look like a baby?

CYRIL: Well, no….

ANTHEA: Until sunset, I suppose?

PSAMMEAD: Quite right, Miss Anthea. *(to* HILARY*)* Now, do be careful not to be on your bicycle when the sun sets.

JANE: Oooh!

HILARY: Then I shall start my search.

*(*HILARY *climbs on the bike.)*

PSAMMEAD: You must be fast: it's nearly sunset already.

HILARY: Good-bye for now.

*(*HILARY *exits stage left, primly riding the bike.)*

CYRIL: *(calls after her)* We will meet you here, Hilary!

HILARY: *(v.o.)* Right. Right here.

CYRIL: *(to the other children)* Come on then.

(With CYRIL *in the lead, the* CHILDREN *exit stage right. After a moment the* PSAMMEAD *sees the pram, takes the handle.)*

PSAMMEAD: *(calls after the children)* You forgot the pram!

(The PSAMMEAD *pushes the pram jauntily and exits stage left.)*

(The BAKER'S BOY *enters from the Sweet Shop, a bag of sweets in his hand. He stops, puts the basket down, unwraps a candy.* HILARY *enters from stage left, dismounts, leans the bike against the bench, and approaches the* BAKER'S BOY.*)*

HILARY: You, I assume, are the Baker's Boy.

BAKER'S BOY: That's me.

HILARY: Ah! Then you are the very person I want to meet.

BAKER'S BOY: I am?

HILARY: There is a little matter I want to settle with you.

BAKER'S BOY: You owe me money?

HILARY: No. It's time you had your come-uppance.

*(*HILARY *grabs the* BAKER'S BOY*'s shirt and punches him.)*

HILARY: *(continuing)* You pushed Robert de Havilland around this morning. Am I not right?

BAKER'S BOY: He was rude to me.

HILARY: Enough to do what you did?

BAKER'S BOY: Let me go!

(The BAKER'S BOY *struggles.* HILARY *chases after him, shoving and punching.)*

HILARY: You don't like being given the same treatment?

BAKER'S BOY: No more! Please!

HILARY: You don't like it, do you?

BAKER'S BOY: Ow! Stop that!

HILARY: Right!

*(*HILARY *pushes hard and the* BAKER'S BOY *falls back onto his basket. It spills bread and a candlestick onto the ground.)*

Ah, ha! What have we here!

*(*HILARY *picks up the candlestick.)*

BAKER'S BOY: Gimme that!

HILARY: Oh, no! This is just what I've been looking for.

*(*HILARY *reaches for the basket, but the* BAKER'S BOY *grabs it and starts to run.* HILARY *shoves the candlestick into her pocket and chases after him. The* BAKER'S BOY *and* HILARY *exit stage right.)*

(A slight pause, then the CHILDREN *enter stage left. The light level has started to decrease.)*

CYRIL: Hilary's not here.

ANTHEA: *(looks up at the sky)* It's getting so late...

*(*HILARY *enters stage right and pulls a candlestick from her pocket. The* PSAMMEAD *enters and pushes the pram in front of her.)*

HILARY: I know who stole the jewelry! It was—

(There is a whooshing and crashing and HILARY *crumples downward, falls over the pram, and disappears. Her voice becomes that of a baby gurgling.)*

JANE: Oooh!

PSAMMEAD: Whew! Just in time.

ROBERT: No. Too soon!

ANTHEA: It's sunset!

(ANTHEA reaches into the pram, pulls out the candlestick, and holds it up; she speaks to the baby.)

You really did find the thief, didn't you?

(There's a gurgle from the baby, like a laugh.)

CYRIL: Doesn't help us now!

(Enter the POLICEMAN *stage right. He sees* ANTHEA *holding the candlestick. The* PSAMMEAD *wheels the bike offstage left.)*

POLICEMAN: Ah-ha! You can give that to me, young lady.

(The POLICEMAN *takes the candlestick.)*

Caught red-handed. Just the evidence I have been looking for.

(The BAKER'S BOY *enters stage right, unseen by the others. He watches the Policeman take the candlestick from Anthea.)*

ANTHEA: It's not ours. We...er...

ROBERT: We found it.

POLICEMAN: A likely story. Now, if you don't mind, I'll look into the pram.

JANE: There's nothing there.

POLICEMAN: I'll be the judge of that, young Miss.

(The POLICEMAN *leans into the pram.)*

ANTHEA: You can't just search without—

(The POLICEMAN *holds the candlestick aloft.)*

POLICEMAN: I have all the evidence I need. Gives me the right to search. I'm sure the other one is in here.

(The POLICEMAN *searches the pram, stands back.*)

JANE: I told you!

POLICEMAN: *(to* CYRIL*)* Where have you hidden it then?

CYRIL: We have nothing to hide.

POLICEMAN: *(indicates candlestick)* What about this?

CYRIL: Not ours.

(The POLICEMAN *shakes his head.*)

ROBERT: But we do know who stole it.

ANTHEA: Well, only one of us knows.

POLICEMAN: And who is that? … Well, who? Tell me!

JANE: *(points to the pram)* The baby.

POLICEMAN: Don't be insolent!

JANE: Well, it's true.

POLICEMAN: I have enough evidence now to arrest you. All of you.

BAKER'S BOY: *(puts his basket down))* And you have a witness.

POLICEMAN: Yes. Yes, I do. Thank you.

ROBERT: *(spits it out)* Him?

(The baby cries. ANTHEA *looks into the pram.*)

ANTHEA: Hush, hush. Hmmm. Let me try something.

(ANTHEA *pushes the pram stage right, in the general direction of the* BAKER'S BOY*; the baby stops crying and starts to gurgle and chuckle. She turns around and pushes stage left; the baby cries loudly.*)

(The PSAMMEAD *re-enters, unobserved.*)

(ANTHEA *repeats the movements and the baby chuckles and cries as before.*)

Why does she do that?

(CYRIL *shrugs. The* PSAMMEAD *stands by* ANTHEA.)

POLICEMAN: What on earth is that?

CYRIL: A Psammead.

POLICEMAN: A what?

ROBERT: A friend.

ANTHEA: A special friend.

JANE: A very special friend.

(The PSAMMEAD *holds a hand out to the* POLICEMAN.)

PSAMMEAD: How do you do, sir.

POLICEMAN: I can't believe... Uh... How do you do?

(The POLICEMAN *reluctantly shakes hands with the* PSAMMEAD.)

(The PSAMMEAD *turns to the audience.*)

PSAMMEAD: I think Miss Anthea's going to need some help. Don't you?

(He waits for a response.)

Right. Now, do *you* know where the stolen jewelry is? ... Good! Now, when Miss Anthea pushes the baby *away* from the jewelry, I want you to shout 'Wrong way!' And when she pushes the baby *toward* the jewelry, I want you to shout 'Yes! Yes! Yes!' Have you got that?

(He waits for a response.)

Then let's try it. *(calls)* Miss Anthea!

(The PSAMMEAD *signals to* ANTHEA *to move the pram away from the* BAKER'S BOY.)

(He places his hand to his ear, encourages a loud response from the audience.)

Oh, you are clever!

(The PSAMMEAD *signals to* ANTHEA *to turn around and approach the* BAKER'S BOY, *then encourages a louder response from the audience.)*

PSAMMEAD: *(continuing)* That's brilliant! Just lovely! *(to ANTHEA)* Now you're on your own.

ANTHEA: You mean, keep trying?

PSAMMEAD: Absolutely. And listen for help from out there.

(The PSAMMEAD points to the audience. ANTHEA waves to them. The PSAMMEAD steps to one side.)

ANTHEA: Here we go then. Find the stolen jewelry.

(ANTHEA moves in various directions, following prompts from the audience, gradually growing closer to the BAKER'S BOY's basket. CYRIL, ROBERT and JANE crowd around the pram as she moves. Eventually the pram bumps against the BAKER'S BOY's basket, which tips over: bread, jewelry, and a candlestick fall onto the ground. ROBERT reaches into the basket and pulls out and holds up some jewelry. CYRIL holds up the second candlestick.)

CYRIL: Look at this!

JANE: The other candlestick!

ROBERT: *(to the BAKER'S BOY)* So *you* were the thief!

(The BAKER'S BOY turns and runs. The POLICEMAN blows his whistle, chases after him. They exit stage right.)

PSAMMEAD: *(to the audience)* Oh, well done. Thank you.

ANTHEA: *(to the audience)* Yes. Thank you. You were just wonderful.

(LADY C enters stage left; she does not see the PSAMMEAD, who is behind the pram.)

LADY C: I heard the Constable's whistle. *(sees jewelry)* Oh, you have found my jewels!

JANE: And your candlesticks.

LADY C: Oh, thank you, thank you. You are so clever!

*(*ROBERT *hands her the jewelry he is holding.)*

LADY C: *(continuing)* How did you find them?

CYRIL: We, er....

LADY C: Who was the culprit?

CYRIL: The Constable will tell you.

LADY C: Yes. Yes, that would be more appropriate.

*(*CYRIL *and* ROBERT *gather the jewelry and candlesticks into the basket.)*

CYRIL: Shall I carry them home for you?

LADY C: Thank you, but I think I can manage. *(takes hold of the basket)* Tomorrow I shall call on your mother, tell her how pleased I am. Bye-bye.

ROBERT: 'Bye.   )

JANE: See you tomorrow.   ) *(Some*

ANTHEA: Glad you've got your jewelry back.   ) *overlap)*

CYRIL: Good-bye, Lady Chittenden.   )

*(*LADY C *turns toward the stage-left exit.)*

JANE: Now! Story time, I think.

CYRIL: More Peter Pan?

ROBERT: Oh, yes.

ANTHEA: The book is nice, but d'you know what I'd really like?

(The PSAMMEAD *leans toward her.)*

There's a play about Peter Pan on at a theatre in London—

CYRIL: I didn't know that.

ANTHEA: Mother told me. Oh, I would love to see the story acted on the stage.

JANE: Oooh, yes.

ROBERT: Do they fly too?

ANTHEA: Mother says they do.

(The PSAMMEAD *turns toward stage left, holds out his arm with the hand vertical, and 'wills' the nearly offstage* LADY C *to stop.)*

ANTHEA: *(continuing)* I mean, it would be so nice if we could…

(The PSAMMEAD *turns to her.)*

PSAMMEAD: Go on, Miss Anthea: you could make it your last wish.

ANTHEA: Really?

(The PSAMMEAD *nods)*

Oh. Then I wish we could go to see the play Peter Pan.

(The PSAMMEAD *makes a joyous leap.* LADY C *turns around, reaches into the basket, lifts out a bundle of tickets, spreads them into a fan.)*

LADY C: This is so strange! I didn't see these before. *(She fans the tickets)* Four children's tickets—one for each of you, I suppose—and one adult ticket. Presumably for me. And all for tomorrow afternoon's performance of Peter Pan at the Royal Theatre in London.

ANTHEA: My wish came true!

LADY C: What a lovely idea.

JANE: Oh, Psammy!

(The four CHILDREN *hug the* PSAMMEAD.*)*

(Freeze, hold for two seconds, then moderately fast blackout.)

CURTAIN

Character Sketches

Primary Characters

Cyril (14)

He is somewhat reserved; he is aware of his position as senior child, male, 'master of the house' when his father is absent, yet frustrated sometimes because it limits what he can do, makes him feel responsible for his younger siblings' actions. He likes to read both historical and contemporary fiction. Daniel Defoe and Robert Louis Stevenson are his favorite authors (*Treasure Island* is his favorite novel). Currently he is reading the newly published novel *Peter Pan* (J.M. Barrie) and is enthralled by it.

He has excellent reasoning abilities and the capability to see a situation from other people's point of view. Makes very good, rational, well-thought-out decisions, but sometimes takes rather long to do so. Is a dedicated 'B Plus' student, but really has to work at his studies.

Cyril envies Anthea's 'quick-study' learning ability, and sometimes is awed by her strong character and willingness to speak her feelings.

Anthea (12)

She is the 'Big Sister' to Robert, Jane and the baby, and sometimes she feels she is Cyril's big sister too. Forms definite opinions and doesn't hesitate to do or say what she thinks is appropriate. Respects Cyril's ability to think a problem through— sometimes wishes she could be like that—but simultaneously is irked by his seeming indecisiveness.

She is a bit adventurous and a sharp 'A' student with strong memory skills. Learning comes easily to her. When she tackles a task, she pushes through—sometimes too fast—until she achieves what she perceives should be her objective.

Robert (10)

He is practical, lives for the moment, wants things to happen *now*. Idolizes Cyril, but hates it when Cyril patronizes him (or imagines Cyril is patronizing him). Generally, a happy, forthright child, although he is more mercurial than his older brother and sister.

Jane *(8)*

For seven years Jane was the youngest child and became used to being spoiled, particularly by her father and Anthea. (Their mother—an extremely practical woman—refused to bestow more affection on Jane than her other children). But the later arrival of a young sister suddenly put Jane's nose out of joint. She has mostly recovered but, if she sometimes feels less attention is paid to her, she tends to 'act up a bit.' Bright, articulate, speaks above her level, is sometimes too outspoken. Cyril monitors her in situations when she sometimes speaks too openly or acts injudiciously.

Hilary (20)

Hilary is the baby of the family (six months old). She appears briefly as a 20-year-old because Robert 'wished she was grown up' when it became inconvenient for him to push the baby carriage. As a sudden 20-year-old she has airs and considers herself 'above' the 'younger' children in the rest of the family. She decides what she wants to do, expects others to meet her needs, and does not readily listen to advice.

The Psammead (527)

The most enigmatic character in the play, and also why there is a play. Although he is very old, when fully awake he is more lively and active than the most agile and mobile Shakespearean Puck. (Ideally, the Psammead is played by a young actor who also is a gymnast who can execute confident front- and back-flips.) Although he tends to be grumpy when first awakened, the Psammead gradually becomes friendly and sym-pathetic when he realizes the de Havilland children are on a mission. He is 'ok' with the boys, rather likes and understands Anthea, and has a soft heart for Jane

Secondary Characters

The Baker's Boy (17)

He is of medium height and somewhat heavy and oafish. He left school on his 15th birthday, partly to help in his father's bakery and deliver bread, and partly because he was a poor student and recognized he was failing. His parents are very strict and demanding, and bear down on him if he is careless or forgetful. He has two older sisters who are intelligent and have married successfully; his mother is constantly 'getting on his case' because he has not turned out like them.

He tends to resent children who have better circumstances and education than he does. He has resorted to petty thieving to give himself some spending money (his father does not pay him for the work he does and allows him only a small amount of pocket money [allowance]). He knows the de Havilland children only slightly, as summer visitors, and resents them because they seem to have all that he does not.

The Police Constable (50)

A typical village 'Bobby', he normally has to deal with only minor events. The robbery of Lady Chittenden's jewelry is a big event for him. He is generally a kind person and hopes villagers perceive him as such. But his awareness of his position as 'maintainer of law and order' in the village tends to make him seem rather formal and prevents him from being his natural self. He does not really know how to relate or converse comfortably with children. He is married but he and his wife have no children.

Lady Chittenden (55)

Part of the British aristocracy by inheritance. Well-to-do, although not wealthy. A widow, she is self-sufficient and expects people to understand her wishes and requests, and to respond to them in the way she wants; she also expects their respect. In turn, she respects those she deals with and is never condescending. Speaks very good English but does not let her capable use of language to appear as though she is "talking down" to those who occupy a lesser station in life. Neither does she talk down to children. She carries herself with an upright bearing and dresses well, although conservatively.

Captain Hook (45)

A rough, tough captain, he is respected but feared by his crew. His blustery ways are mainly bluff, for he does not know how to manage people with finesse and understanding. Any personal fear is deep-rooted and very carefully concealed. His only confidant is Smee, whom he neither likes nor respects, but keeps him at his side as a source of information about the crew.

Smee (35)

A weak sycophant, Smee is a 'yes' person to the captain's every demand. He has no mind of his own and reflects the views and attitudes of the captain. He uses his supplicant manner to worm himself into Hook's confidence.

The Housekeeper [Woman at Window] (40)

She is the vicar's housekeeper/cook. She left school 25 years ago to join the vicarage staff as a housemaid, and has slowly worked her way up to her present position. She runs the house with a strong will and does not like to be crossed.

Production Notes

Essentially, the play is about the adventures the five de Havilland children have after they meet the Psammead. Yet it is the enigmatic character of the Psammead who draws the audience into the production, and really becomes the key character. For the first production, we were determined to find an actor who was young, acrobatic, and able to reach out to the audience. The choice was 17-year-old James le Lacheur.

Jane Blower, the director, took an unusual step in suggesting to James that he create his own image of the Psammead, select his own acrobatic moves, and devise his own dance sequence to open Act 2. The result was an extraordinarily intuitive performance.

We were fascinated that the production clearly appealed to audiences on two levels. Children quickly accepted the Psammead and then readily related with him and the five children. That the de Havilland children ranged in age from 7 to 14, and the actors were almost exactly the age of the children they were playing, was a particular advantage since it provided a reference point for young audience members of similar ages.

Whereas the action embedded in the events appealed to children, it was the concept and 'warmth' of the story that appealed to adults. They liked the rare imagination inherent in the story, the 'coin' and 'flying' sequences, and the adventure with Captain Hook and Smee. The sequence in which a light represented Tinker Bell also had special appeal.

At first glance the set seemed complicated, but in effect proved otherwise. A raised platform about one meter high at upstage center became the setting for the flying sequence. By sliding a flat in front, with the hull of a ship painted on it, and raising a mast at the center, the platform quickly became the deck of the pirate ship (see page 135). The Sweet Shop (candy store) at stage right was a flat with a door set in the middle and a window with images of jars of sweets (candies) painted behind it. Similarly, a window of the vicarage was a flat with a platform built into it to hold the foods the housekeeper has prepared.

Lady Chittenden and Anthea in front of the Sweet Shop.

(Note the heritage pram/baby carriage.)

Photo: John Fitzgerald

The sandpit in which Anthea is digging at the start of the play, and from which the Psammead emerges, was a sand-colored donut-shaped structure solid enough for the children to climb on and the Psammead to sit on. There were also two flats with artistic images of trees and bushes painted on them.

Before the first performance, I had been concerned that a whimsical play like *Adventures with a Psammead* might not meet the demands of a modern audience. Now, looking back at the audience reaction during and immediately following those early performances, I realize there certainly is room for imaginative renditions of century-old stories.

The poster—and subsequently the program cover—announcing the first production of The Railway Children.

Poster design by the director: John Gaisford.

Play No. 5

The Railway Children

Synopsis

The "Railway Children" are Roberta (14), Peter (10) and Phyllis (7), and they live with their parents in a comfortably furnished home in one of the better parts of London. The ease of their lifestyle is shattered when their father is suddenly and inexplicably taken away by two mysterious men and their mother won't tell them why. Because the family's income will be much lower, she takes them to live in a simple country cottage where they discover a nearby railway line and have a series of adventures. They prevent a rail disaster by warning the train's engine driver of a signal gantry that has fallen across the line (and are given commemorative awards by the railway company); they rescue a lost, very sick Russian and bring him home to their mother to recover (and help him find his wife and child); and they rescue a schoolboy who has been injured in a railway tunnel and is in danger of being run over by an express train.

By waving flags torn from the girls' red petticoats, Roberta, Phyllis and Peter stop the train and prevent a major crash. They are thanked by the train engineer and fireman.

Photo: John Gaisford

207

Along the way they meet the Stationmaster, the train's engine driver and fireman, and—without knowing his importance—a white-haired passenger they label "The Old Gentleman," who happens to be a director of the railway and, coincidentally, the injured boy's grandfather. When Roberta accidentally discovers the reason for her father's disappearance (he has been convicted for selling State secrets, which she refuses to believe is true), she turns to The Old Gentleman for help. He investigates and discovers the children's father has been wrongfully convicted, and arranges for him to be brought back to them.

History

This simple story was written by Edith Nesbit early in the 20th century, yet after more than one hundred years it still captures young readers' interest and imagination. The book is now public domain and, despite its age, still sells well. It was made into a film in the early 1960s, and more recently was remade as a film in 1999. The latter, however, has had fewer viewers because it was made for and presented on Public Television's Masterpiece Theatre—primarily a selective, mainly adult medium.

In 1999 the Folio Society, which publishes reprints of significant books, printed a new hardback memorial volume of The Railway Children. In the Introduction, Helen Cresswell wrote:

> " 'Oh, my daddy, my daddy!' That scream went
> like a knife into the heart of everyone in the
> train...". These lines are amongst the best known in
> English children's literature... The reader is not
> only hugely entertained by the drama of the
> unfolding story, but is emotionally engaged too.

Creswell is referring to a line at the very end of the book, when Roberta sees her father step out of the train and knows he has come back to the family. The whole story leads up to this moment, which becomes the play's climax.

Rationale

Nesbit's story not only encourages its youthful readers to follow the children through their adventures, but also introduces them to the sociological aspects prevalent in early 20th-century society (some of which still apply today). Because it would be too much to cover both aspects in a short play for young people, and still hold their attention, I have concentrated on the adventures the three Railway Children experience.

The three children have walked along the railway line and into the tunnel to rescue a boy whose foot is caught under a rail. They have to work fast because a train is approaching. (An exciting moment in the play!)

Photo: John Gaisford

Unlike stories told in films, a stage drama prepared on a limited budget cannot have a real railway engine and its carriages puffing through the countryside and into an onstage station! (The only exception was a recent production in Yorkshire, London and Toronto, where the platforms on each side of a single line in a rail station were converted into banked seats and a real engine and its entourage of passenger coaches chugged along the line between them.) But a stage play can still capture a youthful audience's imagination by creating the sounds and feel of the railway, and draw its viewers into believing a train really is there.

Many of today's children, even though they are accustomed to electronic technology, still are fascinated by steam trains (after all, many of them have watched Thomas the Tank Engine and his friends on television.) The audience recognizes that the railway lines lie between them and the children on stage, they hear and see the sound and lights of the train, and watch The Railway Children experience the wind it produces as it rushes by, and its lights as they crouch beside the line in the dark depths of the tunnel.

The Characters

The major characters in the play are the three children and their mother, who encounter many others as the story evolves:

Primary Characters

> Roberta, age 14
> Peter, age 10
> Phyllis, age 7
> Mother, age 35-40

Secondary Characters

> The Children's Father, age 40
> The Old Gentleman, Director of the Railway, about 60
> The Stationmaster, age 50
> Jim; a schoolboy. age 15
> The Russian, male, age 45

Characters with Brief Speaking Appearances

> The Train Engineer
> The Train Fireman
> A Doctor
> Two Male Passengers

Non-speaking Roles

> 2 or 3 passengers on the station platform
> Several 12- to 16-year-old schoolboys

The Set

The primary locations occur on and beside the railway line and at the railway station. There are also sequences in the city and country houses where the children live.

The Embankment

This is a raised portion upstage that represents an embankment overlooking the railway line; it stretches across the width of the stage.

The rail-lines are made of 2 x 2 inch lumber laid on 1 x 8 inch cross pieces, and then spray-painted. The signal arm on top of the signal gantry (not yet installed in the photo) clanks from a 45° downward angle to indicate the line is clear, and to horizontal to indicate the train must stop.

The set for scenes at the embankment, photographed during construction; the tunnel entrance is at stage right, the signal gantry is at stage left.
Author Photo

At stage left the rail lines run offstage; at stage right they run into the tunnel, and then offstage. The embankment has a fence along the top behind which the children stand facing the audience, as they watch the trains passing below.

The children watch as the 'hare and hounds' paper-chase passes beneath them. The Stationmaster shouts to the boys to get off the line.

Photo: John Gaisford

The Tunnel

When the children rescue a boy trapped in the tunnel (his foot is caught under one of the lines), the scene is in darkness, with very limited light. The side of the tunnel can simply be a black backdrop between the embankment and the railway line, with a a facsimile of a cut-out area painted on it (see page 209).

The Railway Station

Downstage, the width of the stage represents part of the railway platform. At stage right there is a gate, the corner of the ticket office, and a passenger bench.

The Cottage Kitchen
This is a simply decorated room with a basic table, several chairs, and a china cabinet with drawers. There are two doors: at stage right a door opens onto the stairs to the second level; at stage left a door opens onto the garden.

The City House Drawing Room/Parlor
The opening and closing scenes occur in an elegantly decorated and furnished room with a window at stage right, through which people approaching the front door can be vaguely seen. There are a table with a train on it, several dining chairs, and an armchair. A door at stage right leads into a front hall; a door at stage left leads to the interior of the house.

A Country Path
Several brief conversations occur on a path which can be at the foot of the stage in front of the curtain There is a gate at stage right, to represent the gate at the end of the cottage garden.

Video Bridge
A short video scene of a vintage train can be projected as a bridge between scenes.

Running Time
Overall: 75-80 minutes plus 15-minute interval.
Act 1: 50-55 minutes;   Act 2: 25 minutes.

First Production
The play was produced first by the Guernsey Amateur Dramatic and Operatic Club (GADOC) in the U.K. from 23 to 25 October 2003, and directed by John Gaisford. The cast for the first production comprised:

Roberta	*Caitlin Sullivan*
Peter	*Jack Waterman*
Phyllis	*Rosalie Falla*
Mother	*Paula Harrison*
Father	*Andy McCutcheon*
The Old Gentleman	*Iain Mathieson*
The Stationmaster	*Brian Garner*

The Russian	*Steve Molnar*
Jim	*Darren Alderton*
Engine Driver	*Mack Tachon*
Fireman	*Ollie Garnham*
The Doctor	*Tony Riddle*
The Hare	*Michael Sullivan*
Passengers	*Chris and Dave*
	Northrop
Onlookers	*Sheila Garner*
	Pauline Telford

Some Script Guidelines

Throughout the script, two symbols are used occasionally at the end of a piece of dialogue to indicate how the sentence ends:

- **...** An ellipsis at the end of a statement means the speaker just trails off and leaves his or her thought hanging in the air (possibly accompanied by a shrug).

- — a dash at the end of a statement means the speaker is interrupted by the next speaker and the first speaker's statement is incomplete. Sometimes there is an italicized continuation of the statement *(within brackets)* immediately following the dash, to help the actor sense where the sentence was going.

Additionally, 'v.o.' means 'voice over' (i.e. spoken off-stage)

Here are definitions for some British words and expressions used in the play.

a cheque	a check (bank check)
a torch	a flashlight
tea	it can be just a drink (a cup of tea) or a light meal (known as afternoon tea), held about 4 p.m. and composed of light sandwiches, scones, buttered bread and jam, slices of cake, and (of course) tea.
tea towel	a cloth for drying washed dishes
the post	the mail

Character sketches for the four primary roles start on page 269. Notes made following the first production start on page 271.

Script: *The Railway Children*

© 2003, Ron Blicq

(To set the scene and prepare the audience for the play, either before or immediately after curtain up, a film or video clip of a British steam train pulling passenger carriages, vintage 1905, puffing its way through country hills, is projected onto a screen. This can also become a bridge between some of the scenes.)

Act 1

(The play opens in the drawing room of a large house in London, circa 1905, set on the right side of the stage. There is a table on which PETER *and* PHYLLIS *are playing with a large-scale train (an engine plus two or three passenger carriages) running around a track.* ROBERTA *is leaning over the back of an armchair in which* FATHER *is sitting. He is pointing out something to her in the newspaper. [It's apparent there is close affection between* FATHER *and his elder daughter.] There is a small writing table with* MOTHER *writing at it. At the far right there is a glazed window that looks over the entrance to the front door, through which the audience will see the outline of two men as they enter and leave. It is evening.)*

(In addition to being the children's mother, from time to time MOTHER *becomes a narrator who provides a link between scenes.)*

(From the opening until the train engine explodes, only the MOTHER*'s voice is heard. [*FATHER, ROBERTA, PETER *and* PHYLLIS *mime their interactions as they converse or play]. Most of the information* MOTHER *imparts is taken word-for-word from Nesbit's novel.)*

*(*MOTHER *rises and steps fully downstage, a spotlight on her.)*

The Railway Children

MOTHER: *(to the audience)* They were not railway children to begin with. I don't suppose they had ever thought about railways except as a means of getting to the Pantomime, or to the Zoo, or Madame Tussaud's. They're just ordinary suburban children, and they live in London with their Father and Mother in an ordinary red-brick-fronted villa, with colored glass in the front door, a tiled passage called a hall, a bathroom with hot and cold water, electric bells, French windows, and a good deal of white paint. *(looks at family)* That's Bobbie standing behind Father. *(confidentially)* Actually, her real name is Roberta, but she prefers to be called Bobbie–she'd really like to be a boy. And Peter and Phyllis are playing with Peter's new train. Not an electric train; not even a clockwork one. It has a boiler and a real fire in it, to make steam, just like a real railway engine.

(There's an explosion on the table, just as PHYLLIS is trying to set a toy figure on the last coach of the train. The engine briefly spurts out flame and steam. FATHER lowers his paper. MOTHER turns to look, walks into the scene. Now there is normal dialogue.)

PETER: Look what've you done! Oh, Phyllis!

PHYLLIS: I didn't do it! I didn't touch your engine.

PETER: But I saw you. You were reaching over and—

PHYLLIS: Mother! Tell him I didn't do it.

FATHER: *(approaching; shouts a warning)* Peter, stop! Don't touch it!

(Peter looks up, questioningly.)

The engine will be too hot!

ROBERTA: What happened?

PETER: Phyllis put something on the engine.

PHYLLIS: Tell her, Daddy. I didn't do anything.

FATHER: No, no, no. Whatever happened occurred inside the engine. It was nothing you did.

(FATHER pokes at the engine with a pencil.)

PETER: Is it broken? For ever?

FATHER: No. Oh, no! It just needs a bit of brazing, or some solder and a new valve. Not something I can do tonight. Saturday afternoon, I should think, and you shall all help me.

PETER: *Can* girls help to mend engines?

FATHER: Of course they can. Girls are just as clever as boys, and don't you forget it! How would you like to be an engine-driver, Phyllis?

PHYLLIS: Ugh. My face would always be dirty, wouldn't it?

ROBERTA: I should just love it! Do you think I could when I'm grown up, Daddy? Or even be a stoker?

FATHER: You mean a fireman, Bobbie? Well, if you still wish it, when you're grown up we'll see about it. You would probably be one of the first women to become a...a fire-woman. Now, when I was a boy— *(railways were only just starting)*

(There is a knock at the front door. [During the last piece of dialogue, the shapes of two men are seen through the window as they enter.]

Who on earth could that be, at this time of night?

(FATHER exits, closing the door behind him. He opens the front door [we see a glow of light through the window and we hear strong voices but not necessarily the exact words]. Essentially the voice-over dialogue runs like this:)

MAN 1: Mr. Baldwin?

FATHER: Yes.

MAN 1: We need you to come with us.

FATHER: What on earth for?

MAN 2: I have to remind you that anything you say may be taken in evidence against you.

FATHER: I don't understand...

MAN 1: We have a warrant...

FATHER: Please! Let me call my wife.

*(*MOTHER *moves to the door, tries to hear. The door opens and* FATHER *looks in.)*

FATHER: *(to* MOTHER*)* Would you mind coming out here? *(to the* CHILDREN*)* Just continue playing.

*(*FATHER *and* MOTHER *exit. The children don't play but just look at each other;* ROBERTA *runs to the door and listens.)*

FATHER: *(v.o., to Mother)* These gentlemen are insisting I go with them.

MOTHER: *(v.o.)* But why? Where?

FATHER: *(v.o.)* It doesn't matter. I have no choice. They have a warrant.

MAN 1: *(v.o.)* Come now, we must be off.

(Three male shapes exit past the window.)

PHYLLIS: Where is Father going?

ROBERTA: Ssh! Mother will tell us.

PETER: It seems so strange…

ROBERTA: Look as if we're playing.

(The children scamper back to the table and sit/stand as before. PHYLLIS *picks up the engine.)*

PHYLLIS: Look how it's scorched!

PETER: Oh, Father will be able to repair it. He'll know what to do.

(The door opens and MOTHER *enters. She has been weeping but tries to conceal it; her manner is distracted. The younger children don't notice, but* ROBERTA *does.)*

MOTHER: Er … your Father has had to go out for a while. On business. Come now, it's past everyone's bedtime. Up the stairs with you. *(she shushes the children toward the door stage left)* I'll be up presently to say good night. Bobbie, will you make sure Phyllis brushes her hair thoroughly – and brushes her teeth?

*(*ROBERTA, *the last to leave, looks questioningly back at* MOTHER, *who nods to her in a way that both understand means: "Go on. Please! I'll talk to you later." As the door closes,* MOTHER *composes herself and walks downstage. Although distressed, she regains composure as she speaks.)*

(Spotlight on MOTHER, *blackout on drawing room.)*

MOTHER: *(to the audience)* How am I to tell the children that their father won't be coming back for a long time? That we are going to be poor? That we'll have to move from this lovely house to a little cottage somewhere in the country; it will be all I can afford. And that there will be much less on the table at mealtimes?

(Lights dim on MOTHER. *The video of a train wending its way through the countryside is projected briefly, then the lights come up on the kitchen/living area of a sparsely furnished cottage: a deal table; five chairs; a dresser with plates, cups and cutlery on it; a small table against a wall. Daylight; the sun is coming through the window.* ROBERTA *and* PETER *peer in the window.)*

PETER: I can see the kitchen. Not much in there.

ROBERTA: Well, at least it looks clean.

PHYLLIS: *(v.o.)* I can't see! Lift me up Bobbie.

*(*ROBERTA, *lifts her.* PHYLLIS *looks in the window.)*

Oooh. It's not very big.

ROBERTA: Phyllis: we can't expect everything to be the same.

(Sound of a door being unlocked stage left. MOTHER *pushes it open and more light streams into the room. She enters. She has a light coat on and carries a suitcase and a basket of groceries.)*

MOTHER: Come on. Let's get in and we'll make some tea.

(The CHILDREN *enter. Each wears a light coat and carries a suitcase.* PETER *has his engine tucked under his arm;* PHYLLIS *carries a raggedy teddy bear.* ROBERTA *also carries groceries.)*

PETER: Well, for me the best part of the trip was the rail journey. Not the arrival.

MOTHER: It just looks bare because we haven't spread our things around. When we're settled in, the cottage will look more inviting.

PHYLLIS: It's cold in here.

ROBERTA: I could light the fire. It's been set.

MOTHER: No, I'd rather not. We can't waste coal. Keep the fire for a rainy day.

PETER: Come on, Phyl. Let's see what's upstairs.

MOTHER: *(calls after them)* The bedrooms with two beds in them are for you children. Bobbie and Phyllis in one, Peter in the other.

(PETER and PHYLLIS exit. MOTHER and ROBERTA unpack groceries and set the table as they talk.)

The house is small, but it will do.

ROBERTA: I think I like being in the country. It's much quieter.

MOTHER: Yes, there is something useful in that. *(pause)* Roberta: I'm going to have to depend on you, to keep an eye on Peter and Phyllis; particularly Phyllis.

ROBERTA: Of course.

MOTHER: What I'm really saying is, sometimes I'll need you to "keep them out of my hair." To supplement our income, I'm going to try my hand at writing—poems, short stories.

ROBERTA: You used to write once, didn't you?

MOTHER: A little, before I married your father.

ROBERTA: Well, you do write poems for us, on our birthdays. Funny poems.

MOTHER: After tea you can help me take a table up to my room. That's where I'll write.

ROBERTA: *(after a pause)* Mother: Where *is* daddy?

MOTHER: He's just...away.

ROBERTA: Why won't you tell us what he's doing?

MOTHER: It isn't necessary for you to know anything about it. It's about business, that's all.

ROBERTA: Is it something to do with the Government?

MOTHER: Well, yes, I suppose. But that's all I can tell you right now.

ROBERTA: Daddy will be coming back, won't he?

MOTHER: Of course he will.

ROBERTA: Then why did we have to move to the country?

MOTHER: Oh, Roberta, you really do ask too many questions. It's because we … we couldn't afford to keep up the big house. And I need somewhere quiet to write.

(PETER and PHYLLIS burst into the room.)

PETER: Can we go exploring?

PHYLLIS: I want my tea first.

MOTHER: Quite right, Phyllis. And it's nearly ready.

PETER: I'd like to explore where the trains are.

MOTHER: Will you be going with them, Roberta? *(it's a request, rather than a question)*

PHYLLIS: Oh, yes, Bobbie. Please. You talk to me more than Peter.

ROBERTA: Of course I will. It'll be fun.

(Fade lights on the cottage. MOTHER steps forward to address the audience, highlighted by a spotlight.)

MOTHER: Oh, it's going to be so difficult. I don't want to tell the children. Roberta's old enough, but I don't want to burden her with a secret she must keep from Peter and Phyllis. *(sighs)* And I don't want to hide away from them. But I do have to write, if we are to have bread and butter on our table.

(Fade lights on MOTHER.)

(Lights up on the front of the stage, with a plain backdrop or a country field scene. The children approach from downstage right. PETER is in front, then ROBERTA with PHYLLIS dragging behind.)

PETER: Come on! The railway line's straight ahead.

PHYLLIS: I'm coming as fast as I can!

(Sound of train whistle.)

PETER: Listen! There's a train coming.

ROBERTA: Which way?

PETER: From inside the tunnel, I think.

PHYLLIS: Where's the tunnel?

PETER: *(pointing stage left)* Come on, we don't want to miss it! *(runs off, downstage left)*.

ROBERTA: Come on, Phyl!

PHYLLIS: I'm coming!

(They exit stage left. Sound of a steam train. The scene changes to the embankment with the railway lines in front of it. There is the entrance to a tunnel visible at stage right, and a signal gantry with a working signal at stage left. When trains pass, we hear the whistle and roar and clatter of wheels, and see the smoke and the signal change, and the children feel the wind, but we have to imagine the train is there.)

(PETER runs in from upstage left, on the embankment, A train whistle sounds. He turns and faces stage left.)

PETER: Come on, you two, or you'll miss it!

(PETER runs to the right along the embankment, but stops part way to lean over the fence and peer into the tunnel. ROBERTA and PHYLLIS enter from upstage left, ROBERTA pulling PHYLLIS along. They look toward the tunnel as the engine sounds grow louder, then suddenly the pitch changes and the noise increases from right to left across the stage. As the engine "passes" there are puffs of smoke from the tunnel and then a rush of wind that flutters the girls' dresses. The CHILDREN move their heads from stage right to left, in the direction the train is moving.)

ROBERTA: *(shouts)* Wave!

PHYLLIS: *(shouts)* I am waving!

(The train has passed and the sounds die down.)

PETER: I never thought we should ever get so near to a train as that.

ROBERTA: *(to* PHYLLIS*)* It was like a great dragon tearing by. Did you feel it fan us with its hot wings?

PHYLLIS: *(points to tunnel entrance)* I suppose a dragon's lair might look like that, from the outside.

PETER: That's what we'll call it: The Green Dragon.

*(*PETER *examines his pocket watch.)*

It's 5:47 and it's an express. We'll have to remember that for other nights.

ROBERTA: Better than toy engines, isn't it?

PETER. I don't know. It's different. It seems odd to *feel* the train.

ROBERTA: And so close.

PETER: The engine driver waved at us!

PHYLLIS: I didn't see any passengers wave.

ROBERTA: No, there was one. A white-haired gentleman in a first class compartment. I wonder if the train was going to London. That's where Daddy is.

PETER: Let's go down to the station and find out. I can copy down the timetable, then we'll know when to watch for the trains.

(They walk toward stage left along the embankment, away from the tunnel, and exit. Spotlight comes up on MOTHER *writing at her writing desk. She stops writing and addresses the audience.)*

MOTHER: And that's how it all started; that's how they became The Railway Children. They came home bubbling with excitement, with great plans to wave to trains at different times and to visit the station. *(pause)* Bobbie, I feel, was wistful: hoping perhaps their father one day will wave to them from a train and alight at the station. She does miss him so.

MOTHER: *(continuing, stands and walks toward the audience)* Now a whole month has passed, and they have waved to the trains almost every day. And then, something frightful happened. It makes me nervous even to think about it.

(Spotlight fades on MOTHER and lights come up on the previous scene. The only difference is that the signal gantry has fallen across the line at stage left. The CHILDREN are sitting behind the fence near the tunnel. They haven't noticed the fallen signal. They are part way through an ongoing conversation.)

PHYLLIS: We could buy Mother a basket of fruit.

PETER: What would we use for money, silly?

ROBERTA: Fruit would be nice. You know how mother likes peaches and pears.

PHYLLIS: Strawberries. Mother *loves* strawberries.

PETER: You mean *you* love strawberries!

ROBERTA: It will have to be something that grows wild, something we can pick ourselves.

PETER: Do you remember, farther along the line, there are wild cherry trees growing on the embankment?

ROBERTA: Yes, they were in blossom when we first came here. They should be ripe by now.

PETER: Let's go and see.

PHYLLIS: What about the train?

PETER: We've enough time. We'll walk along the top. Come on.

ROBERTA: Come on, Phyl.

(They are half way along the embankment when PETER, who is ahead, sees and points at the fallen signal gantry.)

PETER: Just look at that!

PHYLLIS: It's fallen on the line!

ROBERTA: It must've been the wind, last night.

PHYLLIS: Could we move it, do you think?

ROBERTA: It'd be too heavy.

(PETER starts to climb over the fence.)

PETER: Perhaps we could drag it.

PHYLLIS: You know what mother said! We promised *never* to walk on the line.

(PETER pauses.)

PETER: Well, how else are we going to move it?

PHYLLIS: Can't we stop the train?

PETER: How? It will be here in just minutes!

(Sound of a train whistle.)

ROBERTA: Peter's right, Phyl. We've got to move it before the train comes. Or there'll be a crash.

(ROBERTA starts to climb the fence.)

You stay here.

PHYLLIS: No! I'm coming too.

(The CHILDREN either scramble down the embankment or exit stage left and re-enter at rail-line level.)

PETER: *(to ROBERTA)* You grab that part. I'll take this. Now, pull!

(They make several efforts but it's too heavy. They shake their heads. The train whistle is heard again.)

PHYLLIS: O-o-o-h...

PETER: That's the 11:15! The engine driver won't notice the signal's on the line until it's too late. If he even sees it.

ROBERTA: What about the signal box? Could we run there, get the signalman to put up a stop signal?

PETER: It's too far. There's not enough time.

PHYLLIS: Will there be a crash?

PETER: We've got to do something!

ROBERTA: We'll have to wave to him to stop.

PHYLLIS: The engine driver will think we're just being friendly. He's used to seeing us wave.

ROBERTA: He'll probably just wave back!

(The train whistle is heard again.)

PETER: If we had something red, we could stand by the line and wave it.

PHYLLIS: Red means danger.

PETER: But there's nothing— *(red around here)*

ROBERTA: Yes! Yes there is. Our flannel petticoats. They're red. *(to* PHYLLIS*)* Come on, we'll take them off. *(*PHYLLIS *shakes her head "no")* Come on!

*(*PETER *walks toward the tunnel, peers into it, returns. The* GIRLS *reach under their long dresses and slip red flannel petticoats down their legs to their ankles and step out of them.)*

PETER: Now. Tear them into large squares, with thin ends.

*(*ROBERTA *and* PETER *tear the petticoats apart.)*

PHYLLIS: We're not...we're not going to *tear* them?

PETER: Just do it!

ROBERTA: Yes, Phyl. We have to. If we can't stop the train there'll be an accident and people will be killed.

PHYLLIS: Oooh!

PETER: Here: I'll do it.

*(*PETER *takes* PHYLLIS*'s petticoat, starts to tear it but has a tough time at the seam.)*

ROBERTA: Like this, Peter! You can't tear it through the band.

*(*ROBERTA *tears the band off in one long strip, then tears a big square out of the remainder. The sound of the train is much more noticeable.)*

PETER: We'll wave from up on the embankment. Come on. Quick!

(THEY climb the embankment [or exit and re-enter stage left], then space themselves two feet apart.)

PETER: Now, *wave!*

(THEY wave the flags, facing stage right. They shout to each other above the engine noise.)

ROBERTA: They don't understand! The engine driver's just waving back at us.

PETER: Wave harder, then!

(THEY wave frantically.)

ROBERTA: It's no good! I'm going down on the line. Wave your flags and point to me.

PETER: No, Bobbie! That's too dangerous!

(ROBERTA climbs down the embankment or exits and re-enters stage left. She stands on the rail line facing toward the tunnel and waves her flag, looking into the tunnel entrance.)

ROBERTA: Now, please, engine driver! Look this way.

PHYLLIS: Bobbie! Come back. Oh, please come back!

ROBERTA: *Please!* Look at me.

(There is a squealing as the engine driver applies the brakes and sounds the whistle; the noise is deafening. PETER and ROBERTA wave harder and harder. PHYLLIS sobs and lets her flag drop.)

PHYLLIS: Oh, stop, train! Get out of the way, Bobbie!

(From the edge of the tunnel the front of the engine appears, accompanied by steam, the wheels locked. It projects 0.8 to 1 meter (2 to 3 feet) into the scene and stops just two feet in front of ROBERTA.)

(PETER and PHYLLIS each run down to the line and give ROBERTA a hug.)

(The ENGINE DRIVER and FIREMAN run in from stage right [from out of the tunnel].)

ENGINE DRIVER: Oh, miss! I was so afraid we wouldn't stop in time!

ROBERTA: Well, you did. Good for you.

ENGINE DRIVER: You could have been hurt. Worse!

(The FIREMAN *points to the fallen signal gantry.)*

FIREMAN: Oh, Lor, Dennis. If we'd run into that at full speed…

ENGINE DRIVER: It would have been a catastrophe! The train would have been derailed for sure. You children… Your quick thinking has prevented a terrible accident!

(Fade lights to blackout. Spotlight on MOTHER *downstage; she addresses the audience.)*

MOTHER: I tell my children *never* to venture onto the railway line; it's much too dangerous. And then they do! But it was for a good reason. So what do I say to them? I had to be cross and pleased, both at the same time! Have your parents ever had to do that? Sometimes children have to be so understanding. *(pause)* But I *was* proud of them. It was such a brave thing to do. *(pause; crosses to another point on the stage)* Now, three more weeks have passed, and I know for sure they haven't broken the rule since then.

(Lights come up on the cottage kitchen. The CHILDREN *are clearing the breakfast table and washing dishes.* MOTHER *is in her room, writing [not visible].)*

ROBERTA: *(to* PETER*)* I'll wash and you dry.

PETER: No! It's my turn to wash. You washed yesterday.

ROBERTA: No, I didn't, Peter. Remember, you had to scrape the stew pot.

PETER: Alright; alright! Why are you always *right*?

ROBERTA: Well, it's— *(being correct, rather than right)*

(Letters drop through the slot in the front door.)

Can you get the letters, Phyl?

*(*PHYLLIS *picks up the letters, opens the inner door.)*

PHYLLIS: *(shouts)* Mother! The post is here!

(PHYLLIS puts the letters on the table, then carries a dish to ROBERTA.)

ROBERTA: Thank you. *(to PETER)* Get a new tea-towel out of the drawer. That one's too wet.

PETER: Shall we go to the station first, or the tunnel?

ROBERTA: Oh, the station, I think. Talk to the Stationmaster.

PHYLLIS: I want to see The Green Dragon.

PETER: It doesn't come until after tea.

MOTHER: *(entering stage right)* Well, what have we here?

(MOTHER sits at the table, opens a large envelope; the CHILDREN gather around her.)

Oh, dear. Another story come home to roost.

PHYLLIS: Didn't they like it, Mummy?

MOTHER: Not quite to their taste, I expect.

(She opens another large envelope.)

Ah! Here's a sensible editor. He's taken my story and this is the proof.

ROBERTA: He has to prove it?

MOTHER: No, no. He's set my pages in type and these are the "proof pages." For me to check.

(MOTHER looks deeper into the envelope, slides out a cheque.)

He's going to print it! And here's the payment!

PETER: Buns for tea?

MOTHER: Oh, yes! Cream buns!

PHYLLIS: With jam in the middle?

MOTHER: If that's what you would like. We're going to celebrate! And you shall buy them, on your way back from the station.

(MOTHER examines another, smaller envelope.)

Mother: *(continuing)* Oh, but this one isn't for me!

(She hands the envelope to ROBERTA.*)*

ROBERTA: *(reads)* "To Miss Roberta, Master Peter and Miss Phyllis, at Three Chimneys."

PETER: Who would be writing to us?

*(*ROBERTA *tears open the envelope and pulls out a letter.)*

ROBERTA: *(reads)* "Dear Sir, and Ladies." Ooohh!

*(*PETER *and* PHYLLIS *echo* ROBERTA's *giggle.)*

"It is proposed to make a small presentation to you, in commemoration of your prompt and courageous action in warning the train on the 18th of last month, and thus averting what must, humanly speaking, have been a terrible accident. The presentation will take place at the Station at three o'clock on the 30th of this month, if this time and place will be convenient for you. Yours faithfully, Jabez Inglewood, Secretary, Great Northern and Southern Railway Company."

*(*ROBERTA *passes the letter to* PETER.*)*

Oh, my goodness!

PETER: Does it mean other people will be there, too?

MOTHER: I expect so. It's a very great honor.

ROBERTA: Oh, I know. But what am I to wear? I don't have anything decent.

MOTHER: You'd be surprised what a turn with an iron over your blue dress will do, Bobbie. You'll look lovely.

PHYLLIS: Can I wear the yellow dress I wore for Peter's birthday?

MOTHER: Yes, of course you can. And Peter, you can put on the clothes you wear on Sunday.

PETER: Don't we have to write back? It says: "If this time and place will be convenient for you."

MOTHER: It would be most impolite not to. And Bobbie, you should do it, as you are the eldest and have the best handwriting.

ROBERTA: What am I to say?

MOTHER: Go upstairs and use my desk. And say what you feel is most appropriate.

(The lights extinguish in the kitchen. The video of the train moving through the countryside may be shown briefly. Lights come up downstage, on a section of the railway station, with a gate at stage right, and the door to the booking office. A train whistle is heard, and the sound of a railway engine. The STATIONMASTER *is there, plus the* ENGINE DRIVER *and* FIREMAN *from the train, and [if possible] two or three additional people. The Old Gentleman [O.G.] walks in from stage left [along the platform]. He is dressed formally and wears a prestigious black top hat.)*

STATIONMASTER: Ah! Good afternoon, sir.

O.G.: Good afternoon, Stationmaster.

STATIONMASTER: May I introduce the engine driver and fireman who were driving the train when the children flagged it down?

O.G.: Ah, yes. *(to the* ENGINE DRIVER*)* Mr. Simpson. We have met before, I think.

ENGINE DRIVER: We have indeed, sir.

(They shake hands.)

O.G.: *(shakes hands with the* FIREMAN*)* And you are…?

FIREMAN: Baddersley, sir. Jim Baddersley. Glad to make your acquaintance.

O.G.: And I yours. And very glad to see you both fit and well. It could have been otherwise.

*(*MOTHER *and the* CHILDREN *enter through the gate. The* STATIONMASTER *turns to greet them.)*

STATIONMASTER: *(to* MOTHER*)* Very glad to see you could come too, Madam. You must be very proud of your children.

MOTHER: Well, of course. I certainly am.

STATIONMASTER: Hello, Peter, and Bobbie, and Phyllis.

(PETER shakes hands; the GIRLS curtsy.)

(to MOTHER) We will be a little formal today. Really, I have got to know your children quite well. They visit the station almost every day. We love to see them down here.

(He turns to the CHILDREN.)

Now, if you three will come over here.

(He leads them to a position mid-stage [they wave to the ENGINE DRIVER and FIREMAN as they pass] and then he returns to MOTHER.)

And if you would accompany me, madam.

(He takes MOTHER to stand with the other viewers.)

(to the O.G.) Shall I go ahead, sir?

(The O.G. nods)

Ladies and gentlemen: It gives me great pleasure to introduce you to three young people who courageously took swift action to prevent a serious accident on our railway line six weeks ago. Consequently, the commissioners of the railway have agreed that a special presentation should be made to these young people, who are standing in front of me right now. And the Chairman of the Board has graciously agreed to make the presentations.

O.G.: Thank you, Stationmaster. When one hears about acts of bravery, one tends to think of soldiers and sailors in times of war. But this time we are talking about three children who, I understand, were not merely passers-by but real enthusiasts about the way our railway line works.

(The STATIONMASTER hands a small jeweler's box to the O.G.)

Each award is different, and each contains a message that reads: "From the Directors of the Great Northern and Southern Railway, in grateful recognition of your courageous and prompt action in averting an accident on the 18th of July 1905." Miss Roberta.

(ROBERTA steps forward, curtsies.)

O.G.: *(continuing)* Oh, I have seen you before!

ROBERTA: Yes, sir. I know.

> You and your brother and sister wave to the 9:15 train almost every morning, just after it comes out of the tunnel. Am I not right?

ROBERTA: Yes. And you are one of the only passengers who waves back. Always you do.

O.G.: Well, yes. You three look so *happy* to see the train.

ROBERTA: Oh, we are!

(The O.G. hands the jeweler's box to ROBERTA.)

O.G.: *(to the assembled gathering)* The engine driver tells me that Miss Roberta stood on the line and refused to budge until the train had come to a complete stop. Bravo.

(The gathered audience applauds. The O.G. turns back to ROBERTA.)

You can open the box.

(ROBERTA lifts out a sparkling gold necklace. There are "ooh's" from the onlookers. Mother wipes away a tear.)

ROBERTA: Oh, thank you, sir.

O.G.: No, no. Thank *you*, my dear.

(The STATIONMASTER hands a second box to the O.G. ROBERTA steps back.)

Master Peter!

(PETER steps forward, is about to give a bow, but the O.G. reaches forward and shakes hands with him.)

It is my pleasure to meet you, Peter. I understand you want to be an engineer when you grow up. ... Well, I hope this commemorative piece will encourage you to become an engineer, and perhaps work on our railroad. We would be honored to see you here.

(The O.G. *hands the box to* PETER, *who pulls out a gold watch.)*

PETER: It's a real railway timepiece! Oh, thank you, sir!

O.G.: Now you will have no excuse: there will be no being late to wave to my train!

(Laughter among the onlookers. PETER *backs away; the two* GIRLS *examine the watch. The* STATIONMASTER *hands the* O.G. *a large cardboard box with a broad red ribbon around it.* PHYLLIS *glances at the box and raises her hand to her mouth, realizing it's for her.)*

Miss Phyllis.

*(*PHYLLIS *curtsies, then offers her hand for a shake as well. The* O.G. *takes it.)*

I am very pleased to meet you, Phyllis, for I have seen you waving to me many times.

PHYLLIS: Yes, sir. You're always in the first class carriage.

O.G.: Well, yes. It's easier for me to see you from there. Now, Phyllis, what's in this box will, I hope, help you remember for many years that you helped save our train.

(He hands the box to PHYLLIS, *who struggles to open it.)*

Here: why don't I help you?

(Together they sit on a railway bench and open it. PHYLLIS *lifts out a large, golden-haired teddy bear. There is a stick tied to its right paw, and on the stick is a square red flag [ideally, the flag isn't yet visible to the audience].)*

PHYLLIS: Oh, my! He's lovely! Thank you.

*(*PHYLLIS *reaches up and plonks a kiss on the* O.G.'s *cheek.)*

O.G.: Show them!

*(*PHYLLIS *holds the bear up for the onlookers to see [they applaud] and then she steps forward and shows it to the audience. She takes the paw that holds the flag and*

wags it back and forth as though she is flagging down the train.)

(Fade lights on the Station. A spotlight comes up on MOTHER *as she steps downstage and speaks to the audience.)*

MOTHER: You would think an experience like that would last the children for several years. Wouldn't you? But shortly afterward something else happened—something quite different—and in rather a strange way.

(Blackout on MOTHER.*)*

(Lights come up on the Station. At stage left two PASSENGERS *are holding up a man [*the RUSSIAN*] who is weak at the knees. The* PASSENGERS *steer him to a bench. The* RUSSIAN *has long hair, wild-looking eyes [he is running a fever], and wears shabby clothes. He is trembling and is unshaven.)*

PASSENGER 1: Make way. This man's ill.

PASSENGER 2: Nah! It's a sham! I'll wager 'e didn't buy a ticket.

(The CHILDREN *enter through the gate.)*

PETER: Oh, look. Something's happened. Come on!

(They run forward.)

PASSENGER 2: If you ask me, I'd say it's a case for the police.

PASSENGER 1: The infirmary, more likely!

PETER: What happened?

PASSENGER 2: 'E got off the train and 'e's got no ticket.

PASSENGER 1: To be accurate, he fell out of the train. Right onto the platform.

STATIONMASTER: *(approaching)* Now then, what's all this about? Move along, please. I'll attend to it. *(to the* RUSSIAN*)* Now then, tell me what this is all about.

RUSSIAN: *(in Russian)* Ya poteryal moi billet, a ya bol'noi chelovek.

(He holds his head)

RUSSIAN: *(continuing)* I ya starayus' naiti zhenu I rebenka—

> *(Translation: I have lost my ticket and I am a sick man. ... And I am trying to find my wife and child.)*

STATIONMASTER: Whoa! Does anyone understand what he's saying?

PASSENGER 1: Sounds like French to me.

PETER: No, it's definitely not French.

ROBERTA: German, perhaps. I'm studying German at school. *(to the RUSSIAN)* Sprechen sie Deutsch?

RUSSIAN: *(in Russian)* Pozhaluista, pomogite mne. Okh, ya tak bolen, I goloden, I ya poteryal zhenu I rebenka.

> *(Translation: Please help me. I am, oh, so sick, and I am hungry, and I have lost my wife and child.)*

PASSENGER 2: Maybe it's Italian. Anyone know Italian?

(The onlookers shake their heads.)

(to PETER) Well, why don't you try him in French? If you know so much about it.

PETER: Uh... *(to the RUSSIAN, says in poor French)* Parley voo Frongsay?

THE RUSSIAN: Je parle Francais! *(holds thumb and finger slightly apart)* Un peu!

PETER: Bon!

PASSENGER 1: Oh, well done, lad!

RUSSIAN: *(haltingly, also in poor French but with a Slavic accent)* Je suis désolé. J'ai perdue mon billet, et je suis malade, et j'a pas d'argent. Vous comprenez?

(Pause; PETER looks bewildered.)

STATIONMASTER: Well, Master Peter. Did you understand what he said?

PETER: My French isn't that good!

PHYLLIS: Peter – Do you have that envelope of foreign stamps with you, that you're collecting…?

PETER: What a good idea!

> (PETER *pulls an envelope from his pocket and from it draws a handful of stamps; he holds a stamp up, points to it, then points to the* RUSSIAN, *who shakes his head "no." They repeat the process several times.*)

PETER: Sveridge? – that's Sweden…. Helvetia? – that's Switzerland …. Nederland? … Poland? ….

> (*The* RUSSIAN *grabs several stamps from* PETER, *looks through them, then holds one up and points to himself.*)

PETER: That's Russian! He's from Russia!

RUSSIAN: Moscva! Moscva!

> (*Translation: "Moscow! Moscow!"*)

ROBERTA: I don't think anyone knows Russian. But Mother does know French. She lived in Paris once. I think we should take him home with us. Mother will know what to do.

PASSENGER 1: He's in no condition to walk any distance.

PETER: *(to* STATIONMASTER*)* Can we borrow a trolley? He could lie on it! Roberta and I could take turns—

PASSENGER 1: I'll go with you, lad. Share the load.

> (PASSENGER 2 *wheels in a trolley. The* RUSSIAN *is lifted onto it. The lights fade as the three* CHILDREN *and* PASSENGER 1 *push the trolley through the gate.*)

> (*Lights come up downstage, against a plain backdrop.* MOTHER *and the* DOCTOR *enter from stage right and cross slowly to stage left. He carries a black bag.*)

DOCTOR: Your Russian friend has mild pneumonia, and he's badly undernourished.

MOTHER: He will be all right, though? Won't he, doctor?

DOCTOR: Yes, but it will take time.

MOTHER: Is it all right for him to be in Peter's room? It's the only spare bed I have at the moment.

DOCTOR: Certainly. He's not infectious. And Peter will keep him company, stop him from brooding.

(Unseen by them, ROBERTA enters from stage right, pauses, hears the remainder of the conversation.)

MOTHER: Oh, he *is* brooding. He does so want to find his wife and child. He's desperate with worry.

DOCTOR: First we have to get him well. Lots of rest and good nourishing food. Broth made from calves-foot jelly. Good meats and chicken as he improves. You will know.

MOTHER: Oh, my. A little different to our diet.

(The DOCTOR and MOTHER exit stage left.)

ROBERTA: How do we get food like that? How can mother afford it? *(she paces about)* What can we do? Well, perhaps there is a way….

(She stops at the stage right exit, calls as if calling upstairs.)

Peter! Phyllis! Can you come down. Quickly, please. *(she exits)*

(Lights come up on the kitchen. ROBERTA enters from stage right, walks to the dresser, pulls paper, an envelope and a pencil from a drawer, and sits at the table. PETER and PHYLLIS enter.)

PETER: What's up?

PHYLLIS: The Russian gentleman's asleep. He snores!

ROBERTA: We've got to be quick. Mother will be back in a minute. Doctor Forrest says the Russian man is to have special foods, and we just don't have anything like that. But I've got an idea. Mother won't exactly be pleased, but it's the only way. PETER, will you go up to the attic, see if you can find one of those old, torn white sheets. And one of the big paint brushes and some paint. We'll use it to make a sign – to get the Old Gentleman's attention. He's a kind man and I'm sure he'll want to help—

(Sound of door being opened.)

PETER: Sssh! Mother!

(MOTHER enters stage left, pauses.)

MOTHER: What are you three up to?

PHYLLIS: Oh, nothing. We're just planning a game. Aren't we, Peter?

PETER: Uh, yes. Let's go up and find some…things.

(PETER and PHYLLIS move toward inner door.)

MOTHER: Sssh as you go. Don't disturb our guest.

(PETER and PHYLLIS exit. MOTHER looks questioningly at ROBERTA, who folds the paper she plans to write on. MOTHER crosses to the cabinet, opens a draw and takes out several men's shirts.)

MOTHER: I'll have to iron these.

ROBERTA: Those are Daddy's shirts!

MOTHER: I'm going to let our guest wear them. He hasn't anything—

ROBERTA: Why didn't Daddy take them?

MOTHER: He…er…he doesn't need them.

ROBERTA: Mother…Daddy isn't…he isn't *dead*, is he?

MOTHER: My darling, no! What makes you think of anything so horrible?

ROBERTA: I… I don't know. You don't tell us anything.

MOTHER: There is very little to tell. Look, Daddy was quite, quite well when I heard from him last. He *will* come back to us. One day.

ROBERTA: You're sure?

MOTHER: Yes …Yes, I am sure.

(PETER and PHYLLIS re-enter stage right. PHYLLIS carries a one-inch wide paint brush and a pot of paint, but holds them behind her. PETER carries the sheet, rolled up, tucked under his arm.)

PHYLLIS: Mother: you promised to tell us about the Russian gentleman.

MOTHER: Oh. Yes, I did. Well, it's a long story. Enough for a book!

PETER: A book you could write?

MOTHER: It would be better if he did. He is a writer. A well-known writer in Russia. But some people there—influential people—didn't like what he wrote. So three years ago they... they put him in prison.

ROBERTA: In prison?

MOTHER: A dark, dark dungeon with hardly any light. Damp and dreadful. And no one to talk to. Then after three long years they put him on a train to Siberia. But he jumped from the train—

PETER: He escaped?

MOTHER: Yes, and went home to find his wife and daughter. But when he got there, a neighbor told him that people had helped them get away, and they'd come here, to England.

ROBERTA: He must have been heartbroken.

MOTHER: He stowed away on a ship, from Rostock I think, and then he got sick. Not seasick but pneumonia. Then someone found him and stole his wallet, while he slept.

ROBERTA: Oh, poor man.

MOTHER: And, well, you know the rest.

PHYLLIS: When he gets better, can we help him find his family?

MOTHER: Oh, if only I knew how. He would recover so much more quickly.

ROBERTA: There must be a way...

(ROBERTA *moves toward the outer door, signaling privately for* PETER *and* PHYLLIS *to follow.* PHYLLIS *sidles past* MOTHER *with the brush and paint concealed behind her.* PETER *does the same with the rolled up sheet.* MOTHER *picks up the shirts and walks down-stage.)*

(Lights fade out on the kitchen.)

MOTHER: *(to the audience)* They're up to something, I'm sure. Aren't they? A mother can tell! *(slight pause)* Oh, dear: am I right? Should I be telling them about their Father? I don't want them to worry—Bobbie, especially—she's so intuitive; she senses things. And they are happy here. We may not have much, but we do have each other. *(continuing, lighter)* And they have discovered the railway. they've become my Railway Children! *(exits)*

(Lights up on the embankment; train whistle and wheels can be heard. PETER and PHYLLIS lean against the fence, peer in the direction from which the train will be coming. PETER has the white sheet rolled under his arm which, when opened out, will be about 2.5 meters wide [8 feet] and 0.6 meters high [2 feet].)

PHYLLIS: Is it coming?

PETER: Yes: Help me hold it out.

(THEY unroll the sheet into a banner; each holding an end, and hang it over the fence. On it, in crudely painted letters, are these words:

Look Out at The Station

(The train noise grows louder and suddenly the train is passing. The two CHILDREN wave and point to their sign. When the train has past, PETER and PHYLLIS roll up the banner.)

(Lights fade on the embankment and come up downstage right. ROBERTA is standing by the Station gate, holding an envelope and looking stage left, in the direction of a train that can be heard approaching. She paces.)

(There are train sounds, then the squeal of breaks, and finally silence as the train stops. One or two passengers approach from left to right along the platform. The O.G. enters stage left. ROBERTA runs toward him. They meet downstage center.)

O.G.: Miss Roberta!

ROBERTA: Oh, "Bobbie." Please!

O.G.: Yes, Miss Bobbie. I saw your message. And your brother and sister wave. So energetic!

ROBERTA: I have… Will you be getting back on the same train?

O.G.: If at all possible.

(ROBERTA thrusts the envelope into his hand.)

ROBERTA: It's all explained in here. You can read it on the train.

O.G.: What is this all about?

ROBERTA: There's a Russian prisoner in our house.

O.G.: You have a prisoner?

ROBERTA: *(fast)* Well, no. He was a prisoner in Russia. He escaped. Mother is caring for him. We want to help him find his wife and daughter. They're in England, but he doesn't know where. His name's Szcepansky. I wrote it down. In the letter. Boris Szcepansky.

O.G.: Boris Szcepansky? I've read his book! Translated of course. A fine book!

ROBERTA: You know of him?

O.G.: Oh, definitely. And your mother is looking after him?

(ROBERTA nods. Train whistle sounds.)

ROBERTA: Hurry! That's your train.

(THEY move quickly toward stage left.)

O.G.: I'm glad you came to me. I will try to find out something. I know a great many Russians in London. And they all know his name.

ROBERTA: He's awfully sick. The doctor says he has to have special food, which we don't have at home. *(points to the letter)* I wrote it down.

(Train whistle.)

Quick, your train's about to leave.

(The O.G. *exits hurriedly, stage left. Sound of train pulling out.* ROBERTA *walks backwards toward gate, waves, then turns and runs out of the gate. Lights fade.)*

(Lights up on the kitchen. It is two days later. The RUSSIAN *is sitting in a chair facing the table, a blanket around him;* PHYLLIS *is facing him. They are playing "Snap" with a deck of cards [she has been teaching him].* PHYLLIS *is fast and snaps out "Snap!" The* RUSSIAN *is slower and tends to say "Schnaaap!" They laugh frequently.* PETER *is lying on the floor face down, drawing in a blank-page notebook. There is a knock at the outer door. Peter jumps up and opens it. A large hamper is pushed through the door.)*

PETER: For us?

DELIVERY PERSON: *(v.o.)* This is "Three Chimneys?"

PETER: Yes.

DELIVERY PERSON: *(v.o.)* Then it must be for you.

(He holds an envelope out to PETER.*)*

This is for your mother, young man.

PETER: Oh, yes. Thank you, sir.

DELIVERY PERSON: *(v.o.)* Good day to you.

*(*PETER *closes the door and drags the hamper farther into the room.* PHYLLIS *jumps down and inspects the hamper. Carrying the letter,* PETER *goes to the inner door, opens it, and calls up the stairs.)*

PETER: Mother! There's a letter for you.

PHYLLIS: And a parcel!

PETER: And a parcel.

PHYLLIS: A *big* parcel!

RUSSIAN: It is… surprise?

PHYLLIS: We don't know anything about it. Who it came from, even.

PETER: The letter will say.

(PETER *holds the letter high.* PHYLLIS *jumps, trying to reach it.*)

PETER: *(continuing)* No! Mother has to open it. It's addressed to her.

(MOTHER *enters stage right.* PETER *hands her the letter. She opens and reads it.*)

MOTHER: Oh, dear. … Oh, dear.

RUSSIAN: C'est mal nouvelles?

MOTHER: Mais, oui…. Non! *(points to letter)* Bon!

RUSSIAN: Ah, bon.

MOTHER: Who put him up to this?

PETER: Who is "him"?

MOTHER: The Director of the Railway.

PHYLLIS: The Old Gentleman?

MOTHER: Yes. But this should not happen. Open the hamper.

(PETER *and* PHYLLIS *open the hamper and lift out port wine, cheese, a ham, and similar luxury items, placing some on the floor, some on the table.*)

PETER: *(reads label)* "Calves foot jelly."

MOTHER: All the things the doctor said our guest should have.

(ROBERTA *enters stage left, pauses when she sees the hamper and goods.*)

Is this your doing, Bobbie?

ROBERTA: I just asked the old gentleman if he could help find Mr Szcepansky's family.

MOTHER: Then why did he send food?

ROBERTA: I… I told him what the doctor said. That he needed special food to… to build up his strength.

MOTHER: You know how I feel about accepting charity! We can manage. You all know that.

ROBERTA: Yes, Mother. I…I thought I was helping.

(The RUSSIAN *pulls himself out of his chair, mimes feeling sleepy.)*

RUSSIAN: *(to* MOTHER*)* Je suis fatigué.

MOTHER: Mais oui.

(The RUSSIAN *exits stage right.)*

Peter: I want you to go upstairs and tidy your hobby box. And Phyllis, you straighten up your bed. You didn't do it this morning.

*(*PETER *and* PHYLLIS *exit.* MOTHER *turns to* ROBERTA.*)*

I don't know what to say. I understand you want to help, but really, you should have asked me first.

ROBERTA: But I know what your answer would have been: "We'll manage." You know we couldn't't've bought special foods for Mr Szepansky.

MOTHER: Well, as it was your doing, I suggest you finish unpacking the hamper.

*(*ROBERTA *kneels by the hamper, pulls out several items, places them on the floor, then lifts out a bundle wrapped in newspaper and tied with string. She unties it and magazines fall out.)*

ROBERTA: Look! Magazines for Mr. Szepansky. And they are in Russian!

MOTHER: Your friend—the Old Gentleman as you call him— does seem to think of everything.

*(*ROBERTA, *still kneeling by the hamper, picks up the English-language newspaper used to wrap the magazines. She smoothes it out, and then goes rigid.)*

ROBERTA: *(reads)* "End of Trial. Verdict. Sentence. Five Years Penal Servitude." Mother! Mother! This is about Daddy! He's in prison!

*(*MOTHER *kneels beside her.)*

MOTHER: Bobbie…. Oh, Bobbie…. Don't you believe it. Your father didn't do it. I *know* he didn't.

ROBERTA: But he's in prison. *For five years!*

MOTHER: Believe me, he didn't do anything wrong. He's good and noble and honorable.

ROBERTA: Oh, Daddy. Oh, Daddy.

MOTHER: We have to be proud of him, and just wait.

ROBERTA: Why didn't you tell me, Mummy?

MOTHER: Are you going to tell the others?

ROBERTA: Peter and Phyllis? No...no.

MOTHER: Why not?

ROBERTA: Because... because they shouldn't have to worry.

MOTHER: Exactly. So now you understand why I didn't tell you.

ROBERTA: Please tell me about it? I want to understand.

MOTHER: *(slight pause)* You remember those men who came to our house that night in London? They came to arrest your Father. They charged him with selling State secrets to a foreign country; for being a spy and a traitor.

ROBERTA: Oh, no. Father wouldn't...He's not like that!

MOTHER: Letters were found in your Father's desk. Someone put them there. The person who's really guilty.

ROBERTA: Do you know who?

MOTHER: No. I don't.

ROBERTA: Does, Daddy?

MOTHER: He has a suspicion, but nothing he can prove.

ROBERTA: Couldn't you explain that to someone?

MOTHER: Who would listen to me?

ROBERTA: Well, you could write about it.

MOTHER: Oh, Bobbie! I may be good at writing poems and little stories, but this? No. *(slight pause)* This will be our secret, then?

ROBERTA: *(slowly)* Yes.

MOTHER: And we won't talk about it anymore?

ROBERTA: No. All right.

MOTHER: Then go upstairs and wash your pretty little face. Perhaps we'll ask Peter to fetch some buns for tea. What d'you think?

(Fade lights on kitchen. A spotlight comes up at downstage right, the STATIONMASTER *strolls in.)*

STATIONMASTER: Boys and girls! Ladies and gentlemen! We hope you are enjoying the adventures of The Railway Children. Now we're going to take a short break, so there's time for you to go down to the buffet car and get some refreshments. *(pulls a watch from his pocket)* Mind you, the train will start again in just fifteen minutes.

CURTAIN

Act 2

(The three CHILDREN *are on the embankment, facing the audience; they are standing stage right, above the entrance to the tunnel. We hear the 2:13 train go by, its smoke billowing up from beneath them as a series of puffs. The* CHILDREN *wave, their eyes following its passage.)*

PETER: The train driver saw us! I saw him wave!

ROBERTA: And the Old Gentlemen. With his white handkerchief.

(A BOY *of about 15, dressed in running shorts and white shirt, runs in from stage left downstage beside the rails. He carries a satchel-type bag beside him, with a strap slung across the opposite shoulder. As he runs, he scatters small bits of white paper from his bag. Puffing from his exertions, he exits into the tunnel entrance, first stopping to scatter more paper.)*

PHYLLIS: What's he doing that for?

PETER: He's the hare.

PHYLLIS: The what?

ROBERTA: It's a chase, Phyllis. It's called Hare and Hounds. The hounds are other boys: they have to find the hare.

PHYLLIS: What other boys?

PETER: They're coming up the hill now.

*(*BOYS *run in from stage left, search for bits of paper, cross to the tunnel, and exit into it. All are in shorts and white or grey shirts.)*

They're following the bits of paper.

PHYLLIS: But what if there's a wind. Won't the paper blow away?

PETER: Well, yes. But the hare makes sure he puts down enough paper.

(The STATIONMASTER *enters on the embankment from stage left. He does not see the running boys, who now have exited into the tunnel.)*

STATIONMASTER: Hello, children. Waiting to see the 2:13? It's already been through.

PETER: No, no, sir. We did see it.

PHYLLIS: We're watching the Hare and Hounds.

(More boys run in from stage left. [They can be the same as the first ones, but in different shirts.]) PHYLLIS *points to them. They exit into the tunnel.*

STATIONMASTER: *(shouts at the boys)* Hey, you boys! Come back! You're not allowed on railway property. And definitely not in the tunnel!

*(The boys exit into the tunnel. There is a space, then the last boy [*JIM*] enters. He is obviously tired and the only boy wearing a red shirt.)*

PHYLLIS: What if a train comes?

STATIONMASTER: Quite correct, miss. It's much too dangerous to be in there. *(to* ROBERTA*)* Do you know who they are?

ROBERTA: No. I don't.

(The STATIONMASTER *looks at* PETER, *who shakes his head.* JIM *exits into the tunnel.)*

STATIONMASTER: I'll wager they're from Braydenborough school.

PETER: How long is the tunnel?

STATIONMASTER: Close to half a mile, I should think. It curves round, like a horseshoe.

PETER: Then they should have time. The next train's not till 3:23.

STATIONMASTER: I'm going up to the school; see the Headmaster. I'll bid you good day.

CHILDREN: Good bye, sir. *(etc)*

(The STATIONMASTER *exits stage left.)*

PETER: If we cut across the fields, we could get to the other end of the tunnel before the hounds get there.

ROBERTA: You mean, warn them? About the Stationmaster?

PETER: Of course!

ROBERTA: I don't think it's any of our business.

PETER: Oh, Bobbie! Stop being such a girl! Come on!

(PETER runs along the embankment above the tunnel entrance stage right and exits; he calls v.o.)

Oh, come on!

(ROBERTA takes PHYLLIS's hand and they exit stage right.)

(Lights fade to black; there is a background sound of a train, then the lights come up again on the embankment and railway line. We are now [supposedly] at the other end of the tunnel.)

(ROBERTA, PETER and PHYLLIS enter on the embankment from stage left.)

PETER: Look, there are pieces of paper: the hare has already come out.

(BOYS straggle out of the tunnel entrance [but not Jim]. They exit stage left.)

There're the hounds. What did I tell you?

PHYLLIS: Oh, do let's have lunch. I've got a pain in my front, I'm so hungry.

PETER: Not yet. We've got to watch.

PHYLLIS: I shall die if I don't have something to eat, and then you'll be sorry.

ROBERTA: We're all hungry, Peter.

PETER: Well, give her a sandwich, for goodness' sake.

(ROBERTA opens the bag and hands PHYLLIS a sandwich.)

PHYLLIS: Thank you.

ROBERTA: *(to* PETER*)* Here, we'd better have one each, too.

(Two or three more BOYS *straggle out tiredly, cross to the left, and exit.)*

PHYLLIS: What shall we do now, then?

PETER: Wait. They're not all out yet.

ROBERTA: Oh, they must be.

PETER: No. There's still one. The boy in the red jersey.

ROBERTA: He probably came out before we got here.

PETER: No, he couldn't. He was the last, and you could see he was tired. He wouldn't have passed all the others.

(The CHILDREN *climb down the embankment [or exit and re-enter stage left] and peer into the tunnel entrance.* PETER *calls into the tunnel.)*

Hey! Is anyone still in there?

(They listen.)

He must have had an accident. Perhaps he's lying with his head on the metal rails, an unresisting prey to the next passing express.

PHYLLIS: Oooh!

ROBERTA: Oh, Peter, stop talking like a book! We'd better go in. Come on, Phyl.

PHYLLIS: Do we have to?

ROBERTA: Yes, we must. Keep close behind me. If a train comes, stand flat against the tunnel wall and hold your petticoats close to you, so they don't fly up and catch on something.

PETER: No. I'll go first. It was my idea.

(They enter the tunnel.)

(Fade lights to black; there are echo sounds, train sounds, perhaps water dripping.)

(Minimal light comes up on the inside of the tunnel [painted on a drop between the embankment and the

*railway lines] with the railway lines only just visible.
A light from the entrance offstage right shines dimly
into the tunnel. Toward stage left, and in complete
darkness, the boy in the red jersey [JIM] is lying on
the railway line; his leg is twisted and his foot is
caught under one of the rails. There are shadows of
the children as they enter [now in the tunnel] from
offstage right.)*

PETER: Keep close behind me.

PHYLLIS: It's too dark. I want to go back.

ROBERTA: You'll be all right. Keep a tight grip on my hand.

PETER: *(to* ROBERTA) Did you bring your torch?

ROBERTA: Yes. Just a minute.

*(ROBERTA searches in her shoulder bag; PHYLLIS
reaches for PETER's hand. ROBERTA pulls a torch
[flashlight] out of the bag, hands it to PETER. As they
stumble on, the daylight behind them fades and
extinguishes.)*

PETER: Thanks.

ROBERTA: Here. *(she re-takes* PHYLLIS*'s hand)*

*(They stumble along a few paces, the tunnel light now
fractionally brighter [from the torch].)*

PHYLLIS: It smells so musty. *(she stumbles and falls)* Oh, ouch!

ROBERTA: Easy there, Phyl.

(ROBERTA helps PHYLLIS get up.)

PETER: Oh, come on! We've got to find the boy. I know he's in
here, somewhere.

PHYLLIS: Really, I do want to go back.

PETER: Well, you can't. It'd be much too dangerous. The 3:23
will be here any minute.

PHYLLIS: Oh, please, can't I— *(just go back?)*

ROBERTA: Sshh! Listen!

(They stand still.)

JIM: *(distant, weak)* Help!

PETER: You see: he is in here!

JIM: Can you help me? Please! Can you help me?

ROBERTA: Yes! Yes, we're coming!

> *(The* CHILDREN *stumble forward, searching with the torch until it catches* JIM*'s shape.)*

PETER: There he is!

> *(The* CHILDREN *crowd around* JIM*; their questions overlap.)*

PETER: What happened?

PHYLLIS: What's your name?

ROBERTA: Are you hurt?

JIM: It's my leg. I think I broke it.

ROBERTA: Can you stand up?

JIM: No. I tried. My foot's caught under the rail.

PETER: *(shines the torch onto* JIM*'s foot)* Let's see.

> *(In the distance they hear a train whistle accompanied by a humming sound on the rails. The* CHILDREN *freeze, look back toward the tunnel entrance, stage right.)*

PETER: That's the 3:23.

PHYLLIS: He's stuck on the tracks. He'll be killed!

ROBERTA: We'll have to move him. We must!

PETER: And quickly!

ROBERTA: Give the torch to Phyllis. *(to* PHYLLIS*)* Shine it on his foot. *(to* PETER*)* We'll have to pull his foot out.

> *(They try pulling on the shoe, but it's stuck and the boy cries out in pain. The engine noise is increasing and the engine headlight is beginning to light the tunnel with a wavering flash.)*

PETER: It's stuck hard.

ROBERTA: Try again.

(They pull again. JIM *moans. There is louder engine noise and more light from the train.)*

PHYLLIS: Oh, do be quick.

ROBERTA: We'll have to undo his shoe. The light, Phyllis. Here!

PETER: There's an alcove over there. We'll pull him into it.

ROBERTA: Be ready to pull him clear.

PETER: I'll take his shoulders.

ROBERTA: Oh, there's a knot. The light, Phyl!

PETER: I'll take the torch. Phyl: you run into that alcove.

*(*PHYLLIS *hesitates.)*

Now!

*(*PHYLLIS *runs to and sits in front of an alcove painted on the backdrop. The train noise and wobbling light from the engine are now intense. The engine's whistle shrieks again.)*

ROBERTA: His shoe's tied so tight.

PETER: Oh, do be quick!

ROBERTA: It's coming!

PETER: I think he's fainted!

ROBERTA: I've got it! His foot's free.

PETER: Pull him over, then!

*(*PETER *takes* JIM*'s shoulders and* ROBERTA *takes his legs. They half lift and half drag him over the rail to the alcove. They cower back and pull on* JIM *so he doesn't slip. There is a cloud of steam, immense noise, the reflection from the engine's firebox, then the lights from the windows flash past them, on and off, accompanied by a cacophony of wheel clatter. Then suddenly it's silent and dark, except for the light from the torch lying on the ground.* PETER *picks it up.)*

PETER: Whew! That was close!

PHYLLIS: Oh, I've got grit in my eyes.

ROBERTA: Here, use my handkerchief.

> *(*ROBERTA *leans over* JIM.*)*

PETER: Is he all right?

ROBERTA: Still unconscious.

PETER: We'll have to carry him out.

ROBERTA: We can't: he's too heavy.

PHYLLIS: And he's got a bad leg.

ROBERTA: *(to* PETER*)* You'd better go for help.

PHYLLIS: Me? I can't go alone in the dark.

ROBERTA: *(to* PHYLLIS*)* No. I mean Peter. *(to* PETER*)* How soon's the next train?

PETER: 4:17, I think.

ROBERTA: Then, run! Please!

PHYLLIS: Can I go too?

PETER: You'd slow me down too much.

PHYLLIS: I don't want to stay here. Not in the dark.

PETER: You won't be in the dark. You'll have the torch.

PHYLLIS: The battery won't last long.

ROBERTA: You should take it, Peter.

PETER: No. I can find my way. And I'll be walking toward the light.

> *(*PETER *walks away fast, exiting to stage right.)*

ROBERTA: *(calling after him)* Peter! Take care. And be as fast as you can. The boy's injured. We need to get him out of here.

PETER: *(v.o.)* I know.

PHYLLIS: Will the battery last, do you think?

ROBERTA: *(more confidently than she feels)* Oh, I expect so. *(to* JIM*)* Boy! Can you speak to us?

PHYLLIS: Yes, speak to us. Please!

ROBERTA: We just want to know you're alright.

PHYLLIS: You don't think he's dead, do you?

ROBERTA: Oh, no. He's just fainted.

PHYLLIS: I don't like it down here.

ROBERTA: None of us do, Phyl. Especially the hurt boy.

JIM: *(opens his eyes)* Oh, it does hurt.

PHYLLIS: Oh, he's not dead!

JIM: What's up?

(ROBERTA *takes a small bottle from her satchel.*)

ROBERTA: Here, drink this. Oh, Phil! Will you stop bleating! This very minute.

(PHYLLIS *sniffles.* ROBERTA *lifts the boy's head onto her lap and helps him drink.*)

JIM: That's enough, thank you.

(JIM *tries to sit up and then with a groan lies his head back.*)

It was one of the signal wires. It tripped me up. It was dark and I couldn't see it. Oh! It does hurt, though.

ROBERTA: Just rest. We've sent for help.

PHYLLIS: Peter's gone to the nearest house.

ROBERTA: Peter's our brother.

JIM: But how did you get here?

ROBERTA: We saw you run into the tunnel, but you didn't come out, so we came in to see.

PHYLLIS: Even though it was dark!

ROBERTA: Hold on. I want to straighten your leg, cushion it a bit.

(JIM *groans, shuts his eyes.*)

PHYLLIS: Oh, don't faint again. Please don't.

JIM: No. Ouch! I'll be all right.

PHYLLIS: Oh, I do wish they'd hurry.

(Pause.)

ROBERTA: What's your name?

JIM: Jim.

ROBERTA: Mine's Bobbie.

JIM: But you're a girl!

PHYLLIS: It's short for Roberta.

JIM: *(to* ROBERTA*)* You act like you were a boy.

ROBERTA: I wish I was a boy.

JIM: You're brave, just like a boy. Both of you.

PHYLLIS: My name's Phyllis.

JIM: Oh, hello, Phyllis.

(There are voices from offstage right and then the shine of several torches. PETER enters, followed by two MEN.)

MAN 1: How much farther?

PETER: I think we're nearly there.

MAN 2: It's far enough, that I'll say.

ROBERTA: *(calling)* Peter! Peter! We're over here.

MAN 1: We're coming, young lady.

(The MEN *bend over Jim; there is some ad-libbing.)*

MAN 2: Where does it hurt?

JIM: My leg. Right leg. Broken, I think.

PHYLLIS: He tripped over a wire.

ROBERTA: And his shoe was trapped under the rails.

MAN 2: You mean he was stuck on the rails?

PETER: Bobbie undid his shoe, then we pulled him to the side.

PHYLLIS: And then a train came through.

PETER: The 3:23.

MAN 1: And you were in here? *(The* CHILDREN *nod.)* All of you? Oh, my!

MAN 2: We've got to get them out of here, before the next train.

PETER: The 4:17.

(The two MEN *lift* JIM *between them and start carrying him out.)*

MAN 1: Where to, young man?

PETER: I... I...

ROBERTA: To our house. Mother will know what's best to do.

(Black out.)

(Lights come up on a front drop, with the exterior of the cottage door at stage right. The DOCTOR *and* MOTHER *enter (they exit from the cottage), walk slowly toward center stage.)*

DOCTOR: He'll be in a cast for another six weeks.

MOTHER: It has been painful for him, I think.

DOCTOR: Yes. But your care has helped. He couldn't be in a better place.

MOTHER: Oh, Bobbie has helped, too.

DOCTOR: A nurse in the making!

MOTHER: I think she has been part of his recovery.

(The DOCTOR *moves toward stage left.)*

I'll come with you to the gate.

(They exit. Lights up on the kitchen. From the interior door, stage right, the three children and JIM *enter. He is on crutches.* ROBERTA *helps him onto a chair, lifts his injured leg up onto a second chair.* PETER *takes the crutches.* JIM *is in some pain.)*

PETER: *(to* JIM*)* Where do you live, when you're not at school?

JIM: At Rutley. It's in Northumberland.

PHYLLIS: Do you go home for the holidays?

JIM: Sometimes.

PETER: By train?

JIM: To London first, then from Kings Cross.

PHYLLIS: Peter's going to be an engineer.

JIM: Ouch. A train engineer?

PETER: No. A mechanical engineer. I'll build bridges. Design engines. Things like that.

PHYLLIS: Like daddy.

JIM: Your father's an engineer?

PHYLLIS: Yes. He works for the government.

JIM: When will I meet him?

(Slight pause.)

ROBERTA: Oh...er... it will be a while. He... he's away right now.

PETER: On government business. Mother says I have to be the man of the house.

ROBERTA: Only for the time being.

(The front door opens. MOTHER *enters.)*

MOTHER: Jim has a visitor!

JIM: I do?

MOTHER: I saw him walking up the hill. It's your grandfather, Jim.

*(*MOTHER *ushers in the* O.G.*)*

JIM: Grandpa!

(The O.G. *hands his hat to* PETER. *The* O.G. *does not indicate he knows the children.)*

O.G.: Well, well, James. What have *you* been up to?

*(*JIM *gestures to his leg and to* MOTHER*)*.

It seems to me you're being spoiled more than is warranted!

JIM: Well, I—

O.G.: And you think I'm here to send you back to the school? To the sick ward?

JIM: Oh, do I have to? It can be so lonely there, and they don't feed you well.

O.G.: Or I could arrange to ship you home.

JIM: Yes, but…

O.G.: You would prefer to stay here?

JIM: Well, yes.

O.G.: But your nurse *(indicates* MOTHER*)* really needs to get back to her writing. *(to* MOTHER) Am I not right?

MOTHER: Well, Jim's health does come first.

ROBERTA: But, mother!

O.G.: Aha! I see my three young friends are here.

JIM: You know them, Grandpa?

O.G.: Oh, yes. Definitely. We have met before.

JIM: They saved my life!

O.G.: I am very aware of that. *(to the* CHILDREN*)* Jim and his father will always be indebted to you. As will I.

ROBERTA: Oh, please….

O.G.: I do not mean to embarrass you. But you were very brave. *(slight pause)* Now! I have asked your mother to take on a temporary job for me.

ROBERTA: But, really, mother does have to write.

O.G.: You are quite right. I have already discussed it with your mother, and she has agreed to work for me for six weeks, as Jim's nurse. And, so your Mother will still have time to write, I'm going to ask you, Roberta—Bobbie—to be his assistant nurse.

ROBERTA: Me?

JIM: Oh, yes. She is a good nurse.

O.G.: So I see. *(to* MOTHER*)* That's settled then. Now I must be off. *(to the three* CHILDREN*)* I will still look for you waving from the embankment.

CHILDREN: Oh, yes. We will. We will look for you.

*(*MOTHER *escorts the* O.G. *toward the door stage left.*

ROBERTA *hurries from the room, exiting through the door at stage right.)*

259

O.G.: Mr. Sczepansky: he is still with you?

MOTHER: Yes. And his health is improving. Thanks to you.

O.G.: Think nothing of it. I hope to have news for him soon.

MOTHER: Oh, that would be good for him.

O.G.: I'd keep it to yourself, for the time being. No need to raise false hopes.

(The O.G. *and* MOTHER *exit stage left.* ROBERTA *rushes back into the room, the newspaper cutting about their father in her hand, and exits through the door stage left.)*

(Lights fade to black on the kitchen and come up on a plain backdrop, or of fields, fully downstage. The O.G. *enters stage left, walking toward stage right.* ROBERTA *bursts in and runs after him.)*

ROBERTA: *(calls)* Oh, sir! Please wait. I have something to show you.

(The O.G. *stops.)*

O.G.: Then it must be important.

ROBERTA: Oh, it is! It is!

(She holds the newspaper cutting out to him.)

See what's in this paper. It's about my Father.

O.G.: Mmm, yes. I have heard about his case.

ROBERTA: It's not true, what the paper says! Father never did it! Mother says someone must've put something in Father's desk. But nobody listens to a word she says. And she's getting so thin, she worries about him so much. If only they would *listen*, then perhaps—

O.G: Whoa, Bobbie! I am not unsympathetic to your Father's case. When I read about it at the time, I had my doubts. Your Father's reputation has always been impeccable.

ROBERTA: As you're helping find the Russian gentleman's wife, I thought perhaps…

(Pause; the O.G. waits.)

ROBERTA: *(continuing)* I thought perhaps you could help, find out who did the treason. Because I know it wasn't Father, and no one will listen to Mother.

O.G.: I wasn't going to say anything yet, but ever since I've known who you were, I've been trying to find out things.

ROBERTA: Does Mother know?

O.G.: No. I didn't want to upset your Mother, in case I am unable—

ROBERTA: But there still is hope, isn't there?

O.G.: Yes. I don't think it's a false hope, or I wouldn't have told you.

ROBERTA: You don't think Father did it, do you?

O.G.: My dear, I'm perfectly certain he didn't.

ROBERTA: Oh. Thank you. Thank you.

O.G.: Then will you excuse me? I do have a train to catch.

ROBERTA: Oh, yes. Of course.

(ROBERTA turns to go, then turns back and gives him a kiss on the cheek.)

You won't say anything to Mother, will you? About me asking you?

O.G.: No. It will be our secret.

(They turn to exit, the O.G. stage right and ROBERTA stage left. The O.G. exits first. ROBERTA turns just before the exit, looks back, waves, exits left.)

(Lights fade to black.)

(Lights come up on the embankment. PETER and PHYLLIS enter stage left.)

PHYLLIS: Are we in time?

PETER: *(consults his watch)* Yes. Only just, though.

(Sound of train whistle.)

PHYLLIS: *(calling to off-stage left)* Come on, you two. Or you'll miss it.

(The train can be heard approaching. ROBERTA *and* JIM *enter stage left, on the embankment. He is on crutches.)*

ROBERTA: We're coming as quickly as we can!

PETER: You don't want to miss it, Jim, the first time you're out.

JIM: *(to* ROBERTA, *pointing to tunnel entrance)* This is where we met, isn't it? Down there?

ROBERTA: Yes.

PETER: Here it comes!

(Train whistle, roar, clatter of wheels, wind. The children wave, their heads moving from one side to the other.)

ROBERTA: My goodness, *everyone* was waving today!

JIM: Is it always like this?

PHYLLIS: Hundreds of handkerchieves! Thousands!

ROBERTA: Did you see your Grandpa?

JIM: Yes. Oh, yes.

PETER: He was signaling something to us. Waving his newspaper.

ROBERTA: It's never been like that before.

JIM: I don't understand…

ROBERTA: Something must be up.

PETER: Must be because you're here, Jim.

JIM: They wouldn't know who I am!

PHYLLIS: But *we* know, don't we?

ROBERTA: Come on. We promised Mother we'd bring Jim right back.

PETER: *(gentle sarcasm)* Yes, nurse.

(They turn toward the stage left exit, then ROBERTA *stops abruptly and beckons to* PETER.*)*

ROBERTA: You take Jim and Phyllis back. Please! Something strange is happening. I want to go to the Station.

(To prevent any argument, ROBERTA *sets off stage right and exits.)*

PHYLLIS: Why's Bobbie doing that?

PETER: I don't know. Come on, Jim.

(Lights extinguish over the embankment.)

(Sound of train approaching.)

(Lights up on the station. We hear the train pull in and stop, followed by the banging of carriage doors. ROBERTA *runs up to the gate stage right and looks along the platform. One or two* PASSENGERS *cross the stage toward the gate. When they see* ROBERTA, *they smile and wave. The* STATION-MASTER *enters from behind her.)*

STATIONMASTER: This *is* a special day, Miss Bobbie.

ROBERTA: Oh, it is. But I don't understand…why is everyone waving to me?

*(*FATHER *enters stage left, walking slowly, dressed exactly as before.* ROBERTA *has her back to him.)*

STATIONMASTER: It's the day we have all been waiting for.

(The STATIONMASTER *places his hands on* ROBERTA*'s shoulders and twists her around so she is facing* FATHER. *She stiffens in disbelief.)*

ROBERTA: *(screams)* Oh, my Daddy! My Daddy!

> *(Nesbit's book says: "That scream went like a knife into the heart of everyone in the train.")*

*(*ROBERTA *flings herself at* FATHER. *They separate and he turns and beckons behind him [to off-stage]. The O.G. enters and shakes* FATHER*'s hand. He holds his hand out to* ROBERTA, *who flings her arms around him. While this is happening the train whistle sounds and the noise of the train departing obscures what is said. The party of three heads toward the gate. On their way*

the STATIONMASTER *and any passengers on the
platform shake* FATHER*'s hand. Background train
sounds rise. When the group reaches mid-stage,*
MOTHER, PETER, *and* PHYLLIS *enter stage right.*
PHYLLIS *runs forward and hugs her father. He picks
her up and swings her around. Then* PETER *runs up,
goes to give his father an embrace, then lowers his arms
and shakes hands.)*

*(*MOTHER *and* FATHER *embrace, but not heavily
emotionally because there are other people present [as
would be customary in Victorian times].)*

(The RUSSIAN *and* JIM *enter; the RUSSIAN wears a
suit.* JIM *is on crutches. They are introduced by the* O.G.
and shake father's hand.)

(Background sounds decrease. The STATIONMASTER
*and passengers move away and gradually exit, leaving
the family, the* O.G., *the* RUSSIAN *and* JIM *gathered
around* FATHER. *The* O.G. *and* JIM *sit on the station
bench.)*

FATHER: If it hadn't been for the help of our very dear friend,
here *(gestures to the* O.G.*),* I might still be languishing in
prison.

O.G.: Oh, your innocence was clear—very clear. It just needed
someone in the know to start the wheels in motion.

PETER: Have they captured the real culprit?

O.G.: Shall we say the police have it well in hand? He will get his
come-uppance.

MOTHER: We can't thank you enough. You have done so much
for us.

O.G.: I think we owe a lot to my young friends here—they took
the initiative. But more than anyone, I have to tell you that it
was Roberta—Bobbie—who *really* pushed me into doing
something, *(The* O.G. *turns toward her.)* Not just for your
Father, my dear, although you were magnificent in your
certainty that he had been wrongly convicted. But also for Mr
Sczepansky. And for young Jim here.

JIM: Oh, Grandpa: Can I stay until my leg is healed? Please?

O.G.: As long as your nurse—your nurses—feel you need to be nursed!

(Laughter.)

And now, if you will forgive me, I do have a train to catch.

PHYLLIS: You always seem to have a train to catch!

O.G. You are quite right, my dear. *(to FATHER and MOTHER)* You will be returning to London, I expect.

FATHER: Shortly. In a few weeks.

O.G. Then I shall come and see you before you leave.

(The FAMILY and JIM exit stage right. The O.G. turns to the RUSSIAN.)

Now, Mr. Sczepansky, will you come with me?

(The O.G. and the RUSSIAN walk stage right.)

I am happy to tell you that your wife and daughter have been found, and are well. I am sure they are looking forward to seeing you.

(The RUSSIAN nods, but hasn't really understood.)

Here is a letter from them.

RUSSIAN: *(recognizes the handwriting on the envelope)* Spaseeba! Spaseeba!

(The STATIONMASTER enters.)

O.G.: Ah! Stationmaster! I want you to arrange for a ticket for Mr. Sczepansky here. He will be going to Ludlow, in Shropshire. *(to the RUSSIAN, speaking slowly)* And you may leave whenever you are ready.

RUSSIAN: Ah, Spaseeba! Spaseeba!

(The O.G. and the RUSSIAN exit. The STATIONMASTER turns to the audience.)

STATIONMASTER: Oh, we did miss seeing Bobbie, Peter and Phyllis at the Station, after they returned to London. Then later we heard they received still another surprise! As you will see.

(The STATIONMASTER *exits.)*

(The lights come up on the living room of the big house in London; it is morning. PETER *and* PHYLLIS *are placing the railway carriages on the track.* ROBERTA *is reading.* FATHER *comes in from the inside door, his coat on, a briefcase under his arm. During the following dialogue,* FATHER *goes to and kisses each child in turn [*PETER *is hesitant about the kiss, shakes hands].)*

FATHER: I have to go to work now. Like I do every day. But I'll be back at half past five. I promise you. Like yesterday, and the day before, and the day before that.

PETER: But not tomorrow!

FATHER: No. Not tomorrow. Tomorrow's Saturday—and we'll repair your engine. And then it will be Sunday and your mother and I thought we could all go to Windsor Castle, take a picnic.

PETER: On the train?

FATHER: Of course.

PHYLLIS: I love trains! But not too close.

ROBERTA: You're right, Phyl.

*(*ROBERTA *runs to* FATHER, *who is now at the door, gives him a hug.)*

'Bye, Daddy.

*(*FATHER *exits. Slight pause.)*

PETER: It's nice to be back home, but…

ROBERTA: You miss the trains?

PETER: Yes, and the Station people.

PHYLLIS: And the Old Gentleman.

ROBERTA: Oh, yes. The Old Gentleman.

(There is a shape at the window followed by a knock at the door, which generates a moment of concern for the children. ROBERTA *goes to the outer door, opens it, and exits, leaving the door to the living room open.)*

ROBERTA: *(v.o.)* Oh, it's the post.

POSTMAN: *(v.o.)* Yes, miss. Special delivery. I need your signature.

ROBERTA: *(v.o.)* Oh? Yes, certainly.

(ROBERTA enters carrying a small book-size parcel.)

ROBERTA: It's for mother.

PHYLLIS: Does it rattle?

ROBERTA: *(shakes parcel)* No, I don't think so.

(MOTHER enters through the inner door.)

MOTHER: Did I hear the door?

PHYLLIS: There's a parcel for you!

(ROBERTA hands the parcel to MOTHER. The CHILDREN gather around her as she teasingly delays opening it.)

ROBERTA: Oh, mother!

PHYLLIS: It's only a book.

MOTHER: But a very special one.

PETER: Your name is on it!

MOTHER: Yes. My first book has been published.

ROBERTA: There's a letter with it.

MOTHER: You read it for me.

ROBERTA: *(reads)* "We are rushing to you the very first copy of your book, so that you and your children will be the first to see it. We expect it will become very popular."

(PETER looks at the book.)

PETER: *(slowly, in awe)* It's called The Railway Children!

PHYLLIS: Is it about us?

MOTHER: Yes. Yes, I suppose it is.

PHYLLIS: Oh, could we read some of it now?

MOTHER: Well, we could start.

(MOTHER holds the book out to ROBERTA, implying that Roberta should read it.)

ROBERTA: No. You wrote it. You read it to us.

MOTHER: Alright.

(MOTHER sits in Father's easy chair; the three CHILDREN sit on the floor around her. As she reads, the lights dim slowly on the scene but Mother and the children are highlighted by a spotlight.)

MOTHER: We'll start at the very beginning. *(reads)* "They were not railway children to begin with. I don't suppose they had ever thought about railways except as a means of getting to the Pantomime, or to the Zoo, or Madame Tussaud's. They were just ordinary suburban children, and they lived in London with their Father and Mother in an ordinary red-brick-fronted villa, with colored glass in the front door, a tiled passage called a hall, a bathroom with hot and cold water, electric bells, and a good deal of white paint…"

(As Mother reads, at an appropriate moment the curtain falls slowly—or the spotlight dims to a blackout.)

END

Character Sketches

I have prepared character sketches only for the four main roles, the three children and their mother, since most of the action evolves around them. By the standards of the day, the family would be considered well established and the parents—and hence the children—modern in the attitudes they display, which were prevalent at the time. This knowledge can help us accept the fairly formal relationship that seems to exist between individual members of the family.

Roberta

Although Roberta may be only 14, she acts more like an 18-year-old. We hear her mother say, in her first address to the audience: "Her real name is Roberta, but she prefers to be called Bobbie – she'd really like to be a boy."

She has an interesting mix in her make up: she is definite about what needs to be done and readily takes control of a situation (without being overly authoritative), yet she demonstrates great affection for her father and is deeply upset when he suddenly disappears from her life. That doesn't mean she is distant or difficult with her mother: they have a comfortable, accepting relationship but in a much more businesslike than affectionate way.

Does Roberta resent 10-year-old Peter's standing as "the man of the house" when their father is away? No, not on a personal basis. What she really resents are the limitations that an early 20th century society imposes on her as a young woman rather than a young man. (If she had been born 20 years later, it's likely that, as an adult, she would have become a suffragette.) It's not something she talks about or even thinks about in the way we do now: it's just a subliminal awareness that there seems to be some injustice.

She is compassionate with her young sister Phyllis, who has much more of a 'girl' attitude than she does. For example, whereas Phyllis loves to play with the dolls and soft animal toys she is given, Roberta has consistently said "thank you" and then quietly placed them on a shelf to observe rather than cuddle.

Peter

Peter knows exactly where he is going: he will become an engineer like his father. His attitudes clearly support this: he likes to draw mechanical constructions, he likes the technology associated with his toy train and, more than anything else, he is aware of and to some extent controlled by the need to be on time. It upsets him if he is late for an event (he regularly consults his pocket watch), and can be irritated by the girls who are much less driven by the need to be at a specific place at a specific moment.

Peter doesn't question his father's disappearance in the way that Roberta does: he simply accepts that he is away on a task and will return to the family when the job is finished. To some extent he wishes he really was the eldest child in the family and could be more in control, yet he also is aware that the role will come to him as he approaches his adult years. He likes to read and he likes to design things on paper. He is not an athletic sports-minded boy.

Phyllis

Being the youngest in the family, and a girl, Phyllis tends to be mildly spoiled, not so much by her own family but by her grandparents (whom we do not meet in the play and they are not referred to). She *likes* being a girl and relishes the soft things that go with it. She likes Roberta much more than Peter, because Roberta not only interacts with her but also understands her. She is already aware that Peter simply puts up with her and gets irritated with her if she doesn't do things the way he says they should be done.

Phyllis is a social being who likes interacting with people, particularly playing card games and board games like checkers. She is not a loner and quickly gets bored when left to her own devices.

Mother

The children's mother comes from a reasonably well-to-do family, who considered she "stepped down" when she married a young engineer (which was not seen then as the well-respected career it is now). She is well-educated and was sent to a finishing school in

France in her late teens, then returned there to work with a publishing firm before her marriage.

She could easily have become a career woman but willingly accepted her role as housewife when she married. When her husband is suddenly imprisoned, at first she is overwhelmed that she will now have to be the sole supporter, both physically and financially, of the three children. (She could have turned to her parents for help, but was too independent.) To do this means she has to write stories and sell them to a publisher, which in turn means she has to trust Roberta to look after the other two children.

Why does she choose *not* to tell the children that their father is in prison? It's partly to protect them from the knowledge, but also to prevent them from thinking their father is a criminal: she worries about the effect that the knowledge would have on them. She is essentially a practical person who adapts quickly to the conditions imposed upon her.

As with many parents of that era, she does not show overt affection for her children.

Production Notes

Although I have provided brief character sketches for Roberta, Peter, Phyllis, and their mother, in practice I find it better to suggest that the four actors first read Edith Nesbit's novel, which will give them a much broader insight into the character each is playing. (Paperback editions are available from most bookstores). Then, of course, they point out the differences between the original story and the script, and I have to explain the main reasons I omitted some parts and some of the characters, and made some minor changes, such as these:

- Although some of the omitted events from the book are interesting *to a reader*, they do not contribute sufficiently to the dramatic effect required for a stage play.
- The play would have become unwieldy with even more scenes than it already has.
- A playing time of 80 minutes, even with an interval, is the maximum tenable length for a young audience.

- It would be impractical on stage to have part of the earth bank slide and form a small mountain on the railway lines (as happens in Nesbit's novel); instead, I made a signal gantry fall across the lines.

There were other changes, useful from a director's point of view, some of which I outline below.

I have carried much of the dialogue from Nesbit's book into the script, but for this second edition of the play have changed some of the words and phrases that would seem strange to a modern audience. For example:

- When the model train breaks in the first scene:
  Peter asks his father: *"Is there any hope?"*
  Father replies: *"Hope? Rather! Tons of it. It just needs...."*

I changed these two lines to:
  Peter: *"Is it broken? For ever?"*
  Father: *"No. Oh, no. It just needs...."*

- Similarly, when the children arrive at the country cottage, Mother urges them along by saying *"Come on, my chickadees...."* I have deleted *"my chickadees."*

At the same time I have retained some expressions that are particularly suitable for the era and a British setting. I also expect directors will likely make further changes to suit their particular audience. (Although I wouldn't change "afternoon tea" to "hot dogs"!)

Two exciting events, one in each act of the play, compel audience attention and inevitably cause a round of applause as each is resolved. The first is when the three children, and particularly Roberta, stop an approaching train and prevent a disastrous accident. The second occurs in the depths of a dark tunnel as the children try to release a boy's foot from where it is trapped under a railway line; again, a train is approaching. The boy's foot is released only just in time for the children to press themselves against the tunnel wall as the train rushes past. For a stage play, both seem to imply horrendous production problems.

In effect, the problems can be overcome fairly simply. The impression that a train is passing can be created by combining four effects: increasing and then decreasing the noise of the train as it rattles past from stage right to stage left, having steam (dry ice) drift out of the tunnel; using special lamps that emulate light from train windows traveling from stage right to stage left; and having the children wave to where the train is supposed to be at a particular moment, again facing gradually from right to left.

For the first production, a 5-ft high platform about 18 inches deep was built across the back of the stage, with a low picket fence along its downstage edge, behind which the children stood to wave to the trains. Below the picket fence, light siding was erected and painted to resemble a steep grass bank. Steps were set into the bank for the children to climb down to the railway line (although in practice they were not used because the fence and steps proved dangerous for the girls to negotiate in ankle-length dresses). At upstage right, immediately in front of the trestle, a 7-ft high tunnel entrance was built, from which 2 x 2 inch lumber was nailed down onto cross pieces to resemble a railway line running across the width of the stage, immediately in front of the embankment. Trains supposedly always entered from the tunnel.

For the moment when Roberta stands center stage, between the lines, frantically waving a red flag, the front of the engine emerges from the tunnel and stops directly in front of her. To achieve this, the carpenter built a facsimile of just the first three feet of the engine and mounted it on a trolley which was pushed by two stage hands. (That it sometimes wobbled did not matter, because the engine driver was desperately applying the brakes to stop it.)

For the inside-the-tunnel sequence, a backcloth was painted with a wall and alcove on it, and dropped between the embankment and the upstage railway line. With a very low light level there was a strong impression the children were in the tunnel and the approaching headlight of a train flashing on them from stage right added to the effect.

Because scenes occur in many locations, it's useful to have three backdrops that can be dropped into place and so have smooth transitions between scenes:

1. The drop I have described for the scene inside the tunnel, between the embankment and the railway lines.
2. A drop between the downstage side of the railway lines and in front of the tunnel entrance, downstage of which sets for the living room of the city home and the kitchen of the country cottage, can be rolled in.
3. A drop well downstage, in front of the living room and kitchen sets, for scenes at the railway station and for moments when the cast are walking along a footpath.

Because the story occurs early in the twentieth century, Velcro played an important part in the girls' and their mother's clothing. It was common in the early 1900's for women to wear layers of petticoats and numerous buttons on their clothing; for the female actors to be similarly attired would have presented insurmountable quick-change problems. By using concealed Velcro to hold their clothing together, they were able to pull the layers on and off quickly. Velcro also played an important part in the "stop the train" scene, when the girls took off their red petticoats and tore them apart to make flags they could wave.

Sometimes things can happen at the first performance that take one completely by surprise. As the lights dimmed following the scene close to the end of the play when Father returns and is greeted by the family—and Mr. Sczepansky is told his family has been found—we discovered some people in the audience jumped up ready to leave (thinking it was the end of the play). That's when the director and I decided the Stationmaster must forewarn the audience to expect another surprise when the family returns to London. In the Nesbit novel, the scene does end in the cottage. But for dramatic purposes I wanted to to take the family back to London and so 'complete the circle.'

And a final note: the script refers to stage left and stage right, following the scene as I imagined it when I wrote the script. There are likely to be some changes, however, since each director and designer may create sets that differ in shape and position.

Obtaining Performance Rights

All five plays in this book are fully protected under the copyright laws of Canada, the United States of America, the British Commonwealth, and all other countries forming part of the Copyright Union. No part of this book may be reproduced in any form, either print or electronic, or transmitted to others.

Amateur and professional rights for live stage performance can be obtained by accessing our web site:

www.r-group.ca

Performance rights must be acquired at least six weeks before the first of the planned production dates.

Where royalty rights apply, they are reasonable. They are based on the particular play and according to the production plans of each company, and determined by factors such as the number of performances, seating capacity at the production site, the number of actors and support staff (and whether they are paid or their involvement is voluntary), and the price charged for admission to the performances.

Some further guidelines apply:

1. No changes may be made to the plot, the dialogue, and the stage directions without the prior approval of the author or his representative. If a request for change is necessary, information is available on the web site.

2. The author's name must appear on all documents associated with the production, such as the program and marketing literature, and be placed on a separate line immediately below the play's title

3. Sometimes the author can be available to attend a performance, particularly as part of a media-related marketing event. Alternatively, the author can be available by remote means, such as Skype. Arrangements must be made in advance: see the web site for details.

If difficulties are encountered in reaching the web site, write to rgrouppubs@gmail.com.

About the Author

Ron Blicq was a flyer in the Royal Air Force who later became a technical editor for CAE Industries, and then a teacher of technical communication at Red River College in Winnipeg, Canada.

On his 'retirement,' he tried his hand at writing stories and novels. But when he discovered he preferred writing dialogue than descriptive scenes, he turned to playwriting. Since then he has written 14 plays, 11 of which have been produced. His play *Closure,* in which a key role is played by a nine-year-old boy (see below), won the Samuel French award for Best Canadian Play in 2008, and is now being performed in several countries.

Ron particularly enjoys writing for young audiences. Although he lives in Winnipeg, he frequently travels to the UK and especially to the Island of Guernsey, where he was born and many of his plays have been performed.

In 2005, young Alex Crossan played the role of Gordie in **Closure***. Then in 2009 he was again on stage in a Blicq play, this time in the role of Cyril in* **Adventures with a Psammead***. You can see him at the far left in the lower photograph on the front cover, and as the older boy outside the Sweet Shop on page 133.*
(Photo by the author)

Closure is published by Samuel French and is available from the publisher (Samuel.french.com), Amazon, or most bookstores. The ISBN is 978-0-573-66400-7.

Printed in Canada